*The Meaning of Life*

# The Meaning of Life

## A Reader

*Edited by*

## E. D. Klemke
## Steven M. Cahn

New York     Oxford
OXFORD UNIVERSITY PRESS
2008

Oxford University Press, Inc., publishes works that further Oxford University's
objective of excellence in research, scholarship, and education.

Oxford   New York
Auckland   Cape Town   Dar es Salaam   Hong Kong   Karachi
Kuala Lumpur   Madrid   Melbourne   Mexico City   Nairobi
New Delhi   Shanghai   Taipei   Toronto

With offices in
Argentina   Austria   Brazil   Chile   Czech Republic   France   Greece
Guatemela   Hungary   Italy   Japan   Poland   Portugal   Singapore
South Korea   Switzerland   Thailand   Turkey   Ukraine   Vietnam

Published by Oxford University Press, Inc.
198 Madison Avenue, New York, New York, 10016
http://www.oup.com

**Library of Congress Cataloging-in-Publication Data**
The meaning of life / edited by E. D. Klemke and Steven M. Cahn. — 3rd ed.
    p.   cm.
Includes bibliographical references.
ISBN-13: 978-0-19-532730-4 (pbk.)
1. Life. I. Klemke, E. D., 1926 – II. Cahn, Steven M.
BD431.M4688 2008
128—dc22        2007060088

Printing number: 20 19 18 17 16 15 14 13 12 11 10
Printed in the United States of America
on acid-free paper.

# *Contents*

Contents

PART THREE

*Questioning the Question*                                                           **197**

# *Preface to the Third Edition*

E. D. Klemke (1926–2000) taught at DePauw University, Roosevelt University, and, for more than two decades, at Iowa State University, winning teaching awards at each institution. In addition to his own numerous writings, many of which explored the early development of analytic philosophy, he was a prolific editor, and *The Meaning of Life,* which first appeared in 1981 with a second edition in 2000, is one of his best-known collections.

At the suggestion of Robert Miller, my longtime editor at Oxford University Press, and with the approval of executors of Professor Klemke's estate, I have undertaken a third edition, retaining the book's structure while adding a significant number of essays, mostly of recent vintage, and shortening or omitting others so as not to increase the volume's overall length. With this updating I hope to highlight the continuing significance of Professor Klemke's work.

The introduction remains as he wrote it. A comprehensive bibliography of contemporary books and articles on the meaning of life can be found in the survey article on the subject by Thaddeus Metz in *Ethics,* 112:4 (2002).

I am grateful to Robert Miller for his support and guidance, to Associate Editor Sarah Calabi for her important role in realizing the project, and to the staff of Oxford University Press for its assistance throughout the stages of production.

New York City     S. M. C.
May 2007

# Preface to the Second Edition

Viktor Frankl once wrote: "Man's concern about a meaning of life is the truest expression of the state of being human." Because I agree with this view, I was led some years ago to put together a collection of essays on the topic of the meaning of life. Since that time I have found many new essays on the topic as well as some that I overlooked in working on the first edition.

The selections contained in this revised edition are, I believe, the most important essays (or chapters) that have been written on the topic of the meaning of life. All but two of the selections are by twentieth-century writers, philosophers, theologians, and others. In some collections of essays, the editor provides a brief summary of all of the selections contained in the anthology. I shall not attempt to do that here, for I believe that the readers' delight and stimulation will be enhanced if they turn to the selections and let the authors speak for themselves.

I would like to express my gratitude to all those who have helped with regard to the planning and preparation of this book. Among those to whom I am especially grateful are Gary Comstock, John Donaghy, John Nerness, Edna Wiser, William D. Hein, and Charles K. Benton.

I would also like to express my appreciation to Robert B. Miller, Jeffrey Broesche, and all of the staff at Oxford University Press.

Finally, I would like to express my unfailing gratitude to some friends who have helped me find meaning and purpose in my own life. Among these I must especially acknowledge Dirk Scholten, Bruce Hardy, Bryan Graveline, Robert Gitchell, Bryan Walker, Steve and Pattie Stamy, David Hauser, William Hein, Robert and Karen Ridgway, and finally, Tom Zmolek, Jim Moran, Matt Schulte, and all of the great employees at Peoples.

Ames, Iowa                                                                                          E. D. K.
February 1999

*The Meaning of Life*

# INTRODUCTION

## *The Question of the Meaning of Life*

### E. D. Klemke

In his work "A Confession," Tolstoy gives an account of how, when he was 50 years old and at the height of his career, he became deeply distressed by the conviction that life was meaningless:

> ... [F]ive years ago, something very strange began to happen with me:
> I was overcome by minutes at first of perplexity and then an arrest of life, as though I did not know how to live or what to do, and I lost myself and was dejected. But that passed, and I continued to live as before. Then those moments of perplexity were repeated oftener and oftener, and always in one and the same form. These arrests of life found their expression in ever the same questions: "Why? Well, and then?"
> At first I thought that those were simply aimless, inappropriate questions. It seemed to me that that was all well known and that if I ever wanted to busy myself with their solution, it would not cost me much labour,—that now I had no time to attend to them, but that if I wanted to I should find the proper answers. But the questions began to repeat themselves oftener and oftener, answers were demanded more and more persistently, and, like dots that fall on the same spot, these questions, without any answers, thickened into one black blotch. ...
> I felt that what I was standing on had given way, that I had no foundation to stand on, that that which I lived by no longer existed, and that I had nothing to live by. ...
> "Well, I know," I said to myself, "all which science wants to persistently to know, but there is no answer to the question about the meaning of my life."[1]

Perhaps almost every sensitive and reflective person has had at least some moments when similar fears and questions have arisen in his or her life. Perhaps the experiences were not as extreme as Tolstoy's, but they have nevertheless been troublesome. And surely almost everyone has at some time asked: What is the meaning of life? Is there any meaning at all? What is it all about? What is the point of it all? It seems evident, then, that the question of the meaning of life is one of the most important questions. Also it is important for all persons, not merely for philosophers.

At least one writer has maintained that it is the most urgent question. In *The Myth of Sisyphus*, Camus writes:

> There is but one truly serious philosophical problem, and that is suicide. Judging whether life is or is not worth living amounts to answering the fundamental question of philosophy. All the rest—whether the world has three dimensions, whether the mind has nine or twelve categories—comes afterwards. These are games; one must first answer. . . .
>
> If I ask myself how to judge that this question is more urgent than that, I reply that one judges by the actions it entails. I have never seen anyone die for the ontological argument [for the existence of a god]. Galileo, who held a scientific truth of great importance, abjured it with the greatest of ease as soon as it endangered his life. In a certain sense, he did right. That truth was not worth the stake. Whether the earth or the sun revolves around the other is a matter of profound indifference. To tell the truth, it is a futile question. On the other hand, I see many people die because they judge that life is not worth living. I see others paradoxically getting killed for the ideas or illusions that give them a reason for living (what is called a reason for living is also an excellent reason for dying). I therefore conclude that the meaning of life is the most urgent of questions.[2]

However we may rank the question—as the most urgent of all or as one of the most urgent of all—most of us do find the question to be one that merits our serious attention. Part of its urgency stems from the fact that it is related to many other questions that face us in our daily lives. Many of the decisions we make with regard to careers, leisure time, moral dilemmas, and other matters depend on how we answer the question of the meaning of life.

However, the question may mean several things. Let us attempt to distinguish some of them. The question "What is the meaning of life?" may mean any of the following: (1) Why does the universe exist? Why is there something rather than nothing? Is there some plan for the whole universe? (2) Why do humans (in general) exist? Do they exist for some purpose? If so, what is it? (3) Why do *I* exist? Do I exist for some purpose? If so, how am I to find what it is? If not, how can life have any significance or value?

I do not mean to suggest that these are rigidly distinct questions. They are obviously interrelated. Hence we may interpret the question "What is the meaning of life?" broadly so that it can include any one or any two or all three of these questions. In so doing, we will be following common usage. Perhaps most of those who are deeply concerned with the question interepret it mainly in terms of question (3). However, there are others who include either question (1) or (2) or both along with question (3). Again, we need not be concerned with specifying one of the interpretations as the "correct" one. Rather let us recognize that all of them are often involved when one asks about the meaning of life.

In turning to possible answers to the question of the meaning of life, we find different approaches or stances:

I. The theistic answer

II. The nontheistic alternative

III. The approach that questions the meaningfulness of the question

These three different approaches are represented by the readings found in Parts I, II, and III, respectively, of this volume. Perhaps a brief summary of each would be desirable at this point.

I. According to the theistic answer, the meaning of life is found in the existence of a god—a supremely benevolent and all-powerful being, transcendent to the natural universe, but who created the universe and fashioned man in his image and endowed him with a preordained purpose. In this view, without the existence of God, or at least without faith in God, life has no meaning or purpose and hence is not worth living. It is difficult to find many works in which this position is explicitly defended from a *philosophical* view. However, it is an answer that is held widely by religious believers, and it is apparent that in many cases it is a basis (or part of the basis) for religious belief. Apart from Tolstoy's *Confession*, the other essays found in Part I of this volume do provide a direct theological, existential defense of this view.

II. The nontheistic (or humanistic) alternative, of course, denies the claim that the meaning of life is dependent on the existence of a god. According to this alternative, since there is no good reason to believe in the existence of a transcendent god, there is no good reason to believe that life has any objective meaning or purpose—that is, any meaning that is dependent on anything outside of the natural universe. Rather, the meaning of life, if there is one, must be found within the natural universe. Some adherents of this view go on to claim that there is no good reason to think life has any meaning in *any* objective sense, but there is good reason to believe that it can nevertheless have meaning in a subjective sense. In other words, it is up to each individual to fashion or create his or her own meaning by virtue of his own consciousness and creative activity. A defense of this position is found in the editor's own essay and in other essays in Part II of this volume.

III. There is yet a third approach to the question of the meaning of life. According to this approach, the question "What is the meaning of life?" is a peculiar or at least an ambiguous one. What kind of question are we asking when we ask about the meaning of life? There are some who think that on analysis of terms such as "meaning," "purpose," and "value," the question of the meaning of life turns out to be cognitively meaningless. However, there are others who reject that claim and take the opposing view. According to them, the various questions that make up the larger question of the meaning of life can be given an interpretation that renders them to be intelligible and cognitively significant. Various aspects of and perspectives on this position are presented in the essays in Part III of this volume.

It is my view that the question of the meaning of life is a significant and important one and that it can be given an answer. I believe that the answer does not rest on any theistic or metaphysical assumptions. Since my defense of this position has been given in my essay "Living Without Appeal: An Affirmative Philosophy of Life," contained in this volume, I will not repeat what I have said there except to say this: It will be recalled that in the passage quoted above, Camus maintains that "Judging whether life is or is not worth living amounts to answering the fundamental question of philosophy." The answer I have given to that question is that there is no formula or recipe or slogan to guarantee that life will be worth living; but I believe that it can be worth living. I believe that I shall die, but that in the meantime, I can find a genuine meaning and purpose in life that makes it worth living.

There are some who will object: But how can life have any meaning or worth or value if it must come to an end? Sir Karl Popper has given the best answer I know of to that question. He writes: "There are those who think that life is valueless because it comes to an end. They fail to see that the opposite argument might also be proposed: that if there were no end to life, life would have no value; that it is, in part, the ever-present danger of losing it which helps to bring home to us the value of life."[3]

## NOTES

1. From L. Tolstoy, *My Confession*, trans. Leo Weiner (London: J. M. Dent, 1905), passim.

2. A. Camus, *The Myth of Sisyphus*, trans. J. O'Brien (New York: Alfred A. Knopf, 1955), p. i.

3. Sir Karl Popper, "How I See Philosophy." In A. Mercier and M. Svilar (eds.), *Philosophers on Their Own Work*, Vol. 3 (Berne and Frankfurt am Main: Peter Lang, 1977), p. 148.

PART ONE    # The Theistic Answer

CHAPTER 1          L E O   T O L S T O Y

# My Confession

Although I regarded authorship as a waste of time, I continued to write during those fifteen years. I had tasted of the seduction of authorship, of the seduction of enormous monetary remunerations and applauses for my insignificant labour, and so I submitted to it, as being a means for improving my material condition and for stifling in my soul all questions about the meaning of my life and life in general.

In my writings I advocated, what to me was the only truth, that it was necessary to live in such a way as to derive the greatest comfort for oneself and one's family.

Thus I proceeded to live, but five years ago something very strange began to happen with me: I was overcome by minutes at first of perplexity and then of an arrest of life, as though I did not know how to live or what to do, and I lost myself and was dejected. But that passed, and I continued to live as before. Then those minutes of perplexity were repeated oftener and oftener, and always in one and the same form. These arrests of life found their expression in ever the same questions: "Why? Well, and then?"

At first I thought that those were simply aimless, inappropriate questions. It seemed to me that that was all well known and that if I ever wanted to busy myself with their solution, it would not cost me much labour,—that now I had no time to attend to them, but that if I wanted to I should find the proper answers. But the questions began to repeat themselves oftener and oftener, answers were demanded more and more persistently, and, like dots that fall on the same spot, these questions, without any answers, thickened into one black blotch.

There happened what happens with any person who falls ill with a mortal internal disease. At first there appear insignificant symptoms of indisposition, to which the patient pays no attention; then these symptoms are repeated more and more frequently and blend into one temporally indivisible suffering. The suffering keeps growing, and before the patient has had time to look around, he becomes conscious that what he took for an indisposition is the most significant thing in the world to him,—is death.

The same happened with me. I understood that it was not a passing indisposition, but something very important, and that, if the questions were going to repeat themselves, it would be necessary to find an answer for them. And I tried to answer them. The questions seemed to be so foolish, simple, and childish. But the moment I touched them and tried to solve them, I became convinced, in the first place, that they were not childish and foolish, but very important and profound questions in life, and, in the second, that, no matter how much I might try, I should not be able to answer them. Before attending to my Samára estate, to my son's education, or to the writing of a book, I ought to know why I should do that. So long as I did not know why, I could not do anything. I could not live. Amidst my thoughts of farming, which interested me very much during that time, there would suddenly pass through my head a question like this: "All right, you are going to have six thousand desyatínas of land in the Government of Samára, and three hundred horses,—and then?" And I completely lost my senses and did not know what to think farther. Or, when I thought of the education of my children, I said to myself: "Why?" Or, reflecting on the manner in which the masses might obtain their welfare, I suddenly said to myself: "What is that to me?" Or, thinking of the fame which my works would get me, I said to myself: "All right, you will be more famous than Gógol, Púshkin, Shakespeare, Molière, and all the writers in the world,—what of it?" And I was absolutely unable to make any reply. The questions were not waiting, and I had to answer them at once; if I did not answer them, I could not live.

I felt that what I was standing on had given way, that I had no foundation to stand on, that that which I lived by no longer existed, and that I had nothing to live by. . . .

All that happened with me when I was on every side surrounded by what is considered to be complete happiness. I had a good, loving, and beloved wife, good children, and a large estate, which grew and increased without any labour on my part. I was respected by my neighbours and friends, more than ever before, was praised by strangers, and, without any self-deception, could consider my name famous. With all that, I was not deranged or mentally unsound,—on the contrary, I was in full command of my mental and physical powers, such as I had rarely met with in people of my age: physically I could work in a field, mowing, without falling behind a peasant; mentally I could work from eight to ten hours in succession, without experiencing any consequences from the strain. And while in such condition I arrived at the conclusion that I could not live, and, fearing death, I had to use cunning against myself, in order that I might not take my life.

This mental condition expressed itself to me in this form: my life is a stupid, mean trick played on me by somebody. Although I did not recognize that "somebody" as having created me, the form of the conception that some one had played a mean, stupid trick on me by bringing me into the world was the most natural one that presented itself to me.

Involuntarily I imagined that there, somewhere, there was somebody who was now having fun as he looked down upon me and saw me, who had lived for thirty or forty years, learning, developing, growing in body and mind, now that I had become strengthened in mind and had reached that summit of life from which it lay all before me, standing as a complete fool on that summit and seeing clearly that there was nothing in life and never would be. And that was fun to him—

But whether there was or was not that somebody who made fun of me, did not make it easier for me. I could not ascribe any sensible meaning to a single act, or to my whole life. I was only surprised that I had not understood that from the start. All that had long ago been known to everybody. Sooner or later there would come diseases and death (they had come already) to my dear ones and to me, and there would be nothing left but stench and worms. All my affairs, no matter what they might be, would sooner or later be forgotten, and I myself should not exist. So why should I worry about all these things? How could a man fail to see that and live,—that was surprising! A person could live only so long as he was drunk; but the moment he sobered up, he could not help seeing that all that was only a deception, and a stupid deception at that! Really, there was nothing funny and ingenious about it, but only something cruel and stupid.

Long ago has been told the Eastern story about the traveller who in the steppe is overtaken by an infuriated beast. Trying to save himself from the animal, the traveller jumps into a waterless well, but at its bottom he sees a dragon who opens his jaws in order to swallow him. And the unfortunate man does not dare climb out, lest he perish from the infuriated beast, and does not dare jump down to the bottom of the well, lest he be devoured by the dragon, and so clutches the twig of a wild bush growing in a cleft of the well and holds on to it. His hands grow weak and he feels that soon he shall have to surrender to the peril which awaits him at either side; but he still holds on and sees two mice, one white, the other black, in even measure making a circle around the main trunk of the bush to which he is clinging, and nibbling at it on all sides. Now, at any moment, the bush will break and tear off, and he will fall into the dragon's jaws. The traveller sees that and knows that he will inevitably perish; but while he is still clinging, he sees some drops of honey hanging on the leaves of the bush, and so reaches out for them with his tongue and licks the leaves. Just so I hold on to the branch of life, knowing that the dragon of death is waiting inevitably for me, ready to tear me to pieces, and I cannot understand why I have fallen on such suffering. And I try to lick that honey which used to give me pleasure; but now it no longer gives me joy, and the white and the black mouse day and night nibble at the branch to which I am holding on. I clearly see the dragon, and the honey is no longer sweet to me. I see only the inevitable dragon and the mice, and am unable to turn my glance away from them. That is not a fable, but a veritable, indisputable, comprehensible truth.

The former deception of the pleasures of life, which stifled the terror of the dragon, no longer deceives me. No matter how much one should say to me, "You cannot understand the meaning of life, do not think, live!" I am unable to do so, because I have been doing it too long before. Now I cannot help seeing day and night, which run and lead me up to death. I see that alone, because that alone is the truth. Everything else is a lie.

The two drops of honey that have longest turned my eyes away from the cruel truth, the love of family and of authorship, which I have called an art, are no longer sweet to me.

"My family—" I said to myself, "but my family, my wife and children, they are also human beings. They are in precisely the same condition that I am in: they must either live in the lie or see the terrible truth. Why should they live? Why should I love them, why guard, raise, and watch them? Is it for the same despair which is in me, or for dulness of perception? Since I love them, I cannot conceal the truth from them,—every step in cognition leads them up to this truth. And the truth is death."

"Art, poetry?" For a long time, under the influence of the success of human praise, I tried to persuade myself that that was a thing which could be done, even though death should come and destroy everything, my deeds, as well as my memory of them; but soon I came to see that that, too, was a deception. It was clear to me that art was an adornment of life, a decoy of life. But life lost all its attractiveness for me. How, then, could I entrap others? So long as I did not live my own life, and a strange life bore me on its waves; so long as I believed that life had some sense, although I was not able to express it,—the reflections of life of every description in poetry and in the arts afforded me pleasure, and I was delighted to look at life through this little mirror of art; but when I began to look for the meaning of life, when I experienced the necessity of living myself, that little mirror became either useless, superfluous, and ridiculous, or painful to me. I could no longer console myself with what I saw in the mirror, namely, that my situation was stupid and desperate. It was all right for me to rejoice so long as I believed in the depth of my soul that life had some sense. At that time the play of lights—of the comical, the tragical, the touching, the beautiful, the terrible in life— afforded me amusement. But when I knew that life was meaningless and terrible, the play in the little mirror could no longer amuse me. No sweetness of honey could be sweet to me, when I saw the dragon and the mice that were nibbling down my support. . . .

In my search after the question of life I experienced the same feeling which a man who has lost his way in the forest may experience.

He comes to a clearing, climbs a tree, and clearly sees an unlimited space before him; at the same time he sees that there are no houses there, and that there can be none; he goes back to the forest, into the darkness, and he sees darkness, and again there are no houses.

Thus I blundered in this forest of human knowledge, between the clearings of the mathematical and experimental sciences, which disclosed to me clear horizons, but such in the direction of which there could be no house, and between the darkness of the speculative sciences, where I sunk into a deeper darkness, the farther I proceeded, and I convinced myself at last that there was no way out and could not be.

By abandoning myself to the bright side of knowledge I saw that I only turned my eyes away from the question. No matter how enticing and clear the horizons were that were disclosed to me, no matter how enticing it was to bury myself in the infinitude of this knowledge, I comprehended that these sciences were the more clear, the less I needed them, the less they answered my question.

"Well, I know," I said to myself, "all which science wants so persistently to know, but there is no answer to the question about the meaning of my life." But in the speculative sphere I saw that, in spite of the fact that the aim of the knowledge was directed straight to the answer of my question, or because of that fact, there could be no other answer than what I was giving to myself: "What is the meaning of my life?"—"None." Or, "What will come of my life?"—"Nothing." Or, "Why does everything which exists exist, and why do I exist?"—"Because it exists."

Putting the question to the one side of human knowledge, I received an endless quantity of exact answers about what I did not ask: about the chemical composition of the stars, about the movement of the sun toward the constellation of Hercules, about the origin of species and of man, about the forms of infinitely small, imponderable particles of ether; but the answer in this sphere of knowledge to my question what the meaning of my life was, was always: "You are what you call your life; you are a temporal, accidental conglomeration of particles. The interrelation, the change of these particles, produces in you that which you call life. This congeries will last for some time; then the interaction of these particles will cease, and that which you call life and all your questions will come to an end. You are an accidentally cohering globule of something. The globule is fermenting. This fermentation the globule calls its life. The globule falls to pieces, and all fermentation and all questions will come to an end." Thus the clear side of knowledge answers, and it cannot say anything else, if only it strictly follows its principles.

With such an answer it appears that the answer is not a reply to the question. I want to know the meaning of my life, but the fact that it is a particle of the infinite not only gives it no meaning, but even destroys every possible meaning.

Those obscure transactions, which this side of the experimental, exact science has with speculation, when it says that the meaning of life consists in evolution and the coöperation with this evolution, because of their obscurity and inexactness cannot be regarded as answers.

The other side of knowledge, the speculative, so long as it sticks strictly to its fundamental principles in giving a direct answer to the question, everywhere and at all times has answered one and the same: "The world is something infinite and incomprehensible. Human life is an incomprehensible part of this incomprehensible *all*. . . ."

I lived for a long time in this madness, which, not in words, but in deeds, is particularly characteristic of us, the most liberal and learned of men. But, thanks either to my strange, physical love for the real working class, which made me understand it and see that it is not so stupid as we suppose, or to the sincerity of my conviction, which was that I could know nothing and that the best that I could do was to hang myself,—I felt that if I wanted to live and understand the meaning of life, I ought naturally to look for it, not among those who had lost the meaning of life and wanted to kill themselves, but among those billions departed and living men who had been carrying their own lives and ours upon their shoulders. And I looked around at the enormous masses of deceased and living men,—not learned and wealthy, but simple men,—and I saw something quite different. I saw that all these billions of men that lived or had lived, all, with rare exceptions, did not fit into my subdivisions,[1] and that I could not recognize them as not understanding the question, because they themselves put it and answered it with surprising clearness. Nor could I recognize them as Epicureans, because their lives were composed rather of privations and suffering than of enjoyment. Still less could I recognize them as senselessly living out their meaningless lives, because every act of theirs and death itself was explained by them. They regarded it as the greatest evil to kill themselves. It appeared, then, that all humanity was in possession of a knowledge of the meaning of life, which I did not recognize and which I condemned. It turned out that rational knowledge did not give any meaning to life, excluded life, while the meaning which by billions of people, by all humanity, was ascribed to life was based on some despised, false knowledge.

The rational knowledge in the person of the learned and the wise denied the meaning of life, but the enormous masses of men, all humanity, recognized this meaning in an irrational knowledge. This irrational knowledge was faith, the same that I could not help but reject. That was God as one and three, the creation in six days, devils and angels, and all that which I could not accept so long as I had not lost my senses.

My situation was a terrible one. I knew that I should not find anything on the path of rational knowledge but the negation of life, and there, in faith, nothing but the negation of reason, which was still more impossible than the negation of life. From the rational knowledge it followed that life was an evil and men knew it,—it depended on men whether they should cease living, and yet they lived and continued to live, and I myself lived, though I had known long ago that life was meaningless and an evil. From faith it followed that, in order to understand life, I must renounce reason, for which alone a meaning was needed.

There resulted a contradiction, from which there were two ways out: either what I called rational was not so rational as I had thought; or that which to me appeared irrational was not so irrational as I had thought. And I began to verify the train of thoughts of my rational knowledge.

In verifying the train of thoughts of my rational knowledge, I found that it was quite correct. The deduction that life was nothing was inevitable; but I saw a mistake. The mistake was that I had not reasoned in conformity with the question put by me. The question was, "Why should I live?" that is, "What real, indestructible essence will come from my phantasmal, destructible life? What meaning has my finite existence in this infinite world?" And in order to answer this question, I studied life.

The solutions of all possible questions of life apparently could not satisfy me, because my question, no matter how simple it appeared in the beginning, included the necessity of explaining the finite through the infinite, and vice versa.

I asked, "What is the extra-temporal, extra-causal, extra-spatial meaning of life?" But I gave an answer to the question, "What is the temporal, causal, spatial meaning of my life?" The result was that after a long labour of mind I answered, "None."

In my reflections I constantly equated, nor could I do otherwise, the finite with the finite, the infinite with the infinite, and so from that resulted precisely what had to result: force was force, matter was matter, will was will, infinity was infinity, nothing was nothing,—and nothing else could come from it.

There happened something like what at times takes place in mathematics: you think you are solving an equation, when you have only an identity. The reasoning is correct, but you receive as a result the answer: $a = a$, or $x = x$, or $o = o$. The same happened with my reflection in respect to the question about the meaning of my life. The answers given by all science to that question are only identities.

Indeed, the strictly scientific knowledge, that knowledge which, as Descartes did, begins with a full doubt in everything, rejects all knowledge which has been taken on trust, and builds everything anew on the laws of reason and experience, cannot give any other answer to the question of life than what I received,—an indefinite answer. It only seemed to me at first that science gave me a positive answer,—Schopenhauer's answer: "Life has no meaning, it is an evil." But when I analyzed the matter, I saw that the answer was not a positive one, but that it was only my feeling which expressed it as such. The answer, strictly expressed, as it is expressed by the Brahmins, by Solomon, and by Schopenhauer, is only an indefinite answer, or an identity, $o = o$, life is nothing. Thus the philosophical knowledge does not negate anything, but only answers that the question cannot be solved by it, that for philosophy the solution remains insoluble.

When I saw that, I understood that it was not right for me to look for an answer to my question in rational knowledge, and that the answer given by rational knowledge was only an indication that the answer might be got if the question were differently put, but only when into the discussion of the question should be introduced the question of the relation of the finite to the infinite. I also understood that, no matter how irrational and monstrous the answers might be that faith gave, they had this advantage that they introduced into each answer the relation of the finite to the infinite, without which there could be no answer.

No matter how I may put the question, "How must I live?" the answer is, "According to God's law." "What real result will there be from my life?"—"Eternal torment or eternal bliss." "What is the meaning which is not destroyed by death?"—"The union with infinite God, paradise."

Thus, outside the rational knowledge, which had to me appeared as the only one, I was inevitably led to recognize that all living humanity had a certain other irrational knowledge, faith, which made it possible to live.

All the irrationality of faith remained the same for me, but I could not help recognizing that it alone gave to humanity answers to the questions of life, and, in consequence of them, the possibility of living.

The rational knowledge brought me to the recognition that life was meaningless,—my life stopped, and I wanted to destroy myself. When I looked around at people, at all humanity, I saw that people lived and asserted that they knew the meaning of life. I looked back at myself: I lived so long as I knew the meaning of life. As to other people, so even to me, did faith give the meaning of life and the possibility of living.

Looking again at the people of other countries, contemporaries of mine and those passed away, I saw again the same. Where life had been, there faith, ever since humanity had existed, had given the possibility of living, and the chief features of faith were everywhere one and the same.

No matter what answers faith may give, its every answer gives to the finite existence of man the sense of the infinite,—a sense which is not destroyed by suffering, privation, and death. Consequently in faith alone could we find the meaning and possibility of life. What, then, was faith? I understood that faith was not merely an evidence of things not seen, and so forth, not revelation (that is only the description of one of the symptoms of faith), not the relation of man to man (faith has to be defined, and then God, and not first God, and faith through him), not merely an agreement with what a man was told, as faith was generally understood,—that faith was the knowledge of the meaning of human life, in consequence of which man did not destroy himself, but lived. Faith is the power of life. If a man lives he believes in something. If he did not believe that he ought to live for some purpose, he would not live. If he does not see and understand the phantasm of the finite, he believes in that finite; if he understands the phantasm of the finite, he must believe in the infinite. Without faith one cannot live. . . .

In order that all humanity may be able to live, in order that they may continue living, giving a meaning to life, they, those billions, must have another, a real knowledge of faith, for not the fact that I, with Solomon and Schopenhauer, did not kill myself convinced me of the existence of faith, but that these billions had lived and had borne us, me and Solomon, on the waves of life.

Then I began to cultivate the acquaintance of the believers from among the poor, the simple and unlettered folk, of pilgrims, monks, dissenters, peasants. The doctrine of these people from among the masses was also the Christian doctrine that the quasi-believers of our circle professed. With the Christian truths were also mixed in very many superstitions, but there was this difference: the superstitions of our circle were quite unnecessary to them, had no connection with their lives, were only a kind of an Epicurean amusement, while the superstitions of the believers from among the labouring classes were to such an extent blended with their life that it would have been impossible to imagine it without these superstitions,—it was a necessary condition of that life. I began to examine closely the lives and beliefs of these people, and the more I examined them, the more did I become convinced that they had the real faith, that their faith was necessary for them, and that it alone gave them a meaning and possibility of life. In contradistinction to what I saw in our circle, where life without faith was possible, and where hardly one in a thousand professed to be a believer, among them there was hardly one in a thousand who was not a believer. In contradistinction to what I saw in our circle, where all life passed in idleness, amusements, and tedium of life, I saw that the whole life of these people was passed in hard work, and that they were satisfied with life. In contradistinction to the people of our circle, who struggled and murmured against fate because of their privations and their suffering, these people accepted diseases and sorrows without any perplexity or opposition, but with the calm and firm conviction that it was all for good. In contradistinction to the fact that the more intelligent we are, the less do we understand the meaning of life and the more do we see a kind of a bad joke in our suffering and death, these people live, suffer, and approach death, and suffer in peace and more often in joy. In contradistinction to the fact that a calm death, a death without terror or despair, is the greatest exception in our circle, a restless, insubmissive, joyless death is one of the greatest exceptions among the masses. And of such people, who are deprived of everything which for Solomon and for me constitutes the only good of life, and who withal experience the greatest happiness, there is an enormous number. I cast a broader glance about me. I examined the life of past and present vast masses of men, and I saw people who in like manner had understood the meaning of life, who had known how to live and die, not two, not three, not ten, but hundreds, thousands, millions. All of them, infinitely diversified as to habits, intellect, culture, situation, all equally and quite contrary to my ignorance knew the meaning of life and of death, worked calmly, bore privations and suffering, lived and died, seeing in that not vanity, but good.

I began to love those people. The more I penetrated into their life, the life of the men now living, and the life of men departed, of whom I had read and heard, the more did I love them, and the easier it became for me to live. Thus I lived for about two years, and within me took place a transformation, which had long been working within me, and the germ of which had always been in me. What happened with me was that the life of our circle,—of the rich and the learned,—not only disgusted me, but even lost all its meaning. All our acts, reflections, sciences, arts,—all that appeared to me in a new light. I saw that all that was mere pampering of the appetites, and that no meaning could be found in it; but the life of all the working masses, of all humanity, which created life, presented itself to me in its real significance. I saw that that was life itself and that the meaning given to this life was truth, and I accepted it.

## NOTE

1. In a passage omitted here, Tolstoy characterized four attitudes that people have toward life: living in ignorance of the problem of the meaning of life; ignoring it and trying to attain as much pleasure as possible; admitting that life is meaningless and committing suicide; admitting that life is meaningless but continuing to live aimlessly. [E. D. K.]

# CHAPTER 2

# DAVID F. SWENSON

## The Dignity of Human Life

Man lives forward, but he thinks backward. As an active being, his task is to press forward to the things that are before, toward the goal where is the prize of the high calling. But as a thinking, active being, his forward movement is conditioned by a retrospect. If there were no past for a man, there could be no future; and if there were no future and no past, but only such an immersion in the present as is characteristic of the brute which perisheth, then there would be nothing eternal in human life, and everything distinctively and essentially human would disappear from our existence.

As a preparation for an existence in the present, the youth of a nation are trained in various skills and along devious lines, according to their capacities and circumstances, for the parts they are to play in existence; their natural talents are developed, some by extended periods of intellectual training, others for participation in various forms of business or technical training; but whatever be the ultimate end of the training, its purpose is to develop those latent powers they possess which will eventually prove of benefit to themselves or to others. But, in addition to this, which we may call a preparation for the external life, a something else is urgently needed, a something so fundamentally important that in its absence every other form of preparation is revealed as imperfect and incomplete, even ineffective and futile.

This so particularly indispensable something is a view of life, and a view of life is not acquired as a direct and immediate result of a course of study, the reading of books, or a communication of results. It is wholly a product of the individual's own knowledge of himself as an individual, of his individual capabilities and aspirations. A view of life is a principle of living, a spirit and an attitude capable of maintaining its unity and identity with itself in all of life's complexities and varying vicissitudes; and yet also capable of being declined, to use the terminology of the grammatical sciences, in all the infinite variety of cases that the language of life affords. Without this preparation the individual life is like a ship without a rudder, a bit of wreckage floating with the current to an uncomprehended destiny. A view of life is not objective knowledge, but subjective conviction. It is a part of a man's own self, the source whence the stream of his life issues. It is the dominant attitude of the spirit which gives to life its direction and its goal. This is why it cannot be directly communicated or conveyed, like an article of commerce, from one person to another. If a view of life were a body of knowledge about life, or a direct and immediate implication from such knowledge, it would be subject to objective communication and systematic instruction. But it is rather a personal expression of what a man essentially is in his own inmost self, and this cannot be learned by rote, or accepted at the hands of some external authority. Knowledge is the answer or answers that things give to the questions we ask of them; a view of life is the reply a person gives to the question that life asks of him. We begin life by scrutinizing our environment, ourselves playing the role of questioners and examiners and critics; but at a later moment, when the soul comes of age and is about to enter upon its majority, it learns that the tables have been turned and the roles reversed; from that moment it confronts a question, a searching and imperative question, in relation to which no evasion can avail, and to which no shifting of responsibility is possible.

In discussing the problem of a view of life which can give it meaning and dignity and worth, I am well aware that no one can acquire a view of life by listening to a speech. Nevertheless, a speech may serve the more modest purpose of stimulating a search, perhaps a more earnest search; and may render more articulate possibly the convictions of those who have already won some such conception, having made it their own by a heart-felt and spontaneous choice.

All men are endowed by nature with a desire for happiness—a principle so obvious as scarcely to need any explanation, and certainly no defense. A human life without happiness or hope of happiness is not a life, but rather a death in life. Happiness is life's vital fluid and the very breath of its nostrils. Happiness and life are so much one and the same thing that the more profoundly any life discovers happiness, the more significant and abundant is that life itself. This is also the principle of the Christian religion, which even dares to formulate the task of life as the duty of being happy; for does not the Apostle Paul say, "Rejoice . . . always: again I will say, Rejoice"? So deeply grounded in human nature is the need for happiness, that the desire for it is not only universal and instinctive, but ineradicable and imperative. Man is made for happiness; an essentially unhappy man has missed his goal, and has failed to realize his humanity.

But for a thinking human being—and God made every man a thinker, whatever may be our estimate of that which men make of themselves—for a thinking human being, happiness cannot consist in the satisfaction of momentary impulse, of blind feeling, of brute immediacy. A pleasant absorption in the present, oblivious of prospect or retrospect, careless of the wider relations or the deeper truth of life, can be called happiness only on the basis of frivolity and thoughtlessness. Just as life is not life unless it is happy, so happiness is not happiness unless it can be justified. In order really to be happiness it requires to be interpenetrated with a sense of meaning, reason, and worth.

For the quest for happiness, like every other human quest, faces a danger. The danger that confronts it is the possibility of error: the error of permitting oneself to be lured into promising paths that lead to no goal, and the error of coming to rest in hollow satisfactions and empty joys. It is possible to believe oneself happy, to seem happy to oneself and to others, and yet in reality to be plunged in the deepest misery; just as, on the other hand, it is possible to stand possessed of the greatest treasure, and yet, in thoughtlessness, to imagine oneself destitute, and through that very thoughtlessness not only neglect and ignore but actually deprive oneself of what one already has. The basic problem of life, the question in response to which a view of life seeks to propound an answer, may therefore be formulated as follows: What is that happiness which is also a genuine and lasting good? In what does it consist, and how may it be attained?

There exists an ancient handbook, an *Art of Rhetoric*, compiled for the guidance and information of orators and other public speakers, written by one of the greatest of Greek philosophers. In this handbook the author formulates the commonly prevailing conceptions of happiness as among the things useful for public speakers to know. This textbook is almost twenty-five hundred years old, and the views it presents on this subject may therefore be expected to seem childish in the light of our greater insight and extraordinary progress in all things. Nevertheless, let us note them in passing, if only for the sake of seeing how far we have advanced beyond them. Happiness is said to be commonly defined as independence of life, as prosperity with virtue, as comfortable circumstances with security, or as the enjoyment of many possessions, together with the power to keep and defend them. Its constituent elements are noble birth, wealth, many good and influential friends, bodily health and beauty, talents and capacities, good fortune, honors, and lastly virtue. We readily perceive how strange and old-fashioned these conceptions are, how foreign to all our modern and enlightened notions. I shall therefore subjoin a more up-to-date consideration of the same subject, derived from a very modern author writing in a journal of today. The author raises the question as to what circumstances and conditions have the power to make him feel really alive, tingling with vitality, instinct with the joy of living. He submits a long list including a variety of things, of which I shall quote the chief: the sense of health; successful creative work, like writing books; good food and drink; pleasant surroundings; praise, not spread on too thick; friends and their company; beautiful things, books, music; athletic exercises and sports; daydreaming; a good fight in a tolerably decent cause; the sense of bodily danger escaped; the consciousness of being a few steps ahead of the wolf of poverty. His social ideal is a community where beauty abounds, where the fear of want is absent, where a man may dress as he pleases, do the work that suits him best; a community where arts and letters flourish, where abundant leisure breaks the remorseless pace of ceaseless work, and, lastly, for those who value religion, a church is provided, with a great nave and a great organ and the sound of vespers across the evening fields. So speaks our modern writer. And now that I have juxtaposed these two accounts, I have to confess to the strange feeling that, despite the interval of more than two thousand years between them, they sound unexpectedly alike, even to the generous inclusion of a place for morality and religion as not an entirely negligible factor in promoting the good and happy life. How strange to find such a similarity! Can it be that after all that has been said and written about the revolutionary and radical changes introduced into life by modern science, modern invention, and modern industry, the influence of the steam engine and the printing press, the telegraph and the radio, the automobile and the airplane, together with the absolutely devastating discoveries of astronomers—can it be, in spite of all this, that the current conceptions of life and its meaning have remained essentially unchanged? Is not this a remarkable testimony to the profound inner resemblance to one another, despite all changes of form and circumstance, exhibited by the countless generations of men, both in their wisdom and in their folly?

However that may be, I do not think that anyone will deny that such views as these are widely held, and constitute the view of life perhaps of the majority of men. The testimony to their prevalence is not merely the articulate confession of the tongue, but the no less revealing though inarticulate direction of the life. I hope not to be misunderstood. The present speaker is human enough to find these objectives, or the majority of them, not only natural but inviting; he finds them desirable, and is by no means schooled in any heroic or stoic indifference to the goods that have rightly been called external, rooted as they are in fortunate circumstances and special privilege. But there are serious difficulties in the way of constructing a view of life out of such considerations.

The constituents of happiness are in both cases a multiplicity of things. As Aristotle so simply says, virtue alone will not make a man happy, but he needs also goods and friends. But the self which sets its heart upon any such multiplicity of external goods, which lives in them and by them and for them, dependent upon them for the only happiness it knows—such a self is captive to the diverse world of its desires. It belongs to the world and does not own itself. It is not in the deepest sense a self, since it is not free and is not a unity. The manifold conditions of its happiness split the self asunder; no ruling passion dominates its life; no concentration gives unity to the personality and single-mindedness to the will. Its name is legion, and its nature is double-mindedness. And if some one thing, like wealth or power, is made the single ambition of an exceptional life, it still remains true that such things are only apparently single; in reality they are various and manifold. The soul that lives in them is torn by diverse impulses, is drawn in many different directions at once, and cannot find the peace which comes only from single-minded devotion, from the pursuit of an end which is intrinsically and genuinely one.

Reflection discovers yet another difficulty in connection with such views of life. Whoever seeks his happiness in external conditions, of whatever sort, seeks it in that which is in its essential nature precarious. He presumes upon the realization of conditions which are not intrinsic to him, or within his control. This happiness is subject to the law of uncertainty, to the qualification of an unyielding, mysterious *perhaps*. Here lurks the possibility of despair. Give a man the full satisfaction of his wishes and ambitions, and he deems himself happy; withdraw from him the smile of fortune's favor, and disappoint his expectation and his hope, and he will be plunged into despair. The shift from happiness to unhappiness in such a life is every moment imminent. And therefore its despair is latent even in its happiness, and discord lurks imminent in the soul's most beautiful music; its presence is masked only by a brutish self-satisfaction, the habit of thoughtlessness, breathless haste in trifling errands, and darkness in the soul's deepest ground, each and all miserable defenses indeed against the enemy within the gates.

A third consideration. Wealth and power and the like, even bodily health and beauty of person, are not in the strictest sense intrinsic values, but rather representative and comparative, conditional and hypothetical. Money is good—if I have learned how to use it; and so with power and influence, health and strength. But in themselves these things are abstract and neutral, and no man can truthfully say whether the acquirement of them in any individual case will work more good than harm. This is a consideration which applies to nearly every item of what we call progress. A new discovery or invention, like the printing press, promises radically to improve life, to secure for us a hitherto undreamed-of happiness and well-being. We hail it with enthusiasm as inaugurating a new era, and in the distance we descry the dawn of a millennial day. A century or so passes. What then? Why, all the old difficulties and problems, all the old dissatisfactions and complaints, the very difficulties and problems that were to be solved by the new invention, are seen to be still with us, having but slightly changed their outward form and habitat. In addition, the new improvement that was to usher in the millennium, is seen to be the source of so many and so serious abuses (consider the abuse of the printing press!) that the best minds of the race have to be concentrated upon the problem of finding a remedy for these abuses, and keeping them under some sort of control. And so also in the individual life. Every access of power and prosperity, and of outward comfort, brings with it its own griefs and dangers. Every such improvement is only potentially a good, as it is also potentially an evil. It is a mere quantity whose qualitative meaning is indeterminate, awaiting the seal of something else, something from within the soul itself, in order to determine its final significance for weal or woe, for happiness or unhappiness.

Lastly, it must be pointed out that the conditions of happiness as conceived in all such views of life, inevitably imply a privileged status for the happy individual. They rest upon differential capabilities and exceptionally fortunate circumstances. To choose them as the end and aim of life constitutes an injury to the mass of men who are not so privileged. This one thought alone is of so arresting a quality as to give the deepest concern to every man who has the least trace of human sympathy and human feeling. I hope I have a soul not entirely a stranger to happy admiration; I know I feel moved to bend low in respect before exceptional talent and performance, and that I am eager to honor greatness and genius wherever I have the gift to understand it. And I am not so unfeeling as to refuse a tribute of sympathetic joy to those who rejoice in fortune's favors and bask in the smiles of outward success. But as the fundamental source of inspiration of my life, I need something that is not exclusive and differential, but inclusive and universal. I require to drink from a spring at which all men may refresh themselves; I need an aim that reconciles me to high and low, rich and poor, cultured and uncultured, sophisticated and simple; to the countless generations of the past as well as to the men and women of the future. I need a spiritual bond that binds me to all human beings in a common understanding of that which is fundamental and essential to human life. To have my life and happiness in that which is inaccessible to the many or to the few, seems to me an act of treason to humanity, a cowardly and pusillanimous attack upon the brotherhood of man; for without the inner spiritual tie of an essential aim which all can reach and all can understand, the concept of the human race as a spiritual unity is destroyed, and nothing is left of mankind but a biological species, only slightly better equipped than the other animals to cope with the present state of their physical environment. The differences between man and man are indeed inseparable from this our imperfect temporal existence; but I cannot and will not believe that their development constitutes the perfection of life itself. Rather is this to be found in the discovery and expectation of something underlying and absolute, something that can be found by all who seek it in earnest, something to which our lives may give expression, subordinating to its unifying principle the infinite multitude of ends, reducing them to their own relative measure and proportion, and refusing to permit the unimportant to become important, the relative to become absolute. The possibility of making this discovery and of giving it expression is, so it seems to me, the fundamental meaning of life, the source of its dignity and worth. The happiness that is found with this discovery is not invidious and divisive, but unifying and reconciling; it does not abrogate the differences, but it destroys their power to wound and to harm, the fortunate through being puffed up in arrogance and pride, the unfortunate through being depressed in envy and disappointment. For this happiness is not denied to any man, no matter how insignificant and humble.

Our criticism has brought us to the threshold of an ethical view of life. That the essence of life and its happiness is to be sought in the moral consciousness alone is the conviction that animates this address, and gives it its reason for being. This view holds that the individual human self has an infinite worth, that the personality has an eternal validity, that the bringing of this validity to expression in the manifold relations and complications of life is the true task of the self, that this task gives to the individual's historical development an infinite significance, because it is a process through which the personality in its truth and depth comes to its own. "Find your self," says the moral consciousness; "reclaim it in its total and in so far unworthy submergence in relative ends; dare to think the nothingness, the hollowness, the relativity, the precariousness, the lack of intrinsic meaning of that which constitutes the entire realm of the external and the manifold; liberate yourself from slavery to finite ends; have the courage to substitute the one thing needful for the many things wished for, and perhaps desirable, making first things first, and all other things secondary—and you will find that these other things will be added unto you in the measure in which you require them and can use them as servants and ministers of your highest good."

So speaks the voice within us, a still small voice, a soft whisper easily overwhelmed by the noise and traffic of life, but a voice, nevertheless, which no one can permit to be silenced except at the cost of acquiring restlessness instead of peace, anxiety instead of trust and confidence, a distracted spirit instead of harmony with one's self. The moral spirit finds the meaning of life in choice. It finds it in that which proceeds from man and remains with him as his inner essence rather than in the accidents of circumstance and turns of external fortune. The individual has his end in himself. He is no mere instrument in the service of something external, nor is he the slave of some powerful master; nor of a class, a group, or party; nor of the state or nation; nor even of humanity itself, as an abstraction solely external to the individual. Essentially and absolutely he is an end; only accidentally and relatively is he a means. And this is true of the meanest wage slave, so called, in industry's impersonal machine—precisely as true of him as it is of the greatest genius or the most powerful ruler.

Is there anyone so little stout-hearted, so effeminately tender, so extravagantly in love with an illusory and arbitrary freedom, as to feel that the glorious promise of such a view of life is ruined, its majestic grandeur shriveled into cramped pettiness, because the task which it offers the individual is not only an invitation, but also an obligation as well? Shall we confess that we cannot endure this "Thou must" spoken to ourselves,[1] even when the voice proceeds from no external power but from our in-most self, there where the human strikes its roots into the divine? Truly, it is this "Thou must" that is the eternal guarantee of our calling, the savior of our hope, the inspirer of our energy, the preserver of our aim against the shiftings of feeling and the vicissitudes of circumstance. It steels the will and makes it fast; it gives courage to begin after failure; it is the triumph over despondency and despair. For duty is the eternal in a man, or that by which he lays hold of the eternal; and only through the eternal can a man become a conqueror of the life of time. It is in the moral consciousness that a man begins truly to sense the presence of God; and every religion that has omitted the ethical is in so far a misunderstanding of religion, reducing it to myth and poetry, having significance only for the imagination, but not for the whole nature of man as concrete reality. The moral consciousness is a lamp, a wonderful lamp; but not like the famous lamp of Aladdin,[2] which when rubbed had the power to summon a spirit, a willing servant ready and able to fulfill every wish. But whenever a human being rubs the lamp of his moral consciousness with moral passion, a Spirit does appear. This Spirit is God, and the Spirit is master and lord, and man becomes his servant. But this service is man's true freedom, for a derivative spirit like man, who certainly has not made himself, or given himself his own powers, cannot in truth impose upon himself the law of his own being. It is in the "Thou must" of God and man's "I can" that the divine image of God in human life is contained, to which an ancient book refers when it asserts that God made man in his own image. That is the inner glory, the spiritual garb of man, which transcends the wonderful raiment with which the Author of the universe has clothed the lilies of the field, raiment which in its turn puts to shame the royal purple of Solomon. The lilies of the field[3] cannot hear the voice of duty or obey its call; hence they cannot bring their will into harmony with the divine will. In the capacity to do this lies man's unique distinction among all creatures; here is his self, his independence, his glory and his crown.

I know that all men do not share this conviction. Youth is often too sure of its future. The imagination paints the vision of success and fortune in the rosiest tints; the sufferings and disappointments of which one hears are for youth but the exception that proves the rule; the instinctive and blind faith of youth is in the relative happiness of some form of external success. Maturity, on the other hand, has often learned to be content with scraps and fragments, wretched crumbs saved out of the disasters on which its early hopes suffered shipwreck. Youth pursues an ideal that is illusory; age has learned, O wretched wisdom! to do without an ideal altogether. But the ideal is there, implanted in the heart and mind of man by his Maker, and no mirages of happiness or clouds of disappointment, not the stupor of habit or the frivolity of thoughtlessness, can entirely erase the sense of it from the depths of the soul. The present generation of men—particularly in the circles of the cultured and the sophisticated, those who are often called "intellectuals" and who perhaps also think of themselves as constituting a special class, characterized by a particularly acute awareness of life—the present generation exhibits in marked degree a loss of faith and enthusiasm, which it is pleased to call "disillusionment," and which perhaps also is disillusionment. They think of themselves, these moderns, as beset with despair;[4] the values that formerly seemed to be unquestionable have somehow gone dead, and many of them find nothing by which they are enabled to see life as dignified and serious. By and large, this despair is an aesthetic despair, an imperfect despair, which has not yet reached the ethical, or grasped the boundless meaning of the moral realm in its truth. Morality is for them not an infinite spontaneity, an inner life, an emancipation and an ennoblement of the self; it is for them mainly a system of conventions and traditional rules, an arbitrary burden imposed from without by social forces that have been outlived; or it is a mere device for reaching finite ends, whose worth has become doubtful. In so far as this despair is an aesthetic despair, it is all to the good; for this is the road which the spirit of man must take in order to find itself. Let us but learn to perceive that no differential talent, no privileged status, no fortunate eventuality, can at bottom be worth while as a consummation; that all such things are quite incapable of dignifying life; and when the misunderstandings with respect to the nature of a moral consciousness have been cleared away, the road will be open to the discovery of man as man. A preoccupation with the secondary thoughts and interests of life is always exhausting and trivializing, and in the end bewildering. Our true refreshment and invigoration will come through going back to the first and simplest thoughts, the primary and indispensable interests. We have too long lost ourselves in anxious considerations of what it may mean to be a shoemaker or a philosopher, a poet or a millionaire; in order to find ourselves, it is needful that we concentrate our energies upon the infinitely significant problem of what it means simply to be a man, without any transiently qualifying adjectives. When Frederick the Great asked his Court preacher if he knew anything about the future life, the preacher answered, "Yes, Your Majesty, it is absolutely certain that in the future life Your Highness will not be king of Prussia." And so it is; we were men before we became whatever of relative value we became in life, and we shall doubtless be human beings long after what we thus became or acquired will have lost its significance for us. On the stage some actors have roles in which they are royal and important personages; others are simple folk, beggars, workingmen, and the like. But when the play is over and the curtain is rolled down, the actors cast aside their disguises, the differences vanish, and all are once more simply actors. So, when the play of life is over, and the curtain is rolled down upon the scene, the differences and relativities which have disguised the men and women who have taken part will vanish, and all will be simply human beings. But there is this difference between the actors of the stage and the actors of life. On the stage it is imperative that the illusion be maintained to the highest degree possible; an actor who plays the role of king as if he was an actor, or who too often reminds us that he is assuming a role, is precisely a poor actor. But on the stage of life, the reverse is the case. There it is the task, not to preserve, but to expose, the illusion; to win free from it while still retaining one's disguise. The disguising garment ought to flutter loosely about us, so loosely that the least wind of human feeling that blows may reveal the royal purple of humanity beneath. This revelation is the moral task; the moral consciousness is the consciousness of the dignity that invests human life when the personality has discovered itself, and is happy in the will to be itself.

Such is the view of life to which the present speaker is committed. He has sought to make it seem inviting, but not for a moment has he wished to deny that it sets a difficult task for him who would express it in the daily intercourse of life. Perhaps it has long since captured our imaginations; for it is no new gospel worked out to satisfy the imaginary requirements of the most recent fashions in human desire and feeling; on the contrary, it is an old, old view. But it is not enough that the truth of the significance inherent in having such a view of life should be grasped by the imagination, or by the elevated mood of a solemn hour; only the heart's profound movement, the will's decisive commitment,[5] can make that which is truth in general also a truth for me.

# NOTES

1. Suggested by Emerson's "So nigh is grandeur to our dust." *Voluntaries.*
2. S. Kierkegaard, *Postscript,* p. 124.
3. S. Kierkegaard, *The Gospel of Suffering,* pp. 174–177.
4. *Postscript,* pp. 327, 328.
5. *Postscript,* p. 226.

# CHAPTER 3

L O U I S  P.  P O J M A N

## Religion Gives Meaning to Life

If theism is true and there is a benevolent supreme being governing the universe, the following eight theses are true.

1. We have a satisfying explanation of the origins and sustenance of the universe. We are not the product of chance and necessity or an impersonal big bang, but of a Heavenly Being who cares about us. As William James says, if religion is true, "the universe is no longer a mere *It* to us, but a *Thou* . . . and any relation that may be possible from person to person might be possible here." We can take comfort in knowing that the visible world is part of a more spiritual universe from which it draws its meaning and that there is, in spite of evil, an essential harmonious relation between our world and the transcendent reality.

Here is the nub of the matter. Is the universe purposeful or merely a blind collocation of particles in motion? Science does not answer this question, though scientism, the secular naturalism, assumes that the world lacks a telos—it is blind matter in motion. However, theism tells us that all things have a purpose, that the universe was created at a point in time and that it will proceed in a lawlike manner to a prescribed end. Consider the naturalist view of the universe eloquently set forth in Bertrand Russell's classic essay "A Free Man's Worship":

> That man is the product of causes which had no prevision of the end they were achieving; that his origin, his growth, his hopes and fears, his loves and beliefs are but the outcome of accidental collocations of atoms; that no fire, no heroism, no intensity of thought and feeling, can preserve an individual life beyond the grave; that all the labors of the ages, all the devotion, all the inspiration, all the noonday brightness of human genius, are destined to extinction

This article first appeared in "Philosophy: The Quest for Truth" 1st ed. (Wadsworth Publishing Co., 1989), copyright © 2002 by Louis P. Pojman, reprinted by permission of family. Originally published under the pseudonym Lois Hope Walker.

in the vast death of the solar system, and that the whole temple of man's achievement must inevitably be buried beneath the debris of a universe in ruins—all these things, if not quite beyond dispute, are yet so nearly certain that no philosophy which rejects them can hope to stand. Only within the scaffolding of these truths, only on the firm foundation of unyielding despair, can the soul's habitation henceforth be safely built.

This is not the kind of "soul's habitation" that is worth building, let alone which can be safely built. Upon an unstable foundation, a secure edifice cannot be built, and from nothing you can only derive nothing. Our product is only as good as the material from which it is derived. From a valueless universe, objective values will not miraculously appear, nor can purpose derive from purposelessness. On the "firm foundation of unyielding despair" we can only build that which is desperate.

2. Theism holds that the universe is suffused in goodness and that good will win out over evil. We are not fighting a desperate battle alone, but God is on our side—or rather, it is possible to be on God's side in the struggle of good over evil. So you and I need not fight in vain. If the universe is meaningless, nothing will ultimately matter. Plato, Shakespeare, Mozart, Michelangelo, the Cathedral of Notre Dame, and the Sun itself will perish in oblivion. But if an Eternal Goodness exists, all will be well, all will be somehow remembered, nothing worthwhile will have been in vain.

The thought of the ultimate victory of goodness over evil, of justice over injustice, gives us confidence to carry on the fight against injustice, cruelty, and hatred, when others calculate that the odds against righteousness are too great to fight against.

3. God loves and cares for us. His love compels us, so that we have a deeper motive for morally good actions, including high altruism. We live deeply moral lives, not out of fear of hell, but out of deep gratitude to One who loves us and whom we love. We live not by impersonal rules but in relation with a Cosmic Lover, one who has our best interests in mind and is powerful enough to ensure that we are as happy as we are good.

Secularism lacks this sense of cosmic love, and it is, therefore, no accident that it fails to produce moral saints like Jesus, Maimonides, St. Francis, Father Damien, Teresa of Avila, Gandhi, Martin Luther King, Jr., and Mother Teresa. You need special love to leave a world of comfort in order to go to a desolate island to minister to lepers, as Father Damien did, or to lay down your life for another as Father Kolbe did when he took the place of a fellow prisoner in the Nazi death cell. Perhaps Ayn Rand is correct. From a secular point of view altruism is not only stupid, it is antilife, for it gives up the only thing we have, our little ego in an impersonal, indifferent world.

4. Theists have an answer to the question Why be moral? Why? Because of the love of God and because that love guarantees justice, so that you will

get what you deserve—good for good and bad for bad. The good really is good for you. Secular ethics has a severe problem with the question Why should I be moral when I can profit from wrongdoing (cheating, lying, stealing, harming another)? When I can advance myself by being an egoist, why should I obey moral rules? A hard question, to which I have never seen an entirely satisfactory secular answer. But the question is quickly satisfied by theism: a kind of karma—what you do to others will be visited upon you. If you do good, you will receive good. If you do evil, you will receive evil. Immorality is really imprudent and self-interest and altruism coincide. I don't have to worry about whether I reap exactly what I put into life's soil now, for I am confident that in the long term, I will reap as I have sown.

5. Cosmic Justice reigns in the universe. The scales are perfectly balanced so that everyone will get what he or she deserves, according to their moral merit. There is no moral luck (unless you interpret the grace which will finally prevail as a type of "luck"), but each will be judged according to how one has used one's talents (Matthew, chapter 25).

6. All persons are of equal worth. Since we have all been created in the image of God and are His children, we are all brothers and sisters. We are family and ought to treat each other benevolently as we would family members of equal worth. Indeed, modern secular moral and political systems often assume this equal worth of the individual without justifying it. But without the Parenthood of God it makes no sense to say that all persons are innately of equal value. From a perspective of intelligence and utility, Aristotle and Nietzsche are right, there are enormous inequalities, and why shouldn't the superior persons use the baser types to their advantage? In this regard, secularism, in rejecting inegalitarianism, seems to be living off of the interest of a religious capital which it has relinquished.

7. Grace and forgiveness—a happy ending for all. All's well that ends well (the divine comedy). The moral guilt which we experience, even for the most heinous acts, can be removed, and we can be redeemed and given a new start. This is true moral liberation.

8. There is life after death. Death is not the end of the matter, but we shall live on, recognizing each other in a better world. We have eternity in our souls and are destined for a higher existence.[1] So if Hebraic-Christian theism is true, the world is a friendly home in which we are all related as siblings in one family, destined to live forever in cosmic bliss in a reality in which good defeats evil.

If theism is false and secularism is true, then there is no obvious basis for human equality, no reason to treat all people with equal respect, no simple and clear answer to the question, Why be moral even when it is not in my best interest? no sense of harmony and purpose in the universe, but "Whirl has replaced Zeus and is King" (Sophocles).

Add to this the fact that theism doesn't deprive us of any autonomy that we have in nontheistic systems. We are equally free to choose the good or the evil whether or not God exists (assuming that the notions of good and evil make sense in a non-theistic universe)—then it seems clear that the world of the theist is far better and more satisfying to us than one in which God does not exist.

Of course, the problem is that we probably do not know if theism, let alone our particular religious version of it, is true. Here I must use a Pascalean argument to press my third point that we may have an obligation or, at least, it may be a good thing, to live *as if* theism is true. That is, unless you think that theism is so improbable that we should not even consider it as a candidate for truth, we should live in such a way as to allow the virtues of theism to inspire our lives and our culture. The theistic world view is so far superior to the secular that—even though we might be agnostics or weak atheists—it is in our interest to live as though it were true, to consider each person as a child of God, of high value, to work as though God is working with us in the battle of Good over evil, and to build a society based on these ideas. It is good then to gamble on God. Religion gives us a purpose to life and a basis for morality that is too valuable to dismiss lightly. It is a heritage that we may use to build a better civilization and one which we neglect at our own peril.

## NOTE

1. Of course, hell is a problem here—which vitiates the whole idea somewhat, but many variations of theism (e.g., varieties of theistic Hinduism and the Christian theologians Origen, F. Maurice, and Karl Barth) hold to universal salvation in the end. Hell is only a temporary school in moral education—I think that this is a plausible view.

CHAPTER 4　　　　　EMIL L. FACKENHEIM

# Judaism and the Meaning of Life

## I

Religions—which differ in much else—differ in substance according to their experience and understanding of the meeting between the Divine and the human: whether, when, and how it occurs, and what happens in and through it. In Judaism, the fundamental and all-penetrating occurrence is a primordial mystery, and a miracle of miracles: the Divine, though dwelling on high and infinitely above man, yet bends down low so as to accept and confirm man in his finite humanity; and man, though met by Divine Infinity, yet may and must respond to this meeting in and through his finitude. . . .

As a consequence of the miracle of miracles which lies at the core of Judaism, Jewish life and thought are marked by a fundamental tension. This tension might have been evaded in either of two ways. It might have been held—as ancient Epicureanism and modern Deism, for example, do in fact hold—that the Divine and the human are after all incapable of meeting. But this view is consistently rejected in Jewish tradition, which considers Epicureanism tantamount to atheism. Or, on the other side, it might have been held that the meeting is a mystical conflux, in which the finite dissolves into the Infinite and man suffers the loss of his very humanity. But this view, too, although a profound religious possibility and a serious challenge, is rejected in Jewish tradition. Such thinkers as Maimonides, Isaac Luria, and the Baal Shem-Tov all stop short—on occasion, to be sure, only barely—of embracing mysticism. And those who do not—such as Spinoza—pass beyond the bounds of Judaism. The Infinity of the Divine, the finitude of the human, and the meeting between them: these all remain, then, wherever Judaism preserves its substance; and the mystery and tension of this meeting permeate all else.

In the eyes of Judaism, whatever meaning life acquires derives from this encounter: the Divine accepts and confirms the human in the moment of meeting. But the meaning conferred upon human life by the Divine-human encounter cannot be understood in terms of some finite human purpose, supposedly more ultimate than the meeting itself. For what could be more ultimate than the Presence of God? The Presence of God, then, as Martin Buber puts it, is an *"inexpressible* confirmation of meaning. . . . The question of the meaning of life is no longer there. But were it there, it would not have to be answered."

## II

In Judaism, however, this *"inexpressible* confirmation of meaning" *does,* after all, assume expression; and this is because the Divine-human meeting assumes structure and content.

First, it is a universal human experience that times of Divine Presence do not last forever. But this experience does not everywhere have the same significance or even reality. Conceivably mythological religions—for which the world is "full of gods" (Thales)—may find divinity even in the most worldly preoccupation with the most finite ends: this is not possible if the Divine is an Infinity and radically other than all things finite. Mystical religions, for their part, may dismiss all such worldly preoccupations as mere appearance, and confine reality to the moment in which the human dissolves into the Divine: this is not possible if the moment of Divine-human encounter itself confirms man in his human finitude. In Judaism, man is real at every moment of his finite existence—including those moments when he is divorced from the Divine. The God of Judaism, while "near" at times, is—for whatever reason—"far" at other times. But times of Divine farness must also have meaning; for the far God remains an existing God, and nearness remains an ever-live possibility. These times of Divine farness, however, derive their meaning from times of Divine nearness. The dialectic between Divine nearness and Divine farness is all-pervasive in Jewish experience; and it points to an eschatological future in which it is overcome.

Secondly, the Divine-human meeting assumes structure and content in Judaism through the way man is accepted and confirmed as a consequence of this meeting. In Judaism God accepts and confirms man by *commanding* him in his humanity; and the response called for is *obedience* to God—an obedience to be expressed in finite human form. Here lies the ground for the Jewish rejection of the mystic surrender. Man *must* remain human because in commanding him *as* human, God accepts him in his humanity and makes him responsible in His very presence. In Judaism, Divine Grace is not superadded and subservient to Divine Commandment. Divine Grace already is, primordially, *in* the commandment; and were it not so, the commandment would be radically incapable of human performance. It is in the Divine Law itself that the Psalmist finds his delight, not only in a Divine action subsequent to observance of the Law; and if the Law saves him from perishing in his affliction, it is because Divine Love has handed it over to humans—not to angels—thereby making it in principle capable of human fulfillment.

Because the Divine acceptance of the human is a commanding acceptance, the inexpressible meaning of the Divine-human encounter assumes four interrelated expressions of which two are immediately contained within the commandment itself. First, there is a dimension of meaning in the very fact of being commanded as a human by the Divine: to be thus commanded is to be accepted as humanly responsible. And before long the undifferentiated commanding Presence will give utterance to many specific commandments, which particularize Divine acceptance and human responsibility according to the exigencies of a finite human existence on earth.

Secondly, if to be commanded by God is to be both obligated and enabled to obey, then meaning must be capable of human realization, and this meaning must be real even in the sight of Divinity. The fear induced in the finite human by the Infinite Divine Presence may seem to destroy any such presumption. Yet the acceptance of the human by the commanding Love makes possible, and indeed mandatory, human self-acceptance.

A third aspect of meaning comes into view because the Divine commandment initiates a relation of *mutuality* between God and man. The God of Judaism is no Deistic First Cause which, having caused the world, goes into perpetual retirement. Neither is He a Law-giver who, having given laws, leaves man to respond in human solitariness. Along with the commandment, handed over for human action, goes the promise of *Divine* action. And because Divine action makes itself contingent upon human action, a relationship of mutuality is established. God gives to man a *covenant*—that is, a contract; He binds Himself by its terms and becomes a partner.

The meaning of the Divine-human encounter, however, has yet a fourth expression; and if this had not gradually emerged, the Jewish faith could hardly have survived through the centuries. Because a pristine Divine Love accepted the human, a relation of mutuality between an Infinite Divinity and a finite humanity—something that would seem to be impossible—nevertheless became possible. Yet that relation remains destructible at finite hands; indeed, were it *simply* mutual, it would be destroyed by man almost the moment it was established. Even in earlier forms of Jewish faith God is long-suffering enough to put up with persistent human failures; and at length it becomes clear that the covenant can survive only if God's patience is absolute. The covenant, to be sure, *remains* mutual; and Divine action remains part of this mutuality, as a response to human deeds. But Divine action also breaks through this limitation and maintains the covenant in *unilateral* love. The human race after Noah, and Israel at least since the time of Jeremiah, still can—and do—rebel against their respective covenants with God. But they can no longer destroy them. Sin still causes God to punish Israel; but no conceivable sin on Israel's part can cause Him to forsake her. Divine Love has made the covenant indestructible.

In Judaism, covenantal existence becomes a continuous, uninterrupted way of life. A Divine-human relation unstructured by commandment would alternate between times of inexpressible meaning and times of sheer waiting for such meaning. A relationship so structured by commandment, yet failing to encompass both Divine nearness and farness, could not extend its scope over the whole of human life. For if it were confined to times of Divine nearness, covenantal existence would be shattered into as many fragments as there are moments of Divine nearness, with empty spaces between them. If, on the other hand, it were confined to Divine farness, it would degenerate, on the Divine side, into an external law sanctioned by an absent God and, on the human side, into legalistic exercises practiced in His absence. But as understood and lived in Judaism, covenantal existence persists in times of Divine farness. The commandment is still present, as is the Divine promise, however obscured for the moment. The human power to perform the commandment, while impaired, is not destroyed; and he who cannot perform the commandment for the sake of God, as he is supposed to do, is bidden to perform it anyway—for performance which is not for His sake will lead to performance which *is* for His sake. Times of Divine nearness, then, do not light up themselves alone. Their meaning extends over all of life.

CHAPTER 5          PHILIP L. QUINN

# The Meaning of Life
# According to Christianity

In the heyday of logical positivism, philosophical discussion of the meaning of life fell under a cloud of suspicion. When I was younger, more than once I heard the reason for suspicion put this way. The bearers of meaning are linguistic entities such as texts or utterances. But a human life is not a linguistic entity. Hence attributing meaning to a human life involves a category mistake. To ask what a human life means is therefore to ask a pseudoquestion.

In our own postpositivistic and postmodern era, this argument is apt to seem too quick and dirty to produce conviction. It is possible to define with tolerable clarity and precision several concepts of the meaning a human life might possess. Two such definitions are of particular importance in the discussion of religious views of the meaning of life. . . . They are as follows:

> (AM)  A human life has positive axiological meaning if and only if (i) it has positive intrinsic value, and (ii) it is on the whole good for the person who leads it; and
>
> (TM)  A human life has positive teleological meaning if and only if (i) it contains some purposes the person who lives it takes to be nontrivial and achievable, (ii) these purposes have positive value, and (iii) it also contains actions that are directed toward achieving these purposes and are performed with zest.

Though I do not know how to prove it, I think the axiological and the teleological are logically independent kinds of meaning, and so I hold that a human life can have more than one sort of meaning. To me it seems possible

From "How Christianity Secures Life's Meaning," in the *Proceedings of the 1997 Chapman University Conference on The Meaning of Life in the World Religions,* edited by Joseph Runzo and Nancy M. Martin. This essay is a lightly revised version of the third section of that paper.

that a premortem human life should have positive axiological meaning and lack positive teleological meaning and possible that a premortem human life should lack positive axiological meaning and have positive teleological meaning; it also seems possible that a human life should lack both sorts of meaning and possible that a human life should have both sorts of meaning. To explicate the last of these possibilities, I propose the following definition:

> (CM)   A human life has positive complete meaning if and only if it has both positive axiological meaning and positive teleological meaning.

In this essay, I propose to discuss some Christian views of the meaning of life in these three senses.

What is more, though a human life is not itself a text or an utterance, the events of which it is composed can be narrated, and narratives of human lives are meaningful linguistic entities. The history of the human race is also at least the potential subject of a meaningful linguistic metanarrative. Of course, not all narratives of human lives exhibit them as having positive meaning in any of the senses previously defined. A narrative might, for example, portray a human life in terms of "a tale, told by an idiot, full of sound and fury, signifying nothing."[1] Or a narrative might depict a human life as lacking positive meaning of the three kinds previously enumerated. Nevertheless, some narratives do present human lives that have these three kinds of meanings. Because Christianity is a religion in which history is important, narratives loom large in its traditions. The gospel stories of the life of Jesus are, for instance, narratives of a human life that has special significance for Christians.

Adopting a suggestion recently made by Nicholas Wolterstorff, I think the gospel narratives "are best understood as *portraits* of Jesus, designed to reveal who he really was and what was really happening in his life, death and resurrection."[2] And like the part of Simon Schama's recent *Dead Certainties* about the death of General James Wolfe on the plains of Abraham, what they assert at some points is "not that things *did go* thus and so but that, whether or not they did, they *might well have gone* thus and so."[3] The importance of the portrait of Jesus thus narrated for his Christian followers is that it furnishes them with a paradigm to which the narratives of their own lives should be made to conform as closely as circumstances permit. The idea that the lives of Christians should imitate the life of Jesus is, of course, a familiar theme in Christian spirituality; it is developed with particular cogency in Thomas à Kempis's *The Imitation of Christ*. Søren Kierkegaard discusses it in terms of a striking contrast between admiring Christ and imitating Christ in his *Practice in Christianity*.

According to Anti-Climacus, the pseudonymous author of *Practice*, "Christ's life here on earth is the paradigm; I and every Christian are to strive to model our lives in likeness to it."[4] The demand is stringent because the likeness is to be as close as possible. "To be an imitator," he tells us, "means that your life has as much similarity to his as is possible for a human life to have."[5] The Christ who is to be imitated is not the glorious Christ of the second coming but is instead the crucified Christ of human history. Hence the imitator of Christ must come to terms with Christ in his lowliness and abasement.

One thing this means is being prepared to suffer as Christ suffered. Anti-Climacus says that Christ freely willed to be the lowly one because he "wanted to express what *the truth* would have to suffer and what the truth must suffer in every generation."[6] Imitators of Christ must therefore be willing to endure suffering akin to his suffering. Anti-Climacus explains what this involves: "To suffer in a way akin to Christ's suffering is not to put up patiently with the inescapable, but it is to suffer evil at the hands of people because as a Christian or in being a Christian one wills and endeavors to do the good: thus one could avoid this suffering by giving up willing the good."[7] Since the Christian is not supposed to give up willing the good, however, he or she must willingly suffer evil precisely because of the endeavor to do the good.

Coming to terms with Christ in his lowliness and abasement also means being "halted by the possibility of offense."[8] Anti-Climacus wittily describes how respectable people of various sorts might have been offended if they had been Christ's contemporaries. A sagacious and sensible person might have said: "What has he done about his future? Nothing. Does he have a permanent job? No. What are his prospects? None."[9] A clergyman might have denounced him as "an impostor and demagogue."[10] A philosopher might have criticized him for lacking a system and having only "a few aphorisms, some maxims, and a couple of parables, which he goes on repeating or revising, whereby he blinds the masses."[11] And others might have scoffed at him and reviled him in other ways. Yet Anti-Climacus insists that no one can arrive at mature Christian faith without first confronting the possibility of offense. He says that "from the possibility of offense, one turns either to offense or to faith, but one never comes to faith except from the possibility of offense."[12] Thus imitators of Christ can also count on being found offensive by those who have chosen to turn to offense rather than to faith.

Imitators of Christ should, therefore, anticipate suffering evils for trying to do good and expect to be found offensive. To join Christ as a follower, it is necessary to have a realistic awareness of the conditions on which discipleship is offered. According to Anti-Climacus, they are "to become just as poor, despised, insulted, mocked, and if possible even a little more, considering that in addition one was an adherent of such a despised individual, whom every sensible person shunned."[13] If any imitators of Christ are not subject to such treatment, it must be the result of good fortune they cannot count on or expect. No mere admirer would want to join Christ on these conditions.

What is the difference between an imitator and a mere admirer? "An imitator *is* or strives *to be* what he admires," Anti-Climacus says, "and an admirer keeps himself personally detached, consciously or unconsciously does not discover that what is admired involves a claim upon him, to be or at least to strive to be what is admired."[14] The difference is to be seen most clearly in their contrasting responses to the stringent practical demands of discipleship. The mere admirer is only willing to pay them lip-service. According to Anti-Climacus, "the admirer will make no sacrifices, renounce nothing, give up nothing earthly, will not transform his life, will not be what is admired, will not let his life express it—but in words, phrases, assurances he is inexhaustible about how highly he prizes Christianity."[15] Unlike the mere admirer, the imitator, who also acknowledges in words the truth of Christianity, acts decisively to obey "Christian teaching about ethics and obligation, Christianity's requirement to die to the world, to surrender the earthly, its requirement of self-denial."[16] And, Anti-Climacus adds wryly, mere admirers are sure to become exasperated with a genuine imitator.

Not all Christians will accept this radical Kierkegaardian view of the demands of discipleship. There is, however, a lesson to be learned about the meanings of a distinctively Christian life if we take it to approximate the most demanding interpretation of what is involved in the call to Christians to conform the narratives of their lives to the portrait of Jesus embedded in the gospel narratives. There seems to be no difficulty in supposing that the life of a successful Kierkegaardian imitator of Christ, devoted to willing and endeavoring to do the good, will have positive teleological meaning, despite the suffering it is likely to contain. But there is a problem in supposing that every such life will also have positive axiological meaning if it terminates in bodily death, because some of these lives appear not to be good on the whole for those who lead them. But, of course, the earthly life of Jesus, which ended in horrible suffering and ignominious death, gives rise to the very same problem. It is part of traditional Christian faith, however, that the life of Jesus did not terminate in bodily death but continued after his resurrection and will continue until he comes again in glory; hence it is on the whole a good life for him. Like the life of Jesus himself, the lives of at least some successful Kierkegaardian imitators of Christ will on the whole be good for them only if they extend beyond death into an afterlife of some sort. Hence survival of bodily death seems required to secure positive axiological meaning and thus positive complete meaning for the lives of all those whose narratives conform as closely as is humanly possible, as Kierkegaard understands what is involved in such conformity, to the paradigm or prototype presented in the gospel narratives of the life of Jesus.

Christianity also tells a tale of the destiny of the human race through the cosmic metanarrative of salvation history. It begins with the creation of humans in God's image and likeness. The Incarnation, in which God the Son becomes fully human and redeems sinful humanity, is a crucial episode. It will culminate with the promised coming of the Kingdom of God. Christians have been divided over some questions about the details of salvation history. Will all humans ultimately be saved? If some will not, did God predestine them to reprobation? But the broad outlines of the story make manifest God's loving concern for humanity and the providential care in which it is expressed. The story's emphasis on what God has done for humans also makes it clear that they are important from a God's eye point of view.

The narrative of salvation history reveals some of God's purposes both for individual humans and for humanity as a whole. Christians are expected to align themselves with these purposes and to act to further them to the extent that their circumstances permit. Such purposes can thus be among those that give positive teleological meaning and thereby contribute to giving positive complete meaning to a Christian's life. We may safely assume that every Christian and, indeed, every human being has a meaningful role to play in the great drama of salvation history if Christianity's view of its shape is even approximately correct.

But what are we to say about those who refuse to align themselves with God's purposes? Mark 14:21 quotes Jesus as saying, "For the Son of Man goes as it is written of him, but woe to that one by whom the Son of Man is betrayed! It would have been better for that one not to have been born." If it would have been better for Judas not to have been born, then his life is not on the whole good for him and so lacks positive axiological meaning. This will be true of Judas on the traditional assumption that he dies fixed in his rejection of God's purposes and so suffers everlastingly in hell. On the universalist assumption, however, even Judas will eventually turn to God, align himself with God's purposes, and be saved. Were this to happen, even the life of Judas would ultimately have both positive axiological meaning and positive teleological meaning. In that case, it would not be true that it would be better for Judas not to have been born.

In a stimulating discussion of the meaning of life, Thomas Nagel argues that from a detached, objective point of view human lives lack importance or significance. He says: "When you look at your struggles as if from a great height, in abstraction from the engagement you have with this life because it is yours—perhaps even in abstraction from your identification with the human race—you may feel a certain sympathy for the poor beggar, a pale pleasure in his triumphs and a mild concern for his disappointments."[17] But, he continues, "it wouldn't matter all that much if he failed, and it would matter perhaps even less if he didn't exist at all."[18] Christians would do well, I think, to resist the seductions of this picture of the objective standpoint. For them, the objective standpoint is the point of view of an omniscient and perfectly good God. Their faith informs them humanity is so important to such a God that he freely chose to become incarnate and to suffer and die for its sake.

The snare Christians need to avoid is assuming that humanity is the most important thing or the only important thing from a God's eye point of view. Such assumptions would bespeak a prideful cosmic anthropocentrism. Nagel claims that "the most general effect of the objective stance ought to be a form of humility: the recognition that you are no more important than you are, and that the fact that something is of importance to you, or that it would be good or bad if you did or suffered something, is a fact of purely local significance."[19] Christians have reasons to believe that facts of the sorts Nagel mentions are of more than purely local significance, but they should have the humility to recognize that such facts may well have less cosmic significance than other facts of which God is aware. Within a balanced Christian perspective, in other words, facts about what it is good or bad for humans to do or suffer have some cosmic importance because God cares about them, but Christians would be unwarranted if they supposed that God cares more about such facts than about anything else that transpires in the created cosmos. Human lives and human life generally are objectively important. Their importance should, however, not be exaggerated.

Nor should Christians exaggerate the certainty about life's meanings to be derived from their narratives. The gospel narratives permit, and historically have received, diverse and often conflicting interpretations. When reasonable interpretations clash, confidence in the exclusive rightness of any one of them should diminish. What is more, other religions have reasonable stories to tell about life's meanings, as do some nonreligious worldviews. Confronted with the twin challenges of reasonable intra-Christian pluralism and reasonable interreligious pluralism, Christians ought to adopt an attitude of epistemic modesty when making claims about life's meanings. They can be, I think, entitled to believe that Christian narratives provide the best story we have about life's meanings. But claims to furnish the complete story should, I believe, be advanced only with fear and trembling. When Christianity secures life's meanings, it should not offer Christians so much security that they acquire the arrogant tendency to set their story apart from and above all other sources of insight into life's meanings.[20]

## NOTES

1. William Shakespeare, *Macbeth* V. v. 26–28.

2. Nicholas Wolterstorff, *Divine Discourse* (Cambridge: Cambridge University Press, 1995), p. 259.

3. Ibid., p. 257.

4. Søren Kierkegaard, *Practice in Christianity,* ed. trans. Howard V. Hong and Edna H. Hong (Princeton: Princeton University Press, 1991), p. 107.

5. Ibid., p. 106.

6. Ibid., pp. 34–35.

7. Ibid., p. 173.

8. Ibid., p. 39.

9. Ibid., p. 43.

10. Ibid., p. 46.

11. Ibid., p. 48.

12. Ibid., p. 81.

13. Ibid., p. 241.

14. Ibid.

15. Ibid., p. 252.

16. Ibid.

17. Thomas Nagel, *The View from Nowhere* (New York and Oxford: Oxford University Press, 1986), p. 216.

18. Ibid., p. 216.

19. Ibid., p. 222.

20. I am grateful to Bill Wainwright and Kate McCarthy for helpful comments on the material in this essay.

PART TWO     # The Nontheistic
Alternative

# CHAPTER 6

# ARTHUR SCHOPENHAUER

## *On the Sufferings of the World*

Unless *suffering* is the direct and immediate object of life, our existence must entirely fail of its aim. It is absurd to look upon the enormous amount of pain that abounds everywhere in the world, and originates in needs and necessities inseparable from life itself, as serving no purpose at all and the result of mere chance. Each separate misfortune, as it comes, seems, no doubt, to be something exceptional; but misfortune in general is the rule.

I know of no greater absurdity than that propounded by most systems of philosophy in declaring evil to be negative in its character. Evil is just what is positive; it makes its own existence felt. Leibnitz is particularly concerned to defend this absurdity; and he seeks to strengthen his position by using a palpable and paltry sophism. It is the good which is negative; in other words, happiness and satisfaction always imply some desire fulfilled, some state of pain brought to an end.

This explains the fact that we generally find pleasure to be not nearly so pleasant as we expected, and pain very much more painful.

The pleasure in this world, it has been said, outweighs the pain; or, at any rate, there is an even balance between the two. If the reader wishes to see shortly whether this statement is true, let him compare the respective feelings of two animals, one of which is engaged in eating the other.

The best consolation in misfortune or affliction of any kind will be the thought of other people who are in a still worse plight than yourself; and this is a form of consolation open to every one. But what an awful fate this means for mankind as a whole!

We are like lambs in a field, disporting themselves under the eye of the butcher, who chooses out first one and then another for his prey. So it is that in our good days we are all unconscious of the evil Fate may have presently in store for us—sickness, poverty, mutilation, loss of sight or reason.

From *Parerga and Paralipomena* (1851), translated by T. Bailey Saunders.

No little part of the torment of existence lies in this, that Time is continually pressing upon us, never letting us take breath, but always coming after us, like a taskmaster with a whip. If at any moment Time stays his hand, it is only when we are delivered over to the misery of boredom.

But misfortune has its uses; for, as our bodily frame would burst asunder if the pressure of the atmosphere was removed, so, if the lives of men were relieved of all need, hardship and adversity; if everything they took in hand were successful, they would be so swollen with arrogance that, though they might not burst, they would present the spectacle of unbridled folly—nay, they would go mad. And I may say, further, that a certain amount of care or pain or trouble is necessary for every man at all times. A ship without ballast is unstable and will not go straight.

Certain it is that *work, worry, labor* and *trouble*, form the lot of almost all men their whole life long. But if all wishes were fulfilled as soon as they arose, how would men occupy their lives? what would they do with their time? If the world were a paradise of luxury and ease, a land flowing with milk and honey, where every Jack obtained his Jill at once and without any difficulty, men would either die of boredom or hang themselves; or there would be wars, massacres, and murders; so that in the end mankind would inflict more suffering on itself than it has now to accept at the hands of Nature.

In early youth, as we contemplate our coming life, we are like children in a theatre before the curtain is raised, sitting there in high spirits and eagerly waiting for the play to begin. It is a blessing that we do not know what is really going to happen. Could we foresee it, there are times when children might seem like innocent prisoners, condemned, not to death, but to life, and as yet all unconscious of what their sentence means. Nevertheless, every man desires to reach old age; in other words, a state of life of which it may be said: "It is bad to-day, and it will be worse to-morrow; and so on till the worst of all."

If you try to imagine, as nearly as you can, what an amount of misery, pain and suffering of every kind the sun shines upon in its course, you will admit that it would be much better if, on the earth as little as on the moon, the sun were able to call forth the phenomena of life; and if, here as there, the surface were still in a crystalline state.

Again, you may look upon life as an unprofitable episode, disturbing the blessed calm of non-existence. And, in any case, even though things have gone with you tolerably well, the longer you live the more clearly you will feel that, on the whole, life is *a disappointment, nay, a cheat.*

If two men who were friends in their youth meet again when they are old, after being separated for a lifetime, the chief feeling they will have at the sight of each other will be one of complete disappointment at life as a whole; because their thoughts will be carried back to that earlier time when life seemed so fair as it lay spread out before them in the rosy light of dawn, promised so much—and then performed so little. This feeling will so completely predominate over every other that they will not even consider it necessary to give it words; but on either side it will be silently assumed, and form the groundwork of all they have to talk about.

He who lives to see two or three generations is like a man who sits some time in the conjurer's booth at a fair, and witnesses the performance twice or thrice in succession. The tricks were meant to be seen only once; and when they are no longer a novelty and cease to deceive, their effect is gone.

While no man is much to be envied for his lot, there are countless numbers whose fate is to be deplored.

Life is a task to be done. It is a fine thing to say *defunctus est;* it means that the man has done his task.

If children were brought into the world by an act of pure reason alone, would the human race continue to exist? Would not a man rather have so much sympathy with the coming generation as to spare it the burden of existence? or at any rate not take it upon himself to impose that burden upon it in cold blood.

I shall be told, I suppose, that my philosophy is comfortless—because I speak the truth; and people prefer to be assured that everything the Lord has made is good. Go to the priests, then, and leave philosophers in peace! At any rate, do not ask us to accommodate our doctrines to the lessons you have been taught. That is what those rascals of sham philosophers will do for you. Ask them for any doctrine you please, and you will get it. Your University professors are bound to preach optimism; and it is an easy and agreeable task to upset their theories.

I have reminded the reader that every state of welfare, every feeling of satisfaction, is negative in its character; that is to say, it consists in freedom from pain, which is the positive element of existence. It follows, therefore, that the happiness of any given life is to be measured, not by its joys and pleasures, but by the extent to which it has been free from suffering—from positive evil. If this is the true standpoint, the lower animals appear to enjoy a happier destiny than man. Let us examine the matter a little more closely.

However varied the forms that human happiness and misery may take, leading a man to seek the one and shun the other, the material basis of it all is bodily pleasure or bodily pain. This basis is very restricted: it is simply health, food, protection from wet and cold, the satisfaction of the sexual instinct; or else the absence of these things. Consequently, as far as real physical pleasure is concerned, the man is not better off than the brute, except in so far as the higher possibilities of his nervous system make him more sensitive to every kind of pleasure, but also, it must be remembered, to every kind of pain. But then compared with the brute, how much stronger are the passions aroused in him! what an immeasurable difference there is in the depth and vehemence of his emotions!—and yet, in the one case, as in the other, all to produce the same result in the end: namely, health, food, clothing, and so on.

The chief source of all this passion is that thought for what is absent and future, which, with man, exercises such a powerful influence upon all he does. It is this that is the real origin of his cares, his hopes, his fears—emotions which affect him much more deeply than could ever be the case with those present joys and sufferings to which the brute is confined. In his powers of reflection, memory and foresight, man possesses, as it were, a machine for condensing and storing up his pleasures and his sorrows. But the brute has nothing of the kind; whenever it is in pain, it is as though it were suffering for the first time, even though the same thing should have previously happened to it times out of number. It has no power of summing up its feelings. Hence its careless and placid temper: how much it is to be envied! But in man reflection comes in, with all the emotions to which it gives rise; and taking up the same elements of pleasure and pain which are common to him and the brute, it develops his susceptibility to happiness and misery to such a degree that, at one moment the man is brought in an instant to a state of delight that may even prove fatal, at another to the depths of despair and suicide.

If we carry our analysis a step farther, we shall find that, in order to increase his pleasures, man has intentionally added to the number and pressure of his needs, which in their original state were not much more difficult to satisfy than those of the brute. Hence luxury in all its forms; delicate food, the use of tobacco and opium, spirituous liquors, fine clothes, and the thousand and one things that he considers necessary to his existence.

And above and beyond all this, there is a separate and peculiar source of pleasure, and consequently of pain, which man has established for himself, also as the result of using his powers of reflection; and this occupies him out of all proportion to its value, nay, almost more than all his other interests put together—I mean ambition and the feeling of honor and shame; in plain words, what he thinks about the opinion other people have of him. Taking a thousand forms, often very strange ones, this becomes the goal of almost all the efforts he makes that are not rooted in physical pleasure or pain. It is true that besides the sources of pleasure which he has in common with the brute, man has the pleasures of the mind as well. These admit of many gradations, from the most innocent trifling or the merest talk up to the highest intellectual achievements; but there is the accompanying boredom to be set against them on the side of suffering. Boredom is a form of suffering unknown to brutes, at any rate in their natural state; it is only the very cleverest of them who show faint traces of it when they are domesticated; whereas in the case of man it has become a downright scourge. The crowd of miserable wretches whose one aim in life is to fill their purses but never to put anything into their heads, offers a singular instance of this torment of boredom. Their wealth becomes a punishment by delivering them up to misery of having nothing to do; for, to escape it, they will rush about in all directions, traveling here, there and everywhere. No sooner do they arrive in a place than they are anxious to know what amusements it affords; just as though they were beggars asking where they could receive a dole! Of a truth, need and boredom are the two poles of human life. Finally, I may mention that as regards the sexual relation, a man is committed to a peculiar arrangement which drives him obstinately to choose one person. This feeling grows, now and then, into a more or less passionate love,[1] which is the source of little pleasure and much suffering.

It is, however, a wonderful thing that the mere addition of thought should serve to raise such a vast and lofty structure of human happiness and misery; resting, too, on the same narrow basis of joy and sorrow as man holds in common with the brute, and exposing him to such violent emotions, to so many storms of passion, so much convulsion of feeling, that what he has suffered stands written and may be read in the lines on his face. And yet, when all is told, he has been struggling ultimately for the very same things as the brute has attained, and with an incomparably smaller expenditure of passion and pain.

But all this contributes to increase the measures of suffering in human life out of all proportion to its pleasures; and the pains of life are made much worse for man by the fact that death is something very real to him. The brute flies from death instinctively without really knowing what it is, and therefore without ever contemplating it in the way natural to a man, who has this prospect always before his eyes. So that even if only a few brutes die a natural death, and most of them live only just long enough to transmit their species, and then, if not earlier, become the prey of some other animal,— whilst man, on the other hand, manages to make so-called natural death the rule, to which, however, there are a good many exceptions,—the advantage is on the side of the brute, for the reason stated above. But the fact is that man attains the natural term of years just as seldom as the brute; because the unnatural way in which he lives, and the strain of work and emotion, lead to a degeneration of the race; and so his goal is not often reached.

The brute is much more content with mere existence than man; the plant is wholly so; and man finds satisfaction in it just in proportion as he is dull and obtuse. Accordingly, the life of the brute carries less of sorrow with it, but also less of joy, when compared with the life of man; and while this may be traced, on the one side, to freedom from the torment of *care* and *anxiety*, it is also due to the fact that *hope*, in any real sense, is unknown to the brute. It is thus deprived of any share in that which gives us the most and best of our joys and pleasures, the mental anticipation of a happy future, and the inspiriting play of phantasy, both of which we owe to our power of imagination. If the brute is free from care, it is also, in this sense, without hope; in either case, because its consciousness is limited to the present moment, to what it can actually see before it. The brute is an embodiment of present impulses, and hence what elements of fear and hope exist in its nature—and they do not go very far—arise only in relation to objects that lie before it and within reach of those impulses: whereas a man's range of vision embraces the whole of his life, and extends far into the past and future.

Following upon this, there is one respect in which brutes show real wisdom when compared with us—I mean, their quiet, placid enjoyment of the present moment. The tranquillity of mind which this seems to give them often puts us to shame for the many times we allow our thoughts and our cares to make us restless and discontented. And, in fact, those pleasures of hope and anticipation which I have been mentioning are not to be had for nothing. The delight which a man has in hoping for and looking forward to some special satisfaction is a part of the real pleasure attaching to it enjoyed in advance. This is afterwards deducted; for the more we look forward to anything, the less satisfaction we find in it when it comes. But the brute's enjoyment is not anticipated, and therefore, suffers no deduction; so that the actual pleasure of the moment comes to it whole and unimpaired. In the same way, too, evil presses upon the brute only with its own intrinsic weight; whereas with us the fear of its coming often makes its burden ten times more grievous.

It is just this characteristic way in which the brute gives itself up entirely to the present moment that contributes so much to the delight we take in our domestic pets. They are the present moment personified, and in some respects they make us feel the value of every hour that is free from trouble and annoyance, which we, with our thoughts and preoccupations, mostly disregard. But man, that selfish and heartless creature, misuses this quality of the brute to be more content than we are with mere existence, and often works it to such an extent that he allows the brute absolutely nothing more than mere, bare life. The bird which was made so that it might rove over half of the world, he shuts up into the space of a cubic foot, there to die a slow death in longing and crying for freedom; for in a cage it does not sing for the pleasure of it. And when I see how man misuses the dog, his best friend; how he ties up this intelligent animal with a chain, I feel the deepest sympathy with the brute and burning indignation against its master.

We shall see later that by taking a very high standpoint it is possible to justify the sufferings of mankind. But this justification cannot apply to animals, whose sufferings, while in a great measure brought about by men, are often considerable even apart from their agency. And so we are forced to ask, Why and for what purpose does all this torment and agony exist? There is nothing here to give the will pause; it is not free to deny itself and so obtain redemption. There is only one consideration that may serve to explain the sufferings of animals. It is this: that the will to live, which underlies the whole world of phenomena, must, in their case satisfy its cravings by feeding upon itself. This it does by forming a gradation of phenomena, every one of which exists at the expense of another. I have shown, however, that the capacity for suffering is less in animals than in man. Any further explanation that may be given of their fate will be in the nature of hypothesis, if not actually mythical in its character; and I may leave the reader to speculate upon the matter for himself.

*Brahma* is said to have produced the world by a kind of fall or mistake; and in order to atone for his folly, he is bound to remain in it himself until he works out his redemption. As an account of the origin of things, that is admirable! According to the doctrines of *Buddhism*, the world came into being as the result of some inexplicable disturbance in the heavenly calm of Nirvana, that blessed state obtained by expiation, which had endured so long a time—the change taking place by a kind of fatality. This explanation must be understood as having at bottom some moral bearing; although it is illustrated by an exactly parallel theory in the domain of physical science, which places the origin of the sun in a primitive streak of mist, formed one knows not how. Subsequently, by a series of moral errors, the world became gradually worse and worse—true of the physical orders as well—until it assumed the dismal aspect it wears to-day. Excellent! The *Greeks* looked upon the world and the gods as the work of an inscrutable necessity. A passable explanation: we may be content with it until we can get a better. Again, *Ormuzd* and *Ahriman* are rival powers, continually at war. That is not bad. But that a God like Jehovah should have created this world of misery and woe, out of pure caprice, and because he enjoyed doing it, and should then have clapped his hands in praise of his own work, and declared everything to be very good—that will not do at all! In its explanation of the origin of the world, Judaism is inferior to any other form of religious doctrine professed by a civilized nation; and it is quite in keeping with this that it is the only one which presents no trace whatever of any belief in the immortality of the soul.

Even though Leibnitz' contention, that this is the best of all possible worlds, were correct, that would not justify God in having created it. For he is the Creator not of the world only, but of possibility itself; and, therefore, he ought to have so ordered possibility as that it would admit of something better.

There are two things which make it impossible to believe that this world is the successful work of an all-wise, all-good, and, at the same time, all-powerful Being; firstly, the misery which abounds in it everywhere; and secondly, the obvious imperfection of its highest product, man, who is a burlesque of what he should be. These things cannot be reconciled with any such belief. On the contrary, they are just the facts which support what I have been saying; they are our authority for viewing the world as the outcome of our own misdeeds, and therefore, as something that had better not have been. Whilst, under the former hypothesis, they amount to a bitter accusation against the Creator, and supply material for sarcasm; under the latter they form an indictment against our own nature, our own will, and teach us a lesson of humility. They lead us to see that, like the children of a libertine, we come into the world with the burden of sin upon us; and that it is only through having continually to atone for this sin that our existence is so miserable, and that its end is death.

There is nothing more certain than the general truth that it is the grievous *sin of the world* which has produced the grievous *suffering of the world*. I am not referring here to the physical connection between these two things lying in the realm of experience; my meaning is metaphysical. Accordingly, the sole thing that reconciles me to the Old Testament is the story of the Fall. In my eyes, it is the only metaphysical truth in that book, even though it appears in the form of an allegory. There seems to me no better explanation of our existence than that it is the result of some false step, some sin of which we are paying the penalty. I cannot refrain from recommending the thoughtful reader a popular, but at the same time, profound treatise on this subject by Claudius which exhibits the essentially pessimistic spirit of Christianity. It is entitled: *Cursed is the ground for thy sake.*

Between the ethics of the Greeks and the ethics of the Hindus, there is a glaring contrast. In the one case (with the exception, it must be confessed, of Plato), the object of ethics is to enable a man to lead a happy life; in the other, it is to free and redeem him from life altogether—as is directly stated in the very first words of the *Sankhya Karika*.

Allied with this is the contrast between the Greek and the Christian idea of death. It is strikingly presented in a visible form on a fine antique sarcophagus in the gallery of Florence, which exhibits, in relief, the whole series of ceremonies attending a wedding in ancient times, from the formal offer to the evening when Hymen's torch lights the happy couple home. Compare with that the Christian coffin, draped in mournful black and surmounted with a crucifix! How much significance there is in these two ways of finding comfort in death. They are opposed to each other, but each is right. The one points to the *affirmation* of the will to live, which remains sure of life for all time, however rapidly its forms may change. The other, in the symbol of suffering and death, points to the *denial* of the will to live, to redemption from this world, the domain of death and devil. And in the question between the affirmation and the denial of the will to live, Christianity is in the last resort right.

The contrast which the New Testament presents when compared with the Old, according to the ecclesiastical view of the matter, is just that existing between my ethical system and the moral philosophy of Europe. The Old Testament represents man as under the dominion of Law, in which, however, there is no redemption. The New Testament declares Law to have failed, frees man from its dominion,[2] and in its stead preaches the kingdom of grace, to be won by faith, love of neighbor and entire sacrifice of self. This is the path of redemption from the evil of the world. The spirit of the New Testament is undoubtedly asceticism, however your protestants and rationalists may twist it to suit their purpose. Asceticism is the denial of the will to live; and the transition from the Old Testament to the New, from the dominion of Law to that of Faith, from justification by works to redemption through the Mediator, from the domain of sin and death to eternal life in Christ, means, when taken in its real sense, the transition from the merely moral virtues to the denial of the will to live. My philosophy shows the metaphysical foundation of justice and the love of mankind, and points to the goal to which these virtues necessarily lead, if they are practised in perfection. At the same time it is candid in confessing that a man must turn his back upon the world, and that the denial of the will to live is the way of redemption. It is therefore really at one with the spirit of the New Testament, whilst all other systems are couched in the spirit of the Old; that is to say, theoretically as well as practically, their result is Judaism—mere despotic theism. In this sense, then, my doctrine might be called the only true Christian philosophy—however paradoxical a statement this may seem to people who take superficial views instead of penetrating to the heart of the matter.

If you want a safe compass to guide you through life, and to banish all doubt as to the right way of looking at it, you cannot do better than accustom yourself to regard this world as a penitentiary, a sort of a penal colony. Amongst the Christian Fathers, Origen, with praiseworthy courage, took this view,[3] which is further justified by certain objective theories of life. I refer, not to my own philosophy alone, but to the wisdom of all ages, as expressed in

Brahmanism and Buddhism, and in the sayings of Greek philosophers like Empedocles and Pythagoras; as also by Cicero, in his remark that the wise men of old used to teach that we come into this world to pay the penalty of crime committed in another state of existence—a doctrine which formed part of the initiation into the mysteries.[4] And Vanini—whom his contemporaries burned, finding that an easier task than to confute him—puts the same thing in a very forcible way. *Man*, he says, *is so full of every kind of misery that, were it not repugnant to the Christian religion, I should venture to affirm that if evil spirits exist at all, they have passed into human form and are now atoning for their crimes.*[5] And true Christianity—using the word in its right sense—also regards our existence as the consequence of sin and error.

If you accustom yourself to this view of life you will regulate your expectations accordingly, and cease to look upon all its disagreeable incidents, great and small, its sufferings, its worries, its misery, as anything unusual or irregular; nay, you will find that everything is as it should be, in a world where each of us pays the penalty of existence in his own peculiar way. Amongst the evils of a penal colony is the society of those who form it; and if the reader is worthy of better company, he will need no words from me to remind him of what he has to put up with at present. If he has a soul above the common, or if he is a man of genius, he will occasionally feel like some noble prisoner of state, condemned to work in the galleys with common criminals; and he will follow his example and try to isolate himself.

In general, however, it should be said that this view of life will enable us to contemplate the so-called imperfections of the great majority of men, their moral and intellectual deficiencies and the resulting base type of countenance, without any surprise, to say nothing of indignation; for we shall never cease to reflect where we are, and that the men about us are beings conceived and born in sin, and living to atone for it. That is what Christianity means in speaking of the sinful nature of man.

*Pardon's the word to all!*[6] Whatever folly men commit, be their shortcomings or their vices what they may, let us exercise forbearance; remembering that when these faults appear in others, it is our follies and vices that we behold. They are the shortcomings of humanity, to which we belong; whose faults, one and all, we share; yes, even those very faults at which we now wax so indignant, merely because they have not yet appeared in ourselves. They are faults that do not lie on the surface. But they exist down there in the depths of our nature; and should anything call them forth, they will come and show themselves, just as we now see them in others. One man, it is true, may have faults that are absent in his fellow; and it is undeniable that the sum total of bad qualities is in some cases very large; for the difference of individuality between man and man passes all measure.

In fact, the conviction that the world and man is something that had better not have been, is of a kind to fill us with indulgence towards one another. Nay, from this point of view, we might well consider the proper form of address to be, not *Monsieur, Sir, mein Herr*, but *my fellow-sufferer, Soci malorum, compagnon de miseres!* This may perhaps sound strange, but it is in keeping with the facts; it puts others in a right light; and it reminds us of that which is after all the most necessary thing in life—the tolerance, patience, regard, and love of neighbor, of which everyone stands in need, and which, therefore, every man owes to his fellow.

## NOTES

1. I have treated this subject at length in "The Metaphysics of the Love of the Sexes," p. 69.

2. Cf. Romans vii; Galations ii, iii.

3. Augustine, *De Civitate Dei*. L, xi, c. 23.

4. Cf. *Fragmenta de philosophia*.

5. *De admirandis naturae arcanis*; dial. L. p. 35.

6. "Cymbeline," Act v, Sc. 5.

# CHAPTER 7

# BERTRAND RUSSELL

## *A Free Man's Worship*

To Dr. Faustus in his study Mephistophelis told the history of the Creation, saying,

> The endless praises of the choirs of angels had begun to grow wearisome; for, after all, did he not deserve their praise? Had he not given them endless joy? Would it not be more amusing to obtain undeserved praise, to be worshiped by beings whom he tortured? He smiled inwardly, and resolved that the great drama should be performed.
>
> For countless ages the hot nebula whirled aimlessly through space. At length it began to take shape, the central mass threw off planets, the planets cooled, boiling seas and burning mountains heaved and tossed, from black masses of cloud hot sheets of rain deluged the barely solid crust. And now the first germ of life grew in the depths of the ocean and developed rapidly in the fructifying warmth into vast forest trees, huge ferns springing from the damp mold, sea monsters breeding, fighting, devouring, and passing away. And from the monsters, as the play unfolded itself, Man was born, with the power of thought, the knowledge of good and evil, and the cruel thirst for worship. And Man saw that all is passing in this mad, monstrous world, that all is struggling to snatch, at any cost, a few brief moments of life before Death's inexorable decree. And Man said, "There is a hidden purpose, could we but fathom it, and the purpose is good; for we must reverence something, and in the visible world there is nothing worthy of reverence." And Man stood aside from the struggle, resolving that God intended harmony to come out of chaos by human efforts. And when he followed the instincts which God had transmitted to him from his ancestry of beasts of prey, he called it Sin, and asked God to forgive him. But he doubted whether he could be justly forgiven, until he invented a divine Plan by which God's wrath was to have been appeased. And seeing the present was bad, he made it yet worse, that thereby the future might

be better. And he gave God thanks for the strength that enabled him to forgo even the joys that were possible. And God smiled; and when he saw that Man had become perfect in renunciation and worship, he sent another sun through the sky, which crashed into Man's sun; and all returned again to nebula.

"Yes," he murmured, "it was a good play; I will have it performed again."

Such, in outline, but even more purposeless, more void of meaning, is the world which science presents for our belief. Amid such a world, if any-where, our ideals henceforward must find a home. That man is the product of causes which had no prevision of the end they were achieving; that his origin, his growth, his hopes and fears, his loves and his beliefs, are but the outcome of accidental collocations of atoms; that no fire, no heroism, no intensity of thought and feeling, can preserve an individual life beyond the grave; that all the labors of the ages, all the devotion, all the inspiration, all the noonday brightness of human genius, are destined to extinction in the vast death of the solar system, and that the whole temple of man's achievement must inevitably be buried beneath the debris of a universe in ruins—all these things, if not quite beyond dispute, are yet so nearly certain that no philoso-phy which rejects them can hope to stand. Only within the scaffolding of these truths, only in the firm foundation of unyielding despair, can the soul's habitation henceforth be safely built.

How, in such an alien and inhuman world, can so powerless a creature as man preserve his aspirations untarnished? A strange mystery it is that nature, omnipotent but blind, in the revolutions of her secular hurryings through the abysses of space, has brought forth at last a child, subject still to her power, but gifted with sight, with knowledge of good and evil, with the capacity of judging all the works of his unthinking mother. In spite of death, the mark and seal of the parental control, man is yet free, during his brief years, to examine, to criticize, to know, and in imagination to create. To him alone, in the world with which he is acquainted, this freedom belongs; and in this lies his superiority to the resistless forces that control his outward life.

The savage, like ourselves, feels the oppression of his impotence before the powers of nature; but having in himself nothing that he respects more than power, he is willing to prostrate himself before his gods, without inquir-ing whether they are worthy of his worship. Pathetic and very terrible is the long history of cruelty and torture, of degradation and human sacrifice, endured in the hope of placating the jealous gods: surely, the trembling believer thinks, when what is most precious has been freely given, their lust for blood must be appeased, and more will not be required. The religion of Moloch—as such creeds may be generically called—is in essence the cringing submission of the slave, who dare not, even in his heart, allow the thought that his master deserves no adulation. Since the independence of ideals is not yet acknowledged, power may be freely worshiped and receive an unlimited respect, despite its wanton infliction of pain.

But gradually, as morality grows bolder, the claim of the ideal world begins to be felt; and worship, if it is not to cease, must be given to gods of another kind than those created by the savage. Some, though they feel the demands of the ideal, will still consciously reject them, still urging that naked power is worthy of worship. Such is the attitude inculcated in God's answer to Job out of the whirlwind: the divine power and knowledge are paraded, but of the divine goodness there is not hint. Such also is the attitude of those who, in our own day, base their morality upon the struggle for survival, maintaining that the survivors are necessarily the fittest. But others, not content with an answer so repugnant to the moral sense, will adopt the position which we have become accustomed to regard as specially religious, maintaining that, in some hidden manner, the world of fact is really harmonious with the world of ideals. Thus man created God, all-powerful and all-good, the mystic unity of what is and what should be.

But the world of fact, after all, is not good; and, in submitting our judgment to it, there is an element of slavishness from which our thoughts must be purged. For in all things it is well to exalt the dignity of man, by freeing him as far as possible from the tyranny of nonhuman power. When we have realized that power is largely bad, that man, with his knowledge of good and evil, is but a helpless atom in a world which has no such knowledge, the choice is again presented to us: Shall we worship force, or shall we worship goodness? Shall our God exist and be evil, or shall he be recognized as the creation of our own conscience?

The answer to this question is very momentous and affects profoundly our whole morality. The worship of force, to which Carlyle and Nietzsche and the creed of militarism have accustomed us, is the result of failure to maintain our own ideals against a hostile universe: it is itself a prostrate submission to evil, a sacrifice of our best to Moloch. If strength indeed is to be respected, let us respect rather the strength of those who refuse that false "recognition of facts" which fails to recognize that facts are often bad. Let us admit that, in the world we know, there are many things that would be better otherwise, and that the ideals to which we do and must adhere are not realized in the realm of matter. Let us preserve our respect for truth, for beauty, for the ideal of perfection which life does not permit us to attain, though none of these things meets with the approval of the unconscious universe. If power is bad, as it seems to be, let us reject it from our hearts. In this lies man's true freedom: in determination to worship only the God created by our own love of the good, to respect only the heaven which inspires the insight of our best moments. In action, in desire, we must submit perpetually to the tyranny of outside forces; but in thought, in aspiration, we are free, free from our fellow men, free from the petty planet on which our bodies impotently crawl, free even, while we live, from the tyranny of death. Let us learn, then, that energy of faith which enables us to live constantly in the vision of the good; and let us descend, in action, into the world of fact, with that vision always before us.

When first the opposition of fact and ideal grows fully visible, a spirit of fiery revolt, of fierce hatred of the gods, seems necessary to the assertion of freedom. To defy with Promethean constancy a hostile universe, to keep its evil always in view, always actively hated, to refuse no pain that the malice of power can invent, appears to be the duty of all who will not bow before the inevitable. But indignation is still a bondage, for it compels our thoughts to be occupied with an evil world; and in the fierceness of desire from which rebellion springs there is a kind of self-assertion which it is necessary for the wise to overcome. Indignation is a submission of our thoughts but not of our desires; the Stoic freedom in which wisdom consists is found in the submission of our desires but not of our thoughts. From the submission of our desires springs the virtue of resignation; from the freedom of our thoughts springs the whole world of art and philosophy, and the vision of beauty by which, at last, we half reconquer the reluctant world. But the vision of beauty is possible only to unfettered contemplation, to thoughts not weighted by the load of eager wishes; and thus freedom comes only to those who no longer ask of life that it shall yield them any of those personal goods that are subject to the mutations of time.

Although the necessity of renunciation is evidence of the existence of evil, yet Christianity, in preaching it, has shown a wisdom exceeding that of the Promethean philosophy of rebellion. It must be admitted that, of the things we desire, some, though they prove impossible, are yet real goods; others, however, as ardently longed for, do not form part of a fully purified ideal. The belief that what must be renounced is bad, though sometimes false, is far less often false than untamed passion supposes; and the creed of religion, by providing a reason for proving that it is never false, has been the means of purifying our hopes by the discovery of many austere truths.

But there is in resignation a further good element: even real goods, when they are unattainable, ought not to be fretfully desired. To every man comes, sooner or later, the great renunciation. For the young, there is nothing unattainable; a good thing desired with the whole force of a passionate will, and yet impossible, is to them not credible. Yet, by death, by illness, by poverty, or by the voice of duty, we must learn, each one of us, that the world was not made for us, and that, however beautiful may be the things we crave, Fate may nevertheless forbid them. It is the part of courage, when misfortune comes, to bear without repining the ruin of our hopes, to turn away our thoughts from vain regrets. This degree of submission to power is not only just and right: it is the very gate of wisdom.

But passive renunciation is not the whole of wisdom; for not by renunciation alone can we build a temple for the worship of our own ideals. Haunting foreshadowings of the temple appear in the realm of imagination, in music, in architecture, in the untroubled kingdom of reason, and in the golden sunset magic of lyrics, where beauty shines and glows, remote from the touch of sorrow, remote from the fear of change, remote from the failures and disenchantments of the world of fact. In the contemplation of these things the vision of heaven will shape itself in our hearts, giving at once a touchstone to judge the world about us and an inspiration by which to fashion to our needs whatever is not incapable of serving as a stone in the sacred temple.

Except for those rare spirits that are born without sin, there is a cavern of darkness to be traversed before that temple can be entered. The gate of the cavern is despair, and its floor is paved with the gravestones of abandoned hopes. There self must die; there the eagerness, the greed of untamed desire, must be slain, for only so can the soul be freed from the empire of Fate. But out of the cavern, the Gate of Renunciation leads again to the daylight of wisdom, by whose radiance a new insight, a new joy, a new tenderness, shine forth to gladden the pilgrim's heart.

When, without the bitterness of impotent rebellion, we have learned both to resign ourselves to the outward rule of Fate and to recognize that the nonhuman world is unworthy of our worship, it becomes possible at last so to transform and refashion the unconscious universe, so to transmute it in the crucible of imagination, that a new image of shining gold replaces the old idol of clay. In all the multiform facts of the world—in the visual shapes of trees and mountains and clouds, in the events of the life of man, even in the very omnipotence of death—the insight of creative idealism can find the reflection of a beauty which its own thoughts first made. In this way mind asserts its subtle mastery over the thoughtless forces of nature. The more evil the material with which it deals, the more thwarting to untrained desire, the greater is its achievement in inducing the reluctant rock to yield up its hidden treasures, the prouder its victory in compelling the opposing forces to swell the pageant of its triumph. Of all the arts, tragedy is the proudest, the most triumphant; for it builds its shining citadel in the very center of the enemy's country, on the very summit of his highest mountain; from its impregnable watchtowers, his camps and arsenals, his columns and forts, are all revealed; within its walls the free life continues, while the legions of death and pain and despair, and all the servile captains of tyrant Fate, afford the burghers of that dauntless city new spectacles of beauty. Happy those sacred ramparts, thrice happy the dwellers on that all-seeing eminence. Honor to those brave warriors who, through countless ages of warfare, have preserved for us the priceless heritage of liberty and have kept undefiled by sacrilegious invaders the home of the unsubdued.

But the beauty of tragedy does but make visible a quality which, in more or less obvious shapes, is present always and everywhere in life. In the spectacle of death, in the endurance of intolerable pain, and in the irrevocableness of a vanished past, there is a sacredness, an overpowering awe, a feeling of the vastness, the depth, the inexhaustible mystery of existence, in which, as by some strange marriage of pain, the sufferer is bound to the world by bonds of sorrow. In these moments of insight, we lose all eagerness of temporary desire, all struggling and striving for petty ends, all care for the little trivial things that, to a superficial view, make up the common life of day by day; we see, surrounding the narrow raft illumined by the flickering light of human comradeship, the dark ocean on whose rolling waves we toss for a brief hour; from the great night without, a chill blast breaks in upon our refuge; all the loneliness of humanity amid hostile forces is concentrated upon the individual soul, which must struggle alone, with what of courage it can command, against the whole weight of a universe that cares nothing for its hopes and fears. Victory, in this struggle with the powers of darkness, is the true baptism into the glorious company of heroes, the true initiation into the overmastering beauty of human existence. From that awful encounter of the soul with the outer world, renunciation, wisdom, and charity are born; and with their birth a new life begins. To take into the inmost shrine of the soul the irresistible forces whose puppets we seem to be—death and change, the irrevocableness of the past, and the powerlessness of man before the blind hurry of the universe from vanity to vanity—to feel these things and know them is to conquer them.

This is the reason why the past has such magical power. The beauty of its motionless and silent pictures is like the enchanted purity of late autumn, when the leaves, though one breath would make them fall, still glow against the sky in golden glory. The past does not change or strive; like Duncan, after life's fitful fever it sleeps well; what was eager and grasping, what was petty and transitory, has faded away; the things that were beautiful and eternal shine out of it like stars in the night. Its beauty, to a soul not worthy of it, is unendurable; but to a soul which has conquered Fate it is the key of religion.

The life of man, viewed outwardly, is but a small thing in comparison with the forces of nature. The slave is doomed to worship Time and Fate and Death, because they are greater than anything he finds in himself, and because all his thoughts are of things which they devour. But, great as they are, to think of them greatly, to feel their passionless splendor, is greater still. And such thought makes us free men; we no longer bow before the inevitable in Oriental subjection, but we absorb it and make it a part of ourselves. To abandon the struggle for private happiness, to expel all eagerness of temporary desire, to burn with passion for eternal things—this is emancipation, and this is the free man's worship. And this liberation is effected by contemplation of Fate; for Fate itself is subdued by the mind which leaves nothing to be purged by the purifying fire of time.

United with his fellow men by the strongest of all ties, the tie of a common doom, the free man finds that a new vision is with him always, shedding over every daily task the light of love. The life of man is a long march through the night, surrounded by invisible foes, tortured by weariness and pain, toward a goal that few can hope to reach, and where none may tarry long. One by one, as they march, our comrades vanish from our sight, seized by the silent orders of omnipotent death. Very brief is the time in which we can help them, in which their happiness or misery is decided. Be it ours to shed sunshine on their path, to lighten their sorrows by the balm of sympathy, to give them the pure joy of a never-tiring affection, to strengthen failing courage, to instill faith in hours of despair. Let us not weigh in grudging scales their merits and demerits, but let us think only of their need—of the sorrows, the difficulties, perhaps the blindness, that make the misery of their lives; let us remember that they are fellow sufferers in the same darkness, actors in the same tragedy with ourselves. And so, when their day is over, when their good and their evil have become eternal by the immortality of the past, be it ours to feel that, where they suffered, where they failed, no deed of ours was the cause; but wherever a spark of the divine fire kindled in their hearts, we were ready with encouragement, with sympathy, with brave words in which high courage glowed.

Brief and powerless is man's life; on him and all his race the slow, sure doom falls pitiless and dark. Blind to good and evil, reckless of destruction, omnipotent matter rolls on its relentless way; for man, condemned today to lose his dearest, tomorrow himself to pass through the gate of darkness, it remains only to cherish, ere yet the blow fall, the lofty thoughts that ennoble his little day; disdaining the coward terrors of the slave of Fate, to worship at the shrine that his own hands have built; undismayed by the empire of chance, to preserve a mind free from the wanton tyranny that rules his outward life; proudly defiant of the irresistible forces that tolerate, for a moment, his knowledge and his condemnation, to sustain alone, a weary but unyielding Atlas, the world that his own ideals have fashioned despite the trampling march of unconscious power.

CHAPTER 8          MORITZ SCHLICK

# On the Meaning of Life

Not everyone is disturbed by the question whether life has a meaning.
Some—and they are not the unhappiest—have the child's mind, which has
*not yet* asked about such things; others *no longer ask*, having unlearnt the question. In between are ourselves, the seekers. We cannot project ourselves back
to the level of the innocent, whom life has not yet looked at with its dark mysterious eyes, and we do not care to join the weary and the blasé, who no
longer believe in any meaning to existence, because they have been able to
find none in their own.

A man who has failed of the goal that his youth was striving for, and
found no substitute, may lament the meaninglessness of his own life; yet he
still may believe in a meaning to existence generally, and think that it continues to be found where a person has reached his goals. But the man who has
wrested from fate the achievement of his purposes, and then finds that his
prize was not so valuable as it seemed, that he has somehow fallen prey to a
deception—that man is quite blankly confronted with the question of life's
value, and before him lies like a darkened wasteland the thought, not only
that all things pass, but also that everything is ultimately in vain.

How are we to discover a unitary meaning, either in the perplexities of a
man's lifetime, or in the stumbling progress of history itself? Existence may
appear to us as a many-hued tapestry, or as a grey veil, but it is equally difficult either way to furl the billowing fabric so that its meaning becomes apparent. It all flaps past and seems to have vanished before we could render an
account of it.

What is the reason for the strange contradiction, that achievement and
enjoyment will not fuse into a proper meaning? Does not an inexorable law
of nature appear to prevail here? Man sets himself goals, and while he is
heading towards them he is buoyed up by hope, indeed, but gnawed at the

Translated by Peter Heath. Published in 1927. From *Philosophical Papers, Vol. 2*, D. Reidel, 1979.
Used by permission of the publisher.

same time by the pain of unsatisfied desire. Once the goal is reached, however, after the first flush of triumph has passed away, there follows inevitably a mood of desolation. A void remains, which can seemingly find an end only through the painful emergence of new longings, the setting of new goals. So the game begins anew, and existence seems doomed to be a restless swinging to and fro between pain and boredom, which ends at last in the nothingness of death. That is the celebrated line of thought which Schopenhauer made the basis of his pessimistic view of life. Is it not possible, somehow, to escape it?

We know how Nietzsche, for example, sought to conquer this pessimism. First by the flight into art: consider the world, he says, as an aesthetic phenomenon, and it is eternally vindicated! Then by the flight into knowledge: look upon life as an experiment of the knower, and the world will be to you the finest of laboratories! But Nietzsche again turned away from these standpoints; in the end, art was no longer his watchword, and nor were science, or beauty, or truth; it is hard to reduce to a brief formula what the wisest Nietzsche, the Nietzsche of *Zarathustra*, saw as the meaning of life. For if it be said that henceforth the ultimate value of life, to him, was *life itself*, that obviously says nothing clear and does not find the right expression for the deep truth which he then perceived or at least suspected. For he saw that life has no meaning, so long as it stands wholly under the domination of purposes:

> Verily, it is a blessing and no blasphemy when I teach: Above all things standeth the heaven of chance, the heaven of innocence, the heaven of hazard, the heaven of sportiveness.
> "Sir Hazard"—his is the most ancient title of nobility in earth: him have I restored to all things, I have saved them from the slavery of ends.
> This freedom and heavenly brightness I set over all things as an azure dome, when I taught that above them and in them there willeth no "eternal will."

In truth, we shall never find an ultimate meaning in existence, if we view it only under the aspect of purpose.

I know not, however, whether the burden of purposes has ever weighed more heavily upon mankind than at the present time. The present idolizes work. But work means goal-seeking activity, direction to a purpose. Plunge into the crowd on a bustling city street and imagine yourself stopping the passers-by, one after another, and crying to them "Where are you off to so fast? What important business do you have?" And if, on learning the immediate goal, you were to ask further about the purpose of this goal, and again for the purpose of that purpose, you would almost always hit on the purpose after just a few steps in the sequence: maintenance of life, earning one's bread. And why maintain life? To this question you could seldom read off an intelligible answer from the information obtained.

And yet an answer has to be found. For mere living, pure existence as such is certainly valueless; it must also have a content, and in that only can the meaning of life reside. But what actually fills up our days almost entirely is activities serving to maintain life. In other words, the content of existence consists in the work that is needed in order to exist. We are therefore moving in a circle, and in this fashion fail to arrive at a meaning for life. Nor is it any better if, in place of work itself, we direct our attention to the fruits of work. The greater part of its products is again subservient to work of some kind and hence indirectly to the maintenance of life, and another large part is undoubtedly meaningless trash. . . . Nor, indeed, can any work-products as such ever be valuable, save insofar as they somehow fulfil and enrich life, by launching man into valuable states and activities. The state of working cannot be one of these, for by work—if we understand this concept in its philosophical generality—we simply mean any activity undertaken solely in order to realize some purpose. It is therefore the characteristic mark of work that it has its purpose outside itself, and is not performed for its own sake. The doctrine that would wish to install work as such at the centre of existence, and exalt it to life's highest meaning, is bound to be in error, because every work-activity as such is always a mere means, and receives its value only from its goals.

The core and ultimate value of life can lie only in such states as exist for their own sake and carry their satisfaction in themselves. Now such states are undoubtedly given in the pleasure-feelings which terminate the fulfilment of a volition and accompany the gratifying of a desire; but if we sought to derive the value of existence from these moments, in which life's pressure is momentarily halted, we should at once become ensnared in that argument of Schopenhauer's, which displays to us, not the meaning, but the absurdity of life.

No, life means movement and action, and if we wish to find a meaning in it we must seek for *activities* which carry their own purpose and value within them, independently of any extraneous goals; activities, therefore, which are not work, in the philosophical sense of the word. If such activities exist, then in them the seemingly divided is reconciled, means and end, action and consequence are fused into one, we have then found ends-in-themselves which are more than mere end-points of acting and resting-points of existence, and it is these alone that can take over the role of a true content to life.

There really are such activities. To be consistent, we must call them *play*, since that is the name for free, purposeless action, that is, action which in fact carries its purpose within itself. We must take the word "play," however, in its broad, true, philosophical meaning—in a deeper sense than is commonly accorded to it in daily life. We are not thereby lending it any new or surprising meaning, but are merely repeating what was perfectly clear to at least one great mind, who apprehended the nature of the human with the eye of a poet—which is to say, in deep truth. For in his *Letters on the Aesthetic Education of Man*, Friedrich Schiller utters the following words:

> For, to declare it once and for all, Man plays only when he is in the full
> sense of the word a man, and *he is only wholly Man when he is playing*. This

proposition, which at the moment perhaps seems paradoxical, will assume great and deep significance when we have once reached the point of applying it to the twofold seriousness of duty and of destiny; it will, I promise you, support the whole fabric of aesthetic art, and the still more difficult art of living. But it is only in science that this statement is unexpected; it has long since been alive and operative in Art, and in the feeling of the Greeks, its most distinguished exponents; only they transferred to Olympus what should have been realized on earth. Guided by its truth, they caused not only the seriousness and the toil which furrow the cheeks of mortals, but also the futile pleasure that smooths the empty face, to vanish from the brows of the blessed gods, and they released these perpetually happy beings from the fetters of every aim, every duty, every care, and made idleness and indifference the enviable portion of divinity; merely a more human name for the freest and sublimest state of being.

These are exalted words, which ring down from the poet's world into a care-dimmed age, and in our own world sound untimely to most ears. The poet sees a state of divine perfection among men, in which all their activities are turned into joyous play, all their working-days become holidays. Only insofar as man shares in this perfection, only in the hours when life smiles at him without the stern frown of purpose, is he really man. And it was sober consideration that led us to this very truth: the meaning of existence is revealed only in play.

But doesn't this notion lead us into mere dreams, does it not loosen every tie with reality, and have we not lost beneath our feet the solid earth of daily life, on which we have ultimately to stay planted, since the question of life is by nature an everyday question? In the harsh reality, especially of the present, there seems no room for such dreams; for our age, for the peoples of a war-racked globe, no other solution seems possible save the word "work," and it appears irresponsible to speak ill of it.

Yet we should not forget that the creation which the hour demands of us is work only in the economic sense, productive activity, that is, which leads to the engendering of values. There is, however, no irreconcilable opposition between play in the philosophical sense and work in the economic meaning of the term. Play, as we see it, is any activity which takes place entirely for its own sake, independently of its effects and consequences. There is nothing to stop these effects from being of a useful or valuable kind. If they are, so much the better; the action still remains play, since it already bears its own value within itself. Valuable goods may proceed from it, just as well as from intrinsically unpleasurable activity that strives to fulfil a purpose. Play too, in other words, can be creative; its outcome can coincide with that of work.

This notion of creative play will be accorded a major part in the life philosophy of the future. If mankind is to go on existing and progressing by way of playful activities, they will have to be creative; the necessary muse somehow be brought forth by means of them. And this is possible, since play is not a form of doing nothing. The more activities, indeed, become play in the philosophical sense, the more work would be accomplished in the economic sense, and the more values would be created in human society. Human action is work, not because it bears fruit, but only when it proceeds from, and is governed by, the thought of its fruit.

Let us look about us: where do we find creative play? The brightest example (which at the same time is more than a mere example), is to be seen in the creation of the artist. His activity, the shaping of his work by inspiration, is itself pleasure, and it is half by accident that enduring values arise from it. The artist may have no thought, as he works, of the benefit of these values, or even of his reward, since otherwise the act of creation is disrupted. Not the golden chain, but the song that pours from the heart, is the guerdon that richly rewards! So feels the poet, and so the artist. And anyone who feels thus in what he does, *is* an artist.

Take, for example, the scientist. *Knowing*, too, is a pure play of the spirit, the wrestling for scientific truth is an end-in-itself for him, he rejoices to measure his powers against the riddles which reality propounds to him, quite regardless of the benefits that may somehow accrue from this (and these, as we know, have often been the most astonishing precisely in the case of purely theoretical discoveries, whose practical utility no one could originally have guessed). The richest blessings flow from the work that is engendered as the child of its creator's happy mood, and in free play, without any anxious concern for its effects.

Not all the activity of the artist or thinker falls, of course, under the concept of creative play. The purely technical, the mere management of the material, as with the painter's colour-mixing, or the composer's setting-down of notes—all this remains, for the most part, toil and work; they are the husks and dross that often still attach to play in real life. Often, but not always; for in the process of execution the working acts involved can either become so mechanized that they hardly enter consciousness, or else develop so much charm and attractiveness that they turn into artistic play themselves.

And that is also true in the end of those actions which engender neither science nor art, but the day's necessities, and which are seemingly altogether devoid of spirit. The tilling of the fields, the weaving of fabrics, the cobbling of shoes, can all become play, and may take on the character of artistic acts. Nor is it even so uncommon for a man to take so much pleasure in such activities, that he forgets the purpose of them. Every true craftsman can experience in his own case this transformation of the means into an end-in-itself, which can take place with almost any activity, and which makes the product into a work of art. It is the joy in sheer creation, the dedication to the activity, the absorption in the movement, which transforms work into play. As we know, there is a great enchantment which almost always brings this transformation about—rhythm. To be sure, it will only work perfectly where it is not brought externally and deliberately to the activity, and artificially coupled with it, but evolves spontaneously from the nature of the action and its natural form. There are some kinds of work where this is impossible; many are of such a nature that they always remain an evil and—except, perhaps, among men entirely blunted and incapable of happiness—are invariably carried out with reluctance and distaste. With such occupations I advise a very careful scrutiny of their fruits: we shall invariably find that such mechanical, brutalizing, degrading forms of work serve ultimately to produce only trash and empty luxury. So away with them! So long, indeed, as our economy is focussed on mere increase of production, instead of on the true enrichment of life, these activities cannot diminish, and thus slavery among mankind (for these alone are true forms of slave-labour) will not be able to decline. But a civilization which maintains artificial breeding-grounds for idle trumpery by means of forced slave-labour, must eventually come to grief through its own absurdity. All that will then remain over will be simply the avocations serving to generate true culture. But in them there dwells a spirit that favours their evolution into true forms of play.

At least there is no law of nature which in any way obstructs such a development of action into an end-in-itself; basically speaking, the road lies open to the realization of Schiller's dream. The idea of a human race thus liberated from all tormenting purposes, all oppressive cares, and cheerfully dedicated to the moment, is at least not a contradictory or inconceivable idea. The individual would lead an existence, as in the profound and beautiful saying of the Bible, like the life of the lilies of the field.

The objection may be raised at this point, that such a life would represent a relapse to a lower level, to the status of plants and animals. For the latter assuredly live for the moment, their consciousness is confined to a brief present, they certainly know pain, but not care. Man, on the contrary, has the privilege of embracing long periods, whole lifetimes, in the span of his consciousness, of coexperiencing them through foresight and hindsight, and that is how he becomes the knowing, supremely self-conscious being, in which capacity he confronts all the rest of nature.

But this objection is easy to meet. Man does not have to forfeit the range of his life, his joy in the moment will not be blind and bestial, but bathed in the clearest light of consciousness. He does not escape the menace of purposes by putting his head in the sand, so as not to see the future at all; it stands before him, calmly and clearly, in the light of hope, just as the past stands behind him in the light of recollection. He can shake off the curse of purposes and liberate his vision from the blight of cares, without lessening the boon of his hopes. He still sees even the remotest consequences of his action clearly before him, and not only the real consequences, but all possible ones as well; but no specific goal stands there as an end to be necessarily attained, so that the whole road would be meaningless if it were not; every point, rather, of the whole road already has its own intrinsic meaning, like a mountain path that offers sublime views at every step and new enchantments at every turn, whether it may lead to a summit or not. The setting of certain goals is admittedly needed in order to produce the tension required for life; even playful activity is constantly setting itself tasks, most palpably in sport and competition, which still remains play so long as it does not degenerate into real fighting. But such goals are harmless, they impose no burden on life and do not dominate it; they are left aside and it does not matter if they are not achieved, since at any moment they can be replaced by others. Stretches of life that stand under the dominion of huge inexorable purposes are like riddles with an answer that we either find or fail at; but a life of play might be compared to an endless crossword puzzle, in which new words are constantly being found and connected, so that an ever larger area is progressively filled in, with no other aim but that of going on further without a halt.

The last liberation of man would be reached if in all his doings he could give himself up entirely to the act itself, inspired to his activity always by love. The end, then, would never justify the means, he might then exalt into his highest rule of action the principle: "What is not worth doing for its own sake, don't do for anything else's sake!" All life would then be truly meaningful, down to its ultimate ramifications; to live would mean: to celebrate the festival of existence.

Plato, in the *Laws* (803c), had already declared that men should make play, song and dance, as the true divine worship, into the proper content of life. But though well over two thousand years have passed in the meantime, perhaps men were closer in those days to such an order of life than they are today. In the present age, assuredly, the daily activity of man can in large part be justified only by distant purposes. In itself such activity is unpleasurable and unjustified, and the deification of work as such, the great gospel of our industrial age, has been exposed as idolatry. The greater part of our existence, filled as it is with goal-seeking work at the behest of others, has no value in itself, but obtains this only by reference to the festive hours of play, for which work provides merely the means and the preconditions.

Unremitting stern fulfilment of duty in the service of an end eventually makes us narrow and takes away the freedom that everyone requires for self-development. We have to be able to breathe freely. Hence arises the task of releasing, for a day, an hour, a minute, at least, the life that is fettered in its entirety to the purposes of utility; and these hours and minutes, however few they may be, form the content for whose sake all the rest is there, and for whose sake all the rest is on occasion sacrificed. At bottom we find man always ready to give up the senseless remainder of life, for an hour that is filled with value.

Man's teachers and benefactors, his seers and leaders, can strive for nothing else but to permeate the broadest possible stretches of existence with meaning. The achievement of a John Ruskin was based on the idea that human life must allow of being shaped into a chain of festive acts; the daily round can be made meaningful if it is filled in every detail with beauty. If it is not possible to lead the whole of life on the bright side, we must at least be able to break surface from time to time. If it is not possible to realize Schiller's dream, there is all the more need to follow Goethe's rule of life: "Work by day, at evening guests, toilsome weeks and joyous feasts." In our own civilization, joyous feasts are not possible without toilsome weeks, but in no age is a lasting life possible without joy and festivities. A life that is constantly focussed only on distant goals eventually loses all power of creation whatsoever. It is like a bow that is always bent: in the end it can no longer loose off the arrow, and with that its tension becomes pointless. Work and toil, so long as they have not themselves become joyous play, should make joy and play possible; therein their meaning lies. But they cannot do it if man has forgotten how to rejoice, if festive hours do not see to it that the knowledge of what joy is, is retained.

Yet let us beware of confusing joy, on which life's value depends, with its surrogate, mere pleasure, that shallow enjoyment of which Schiller said that it smooths the empty face of mortals. Pleasure wearies, while joy refreshes; the latter enriches, the former puts a false sheen upon existence Both indeed, lead us away from daily toil and distract us from care, but they do it in different ways: pleasure by diverting us, joy by pulling us together. Diversion offers the spirit fleeting excitement, without depth or content; for joy there is more needed, a thought or feeling which fills the whole man, an inspiration which sets him soaring above everyday life. He can only joy whole-heartedly about things which completely take hold of him, he has to be utterly devoted to something. Pain is commended for deepening us (perhaps because otherwise we have nothing good to say of it), but true joy has a very much greater effect. Joy is deeper than heartache, says Nietzsche. Pleasure, however, merely ruffles the surface of the soul and leaves it as featureless as before; it even tends to silt up the soul, for it leaves behind a stale after-taste, as symptom of a spiritual turbidity. And by this, indeed, it can be distinguished from exalted joy, which is an affirmation of existence conferring meaning upon life.

Here we can learn from the *child*. Before he has yet been caught in the net of purposes, the cares of work are unknown to him; he needs no diversion or release from the working day. And it is precisely the child that is capable of the purest joy. People everywhere are wont to sing of the happiness of youth, and this is truly more than a mere invention of the poets; youth is really not overshadowed by the dark clouds of purpose.

And with that I come to the heart of what I should here like to say.

It is not in every expression of life, not in the whole breadth of it, that we are able to find a meaning—at least so long as Schiller's dream of divine perfection remains a mere dream; the meaning of the whole is concentrated and collected, rather, into a few short hours of deep, serene joy, into the hours of play. And these hours crowd thickest in *youth*. It is not only that childish games are play even in the philosophical sense of the term; it is also that later youth, which is already well acquainted with aims and purposes, and has been brought up to serve them, still does not stand entirely under their yoke, does not have its gaze fixed on them alone, is not concerned solely with attaining them, as is often the natural attitude later on. Youth, on the contrary, does not really care about purposes; if one collapses, another is quickly built up; goals are merely an invitation to rush in and fight, and this enterprising ardour is the true fulfilment of the youthful spirit. The enthusiasm of youth (it is basically what the Greeks called Eros), is devotion to the deed, not the goal. This act, this way of acting, is true play.

If it is clear in this fashion that what makes up the meaning of existence is nowhere so purely or strongly to be found as it is in youth, some notable questions and clues emerge from this. Youth, after all, is the first phase of life, and it seems incongruous that the meaning of the whole should be found only at its beginning. For according to the traditional view, life is to be regarded as a process of development, whose meaning is constantly unfolding, so that it ought to be most clearly apparent towards the end. What, then, is youth? On the received view it is the time of immaturity, in which mind and body grow, in order later to *have* grown up to their vocation; the time of learning, in which all capacities are exercised, in order to be equipped for work; even the play of youth appears from this angle as merely a preparation for the seriousness of life. It is almost always so regarded, and almost the whole of education is conducted from this point of view: it signifies a training for adulthood. Youth therefore appears as a mere means to the later purposes of life, as a necessary learning period, that would have no meaning of its own.

This view is directly opposed to the insight that we have obtained. It has seldom been remarked, what a paradox it is that the time of preparation appears as the sweetest portion of existence, while the time of fulfilment seems the most toilsome. At times, however, it has been seen. It was primarily Rousseau, and perhaps Montaigne before him, who discovered the intrinsic value of youth. He warns the educator against debasing the youth of the pupil into a mere means and sacrificing his early happiness to later proficiency; the aim should be to fill the days of youth with joy, even for their own sake. At the present day this idea has begun to make a little headway. It is a leading conception of the modern youth movement, that a young life is not only going to receive its value from the future, but bears it within itself. Youth, in fact, is not just a time of growing, learning, ripening and incompleteness, but primarily a time of play, of doing for its own sake, and hence a true bearer of the meaning of life. Anyone denying this, and regarding youth as a mere introduction and prelude to real life, commits the same error that beclouded the mediaeval view of human existence: he shifts life's centre of gravity forwards, into the future. Just as the majority of religions, discontented with earthly life, are wont to transfer the meaning of existence out of this life and into a hereafter, so man in general is inclined always to regard every state, since none of them is wholly perfect, as a mere preparation for a more perfect one.

For modern man there is little doubt that the value and aim of life must either be totally of this world, or else cannot be found at all. And if man were to run through a thousand successive lives, as the theories of transmigration maintain, this would not absolve contemporary thought from seeking in every one of these stages of existence its own special meaning, independent of what has gone before or is yet to follow. Present-day man would have no right to look upon other, metaphysical worlds, if they existed, as superior or more meaningful, and ungratefully to despise our own world by comparison. The meaning of the life that he knows can only be sought in this world, *as* he knows it.

But within life he now commits the same mistake that he committed earlier in thinking of its metaphysical continuation: from immature youth he shifts the value of life into mature adulthood; in his prime, he sees that he is still not yet ripe, that his nature and achievements are not complete, and therefore shifts the meaning of life still further on, and expects it from the peace and mellowness of old age. But on actually arriving at this peace, he then projects the meaning of existence backwards again into the days of acting and striving, and these are by then over and past recovery. And the final result is that man lets his whole life fall under the curse of purposes. It is the unceasing search into the future and concern for the future that casts its shadow over every present and clouds the joy of it.

But if life has a meaning, it must lie in the present, for only the present is real. There is no reason at all, however, why more meaning should lie in the later present, in the middle or final period of life, than in an earlier present, in the first period, known as youth. And now let us consider what "youth" must actually mean for us in this connection. We found its true nature, not in the fact that it is a prelude and first phase of life, but rather in that it is the time of play, the time of activity for the pleasure of acting. And we recognized that all action, even the creative action of the adult, can and must, in its perfect form, take on the same character: it becomes play, self-sufficient action that acquires its value independently of the purpose.

But from this it follows that youth, in our philosophical sense, can by no means be confined to the early stages of life; it is present wherever the state of man has reached a peak, where his action has become play, where he is wholly given over to the moment and the matter in hand. We talk in such cases of youthful enthusiasm, and that is the right expression: enthusiasm is always youthful. The ardour which fires us for a cause, a deed or a man, and the ardour of youth, are one and the same fire. A man who is emotionally immersed in what he does is a youngster, a child. The great confirmation of this is genius, which is always imbued with a child-like quality. All true greatness is full of a deep innocence. The creativity of genius is the play of a child, his joy in the world is the child's pleasure in pretty things. Heraclitus of old it was who compared the creative world-spirit itself to a child at play, building things out of pebbles and bits of wood and tearing them down again. For us, therefore, the word "youth" does not have the external meaning of a specific period of life, a particular span of years; it is a state, a way of leading one's life, which basically has nothing to do with years and the number of them.

It will now no longer be possible to misunderstand me when, as the heart of what I am moved to say, I assert the proposition that the *meaning of life is youth.*

The more youth is realized in a life, the more valuable it is, and if a person dies young, however long he may have lived, his life has had meaning.

CHAPTER 9          ALBERT CAMUS

# The Myth of Sisyphus

## AN ABSURD REASONING

### Absurdity and Suicide

There is but one truly serious philosophical problem, and that is suicide. Judging whether life is or is not worth living amounts to answering the fundamental question of philosophy. All the rest—whether or not the world has three dimensions, whether the mind has nine or twelve categories—comes afterwards. These are games; one must first answer. And if it is true, as Nietzsche claims, that a philosopher, to deserve our respect, must preach by example, you can appreciate the importance of that reply, for it will precede the definitive act. These are facts the heart can feel; yet they call for careful study before they become clear to the intellect.

If I ask myself how to judge that this question is more urgent than that, I reply that one judges by the actions it entails. I have never seen anyone die for the ontological argument. Galileo, who held a scientific truth of great importance, abjured it with the greatest of ease as soon as it endangered his life. In a certain sense, he did right.[1] That truth was not worth the stake. Whether the earth or the sun revolves around the other is a matter of profound indifference. To tell the truth, it is a futile question. On the other hand, I see many people die because they judge that life is not worth living. I see others paradoxically getting killed for the ideas or illusions that give them a reason for living (what is called a reason for living is also an excellent reason for dying). I therefore conclude that the meaning of life is the most urgent of questions. How to answer it? On all essential problems (I mean thereby those that run the risk of leading to death or those that intensify the passion of living) there are probably but two methods of thought: the method of La Palisse and the method of Don Quixote. Solely the balance between evidence and lyricism can allow us to achieve simultaneously emotion and lucidity. In a subject at once so humble and so heavy with emotion, the learned and classical dialectic must yield, one can see, to a more modest attitude of mind deriving at one and the same time from common sense and understanding.

Suicide has never been dealt with except as a social phenomenon. On the contrary, we are concerned here, at the outset, with the relationship between individual thought and suicide. An act like this is prepared within the silence of the heart, as is a great work of art. The man himself is ignorant of it. One evening he pulls the trigger or jumps. Of an apartment-building manager who had killed himself I was told that he had lost his daughter five years before, that he had changed greatly since, and that that experience had "undermined" him. A more exact word cannot be imagined. Beginning to think is beginning to be undermined. Society has but little connection with such beginnings. The worm is in man's heart. That is where it must be sought. One must follow and understand this fatal game that leads from lucidity in the face of existence to flight from light. . . .

But if it is hard to fix the precise instant, the subtle step when the mind opted for death, it is easier to deduce from the act itself the consequences it implies. In a sense, and as in melodrama, killing yourself amounts to confessing. It is confessing that life is too much for you or that you do not understand it. Let's not go too far in such analogies, however, but rather return to everyday words. It is merely confessing that that "is not worth the trouble." Living, naturally, is never easy. You continue making the gestures commanded by existence for many reasons, the first of which is habit. Dying voluntarily implies that you have recognized, even instinctively, the ridiculous character of that habit, the absence of any profound reason for living, the insane character of that daily agitation, and the uselessness of suffering.

What, then, is that incalculable feeling that deprives the mind of the sleep necessary to life? A world that can be explained even with bad reasons is a familiar world. But, on the other hand, in a universe suddenly divested of illusions and lights, man feels an alien, a stranger. His exile is without remedy since he is deprived of the memory of a lost home or the hope of a promised land. This divorce between man and his life, the actor and his setting, is properly the feeling of absurdity. All healthy men having thought of their own suicide, it can be seen, without further explanation, that there is a direct connection between this feeling and the longing for death.

The subject of this essay is precisely this relationship between the absurd and suicide, the exact degree to which suicide is a solution to the absurd. The principle can be established that for a man who does not cheat, what he believes to be true must determine his action. Belief in the absurdity of existence must then dictate his conduct. It is legitimate to wonder, clearly and without false pathos, whether a conclusion of this importance requires forsaking as rapidly as possible an incomprehensible condition. I am speaking, of course, of men inclined to be in harmony with themselves.

Stated clearly, this problem may seem both simple and insoluble. But it is wrongly assumed that simple questions involve answers that are no less simple and that evidence implies evidence. A priori and reversing the terms of the problem, just as one does or does not kill oneself, it seems that there are but two philosophical solutions, either yes or no. This would be too easy. But allowance must be made for those who, without concluding, continue questioning. Here I am only slightly indulging in irony: this is the majority. I notice also that those who answer "no" act as if they thought "yes." As a matter of fact, if I accept the Nietzschean criterion, they think "yes" in one way or another. On the other hand, it often happens that those who commit suicide were assured of the meaning of life. These contradictions are constant. It may even be said that they have never been so keen as on this point where, on the contrary, logic seems so desirable. It is a commonplace to compare philosophical theories and the behavior of those who profess them. . . . Schopenhauer is often cited, as a fit subject for laughter, because he praised suicide while seated at a well-set table. This is no subject for joking. That way of not taking the tragic seriously is not so grievous, but it helps to judge a man.

In the face of such contradictions and obscurities must we conclude that there is no relationship between the opinion one has about life and the act one commits to leave it? Let us not exaggerate in this direction. In a man's attachment to life there is something stronger than all the ills in the world. The body's judgment is as good as the mind's, and the body shrinks from annihilation. We get into the habit of living before acquiring the habit of thinking. In that race which daily hastens us toward death, the body maintains its irreparable lead. In short, the essence of that contradiction lies in what I shall call the act of eluding because it is both less and more than diversion in the Pascalian sense. Eluding is the invariable game. The typical act of eluding, the fatal evasion that constitutes the third theme of this essay, is hope. Hope for another life one must "deserve" or trickery of those who live not for life itself but for some great idea that will transcend it, refine it, give it a meaning, and betray it. . . .

## Absurd Walls

. . . All great deeds and all great thoughts have a ridiculous beginning. Great works are often born on a street-corner or in a restaurant's revolving door. So it is with absurdity. The absurd world more than others derives its nobility from that abject birth. In certain situations, replying "nothing" when asked what one is thinking about may be pretense in a man. Those who are loved are well aware of this. But if that reply is sincere, if it symbolizes that odd state of soul in which the void becomes eloquent, in which the chain of daily gestures is broken, in which the heart vainly seeks the link that will connect it again, then it is as it were the first sign of absurdity.

It happens that the stage sets collapse. Rising, streetcar, four hours in the office or the factory, meal, streetcar, four hours of work, meal, sleep, and

Monday Tuesday Wednesday Thursday Friday and Saturday according to the same rhythm—this path is easily followed most of the time. But one day the "why" arises and everything begins in that weariness tinged with amazement. "Begins"—this is important. Weariness comes at the end of the acts of a mechanical life, but at the same time it inaugurates the impulse of consciousness. It awakens consciousness and provokes what follows. What follows is the gradual return into the chain or it is the definitive awakening. At the end of the awakening comes, in time, the consequence: suicide or recovery. In itself weariness has something sickening about it. Here, I must conclude that it is good. For everything begins with consciousness and nothing is worth anything except through it. . . .

At the heart of all beauty lies something inhuman, and these hills, the softness of the sky, the outline of these trees at this very minute lose the illusory meaning with which we had clothed them, henceforth more remote than a lost paradise. The primitive hostility of the world rises up to face us across millennia. For a second we cease to understand it because for centuries we have understood it in solely the images and designs that we had attributed to it beforehand, because henceforth we lack the power to make use of that artifice. The world evades us because it becomes itself again. That stage scenery masked by habit becomes again what it is. It withdraws at a distance from us. Just as there are days when under the familiar face of a woman, we see as a stranger her we had loved months or years ago, perhaps we shall come even to desire what suddenly leaves us so alone. But the time has not yet come. Just one thing: that denseness and that strangeness of the world is the absurd.

Men, too, secrete the inhuman. At certain moments of lucidity, the mechanical aspect of their gestures, their meaningless pantomine makes silly everything that surrounds them. A man is talking on the telephone behind a glass partition; you cannot hear him, but you see his incomprehensible dumb show: you wonder why he is alive. This discomfort in the face of man's own inhumanity, this incalculable tumble before the image of what we are, this "nausea," as a writer of today calls it, is also the absurd. Likewise, the stranger who at certain seconds comes to meet us in a mirror, the familiar and yet alarming brother we encounter in our own photographs is also the absurd.

I come at last to death and to the attitude we have toward it. On this point everything has been said and it is only proper to avoid pathos. Yet one will never be sufficiently surprised that everyone lives as if no one "knew." This is because in reality there is no experience of death. Properly speaking, nothing has been experienced but what has been lived and made conscious. Here, it is barely possible to speak of the experience of others' deaths. It is a substitute, an illusion, and it never quite convinces us. That melancholy convention cannot be persuasive. The horror comes in reality from the mathematical aspect of the event. If time frightens us, this is because it works out the problem and the solution comes afterward. All the pretty speeches about the soul will have their contrary convincingly proved, at least for a time. From this inert body on which a slap makes no mark the soul has disappeared. This elementary and definitive aspect of the adventure constitutes the absurd feeling. Under the fatal lighting of that destiny, its uselessness becomes evident. No code of ethics and no effort are justifiable a priori in the face of the cruel mathematics that command our condition. . . .

Understanding the world for a man is reducing it to the human, stamping it with his seal. The cat's universe is not the universe of the anthill. The truism "All thought is anthropomorphic" has no other meaning. Likewise, the mind that aims to understand reality can consider itself satisfied only by reducing it to terms of thought. If man realized that the universe like him can love and suffer, he would be reconciled. If thought discovered in the shimmering mirrors of phenomena eternal relations capable of summing them up and summing themselves up in a single principle, then would be seen an intellectual joy of which the myth of the blessed would be but a ridiculous imitation. That nostalgia for unity, that appetite for the absolute illustrates the essential impulse of the human drama. But the fact of that nostalgia's existence does not imply that it is to be immediately satisfied. . . .

With the exception of professional rationalists, today people despair of true knowledge. If the only significant history of human thought were to be written, it would have to be the history of its successive regrets and its impotences.

Of whom and of what indeed can I say: "I know that!" This heart within me I can feel, and I judge that it exists. This world I can touch, and I likewise judge that it exists. There ends all my knowledge, and the rest is construction. For if I try to seize this self of which I feel sure, if I try to define and to summarize it, it is nothing but water slipping through my fingers. I can sketch one by one all the aspects it is able to assume, all those likewise that have been attributed to it, this upbringing, this origin, this ardor of these silences, this nobility or this vileness. But aspects cannot be added up. This very heart which is mine will forever remain indefinable to me. Between the certainty I have of my existence and the content I try to give to that assurance, the gap will never be filled. Forever I shall be a stranger to myself. . . .

Hence the intelligence, too, tells me in its way that this world is absurd. . . . In this unintelligible and limited universe, man's fate hence-forth assumes its meaning. A horde of irrationals has sprung up and surrounds him until his ultimate end. In his recovered and now studied lucidity, the feeling of the absurd becomes clear and definite. I said that the world is absurd, but I was too hasty. This world in itself is not reasonable, that is all that can be said. But what is absurd is the confrontation of this irrational and the wild longing for clarity whose call echoes in the human heart. The absurd depends as much on man as on the world. . . .

## Absurd Freedom

. . . I don't know whether this world has a meaning that transcends it. But I know that I do not know that meaning and that it is impossible for me just now to know it. What can a meaning outside my condition mean to me? I can understand only in human terms. What I touch, what resists me—that is what I understand. And these two certainties—my appetite for the absolute and for unity and the impossibility of reducing this world to a rational and reasonable principle—I also know that I cannot reconcile them. What other truth can I admit without lying, without bringing in a hope I lack and which means nothing within the limits of my condition?

If I were a tree among trees, a cat among animals, this life would have a meaning, or rather this problem would not rise, for I should belong to this world. I should *be* this world to which I am now opposed by my whole consciousness and my whole insistence upon familiarity. This ridiculous reason is what sets me in opposition to all creation. I cannot cross it out with a stroke of the pen. What I believe to be true I must therefore preserve. What seems to me so obvious, even against me, I must support. And what constitutes the basis of that conflict, of that break between the world and my mind, but the awareness of it? If therefore I want to preserve it, I can through a constant awareness, ever revived, ever alert. This is what, for the moment, I must remember. . . .

Let us insist again on the method: it is a matter of persisting. At a certain point on his path the absurd man is tempted. History is not lacking in either religions or prophets, even without gods. He is asked to leap. All he can reply is that he doesn't fully understand, that it is not obvious. Indeed, he does not want to do anything but what he fully understands. He is assured that this is the sin of pride, but he does not understand the notion of sin; that perhaps hell is in store, but he has not enough imagination to visualize that strange future; that he is losing immortal life, but that seems to him an idle consideration. An attempt is made to get him to admit his guilt. He feels innocent. To tell the truth, that is all he feels—his irreparable innocence. This is what allows him everything. Hence, what he demands of himself is to live *solely* with what he knows, to accommodate himself to what is, and to bring in nothing that is not certain. He is told that nothing is. But this at least is a certainty. And it is with this that he is concerned: he wants to find out if it is possible to live *without appeal*. . . .

Before encountering the absurd, the everyday man lives with aims, a concern for the future or for justification (with regard to whom or what is not the question). He weighs his chances, he counts on "someday," his retirement or the labor of his sons. He still thinks that something in his life can be directed. In truth, he acts as if he were free, even if all the facts make a point of contradicting that liberty. But after the absurd, everything is upset. That idea that "I am," my way of acting as if everything has a meaning (even if, on occasion, I said that nothing has)—all that is given the lie in vertiginous fashion by the absurdity of a possible death. Thinking of the future, establishing aims for oneself, having preferences—all this presupposes a belief in freedom, even if one occasionally ascertains that one doesn't feel it. But at that moment I am well aware that that higher liberty, that freedom *to be*, which alone can serve as basis for a truth, does not exist. Death is there as the only reality. . . .

But at the same time the absurd man realizes that hitherto he was bound to that postulate of freedom on the illusion of which he was living. In a certain sense, that hampered him. To the extent to which he imagined a purpose to his life, he adapted himself to the demands of a purpose to be achieved and became the slave of his liberty. Thus I could not act otherwise than as the father (or the engineer or the leader of a nation, or the post-office subclerk) that I am preparing to be. . . .

The absurd enlightens me on this point: there is no future. Henceforth, this is the reason for my inner freedom. . . .

But what does life mean in such a universe? Nothing else for the moment but indifference to the future and a desire to use up everything that is given. Belief in the meaning of life always implies a scale of values, a choice, our preferences. Belief in the absurd, according to our definitions, teaches the contrary. But this is worth examining.

Knowing whether or not one can live *without appeal* is all that interests me. I do not want to get out of my depth. This aspect of life being given me, can I adapt myself to it? Now, faced with this particular concern, belief in the absurd is tantamount to substituting the quantity of experiences for the quality. If I convince myself that this life has no other aspect than that of the absurd, if I feel that its whole equilibrium depends on that perpetual opposition between my conscious revolt and the darkness in which it struggles, if I admit that my freedom has no meaning except in relation to its limited fate, then I must say that what counts is not the best of living but the most living. . . .

For on the one hand the absurd teaches that all experiences are unimportant, and on the other it urges toward the greatest quantity of experiences. How, then, can one fail to do as so many of those men I was speaking of earlier—choose the form of life that brings us the most possible of that human matter, thereby introducing a scale of values that on the other hand one claims to reject?

But again it is the absurd and its contradictory life that teaches us. For the mistake is thinking that that quantity of experiences depends on the circumstances of our life when it depends solely on us. Here we have to be oversimple. To two men living the same number of years, the world always provides the same sum of experiences. It is up to us to be conscious of them. Being aware of one's life, one's revolt, one's freedom, and to the maximum, is living, and to the maximum. Where lucidity dominates, the scale of values becomes useless. . . .

## THE MYTH OF SISYPHUS

The gods had condemned Sisyphus to ceaselessly rolling a rock to the top of a mountain, whence the stone would fall back of its own weight. They had thought with some reason that there is no more dreadful punishment than futile and hopeless labor.

If one believes Homer, Sisyphus was the wisest and most prudent of mortals. According to another tradition, however, he was disposed to practice the profession of highwayman. I see no contradiction in this. Opinions differ as to the reasons why he became the futile laborer of the underworld. To begin with, he is accused of a certain levity in regard to the gods. He stole their secrets. Ægina, the daughter of Æsopus , was carried off by Jupiter. The father was shocked by that disappearance and complained to Sisyphus. He, who knew of the abduction, offered to tell about it on condition that Æsopus would give water to the citadel of Corinth. To the celestial thunderbolts he preferred the benediction of water. He was punished for this in the underworld. Homer tells us also that Sisyphus had put Death in chains. Pluto could not endure the sight of his deserted, silent empire. He dispatched the god of war, who liberated Death from the hands of her conqueror.

It is said also that Sisyphus, being near to death, rashly wanted to test his wife's love. He ordered her to cast his unburied body into the middle of the public square. Sisyphus woke up in the underworld. And there, annoyed by an obedience so contrary to human love, he obtained from Pluto permission to return to earth in order to chastise his wife. But when he had seen again the face of this world, enjoyed water and sun, warm stones and the sea, he no longer wanted to go back to the infernal darkness. Recalls, signs of anger, warnings were of no avail. Many years more he lived facing the curve of the gulf, the sparkling sea, and the smiles of earth. A decree of the gods was necessary. Mercury came and seized the impudent man by the collar and, snatching him from his joys, led him forcibly back to the underworld, where his rock was ready for him.

You have already grasped that Sisyphus is the absurd hero. He is, as much through his passions as through his torture. His scorn of the gods, his hatred of death, and his passion for life won him that unspeakable penalty in which the whole being is exerted toward accomplishing nothing. This is the price that must be paid for the passions of this earth. Nothing is told us about Sisyphus in the underworld. Myths are made for the imagination to breath life into them. As for this myth, one sees merely the whole effort of a body straining to raise the huge stone, to roll it and push it up a slope a hundred times over; one sees the face screwed up, the cheek tight against the stone, the shoulder bracing the clay-covered mass, the foot wedging it, the fresh start with arms outstretched, the wholly human security of two earth-clotted hands. At the very end of his long effort measured by skyless space and time without depth, the purpose is achieved. Then Sisyphus watches the stone rush down in a few moments toward that lower world whence he will have to push it up again towards the summit. He goes back down to the plain.

It is during that return, that pause, that Sisyphus interests me. A face that toils so close to stones is already stone itself! I see that man going back down with a heavy yet measured stop toward that torment of which he will never know the end. That hour like a breathing-space which returns as surely as his suffering, that is the hour of consciousness. At each of those moments when he leaves the heights and gradually sinks toward the lairs of the gods, he is superior to his fate. He is stronger than his rock.

If this myth is tragic, that is because its hero is conscious. Where would his torture be, indeed, if at every step the hope of succeeding upheld him? The workman of today works every day in his life at the same tasks, and this fate is no less absurd. But it is tragic only at the rare moments when it becomes conscious. Sisyphus, proletarian of the gods, powerless and rebellious, knows the whole extent of his wretched condition: it is what he thinks of during his descent. The lucidity that was to constitute his torture at the same time crowns his victory. There is no fate that cannot be surmounted by scorn.

If the descent is thus sometimes performed in sorrow, it can also take place in joy. This word is not too much. Again I fancy Sisyphus returning toward his rock, and the sorrow was in the beginning. When the images of earth cling too tightly to memory, when the call of happiness becomes too insistent, it happens that melancholy rises in man's heart: this is the rock's victory, this is the rock itself. The boundless grief is too heavy to bear. These are our nights of Gethsemane. But crushing truths perish from being acknowledged. Thus, Œdipus at the outset obeys fate without knowing it. But from the moment he knows, his tragedy begins. Yet at the same moment, blind and desperate, he realizes that the only bond linking him to the world is the cool hand of a girl. Then a tremendous remark rings out: "Despite so many ordeals, my advanced age and the nobility of my soul make me conclude that all is well." Sophocles' Œdipus, like Dostoevsky's Kirilov, thus gives the recipe for the absurd victory. Ancient wisdom confirms modern heroism.

One does not discover the absurd without being tempted to write a manual of happiness. "What! by such narrow ways—?" There is but one world, however. Happiness and the absurd are two sons of the same earth. They are inseparable. It would be a mistake to say that happiness necessarily springs from the absurd discovery. It happens as well that the feeling of the absurd springs from happiness. "I conclude that all is well," says Œdipus, and that remark is sacred. It echoes in the wild and limited universe of man. It teaches that all is not, has not been, exhausted. It drives out of this world a god who had come into it with dissatisfaction and a preference for futile sufferings. It makes of fate a human matter, which must be settled among men.

All Sisyphus' silent joy is contained therein. His fate belongs to him. His rock is his thing. Likewise, the absurd man, when he contemplates his torment, silences all the idols. In the universe suddenly restored to its silence, the myriad wondering little voices of the earth rise up. Unconscious, secret calls, invitations from all the faces, they are the necessary reverse and price of victory. There is no sun without shadow, and it is essential to know the night. The absurd man says yes and his effort will henceforth be unceasing. If there is a personal fate, there is no higher destiny, or at least there is but one which he concludes is inevitable and despicable. For the rest, he knows himself to be the master of his days. At that subtle moment when man glances backward over his life, Sisyphus returning toward his rock, in that slight pivoting he contemplates that series of unrelated actions which becomes his fate, created by him, combined under his memory's eye and soon sealed by his death. Thus, convinced of the wholly human origin of all that is human, a blind man eager to see who knows that the night has no end, he is still on the go. The rock is still rolling.

I leave Sisyphus at the foot of the mountain! One always finds one's burden again. But Sisyphus teaches the higher fidelity that negates the gods and raises rocks. He too concludes that all is well. This universe henceforth without a master seems to him neither sterile nor futile. Each atom of that stone, each mineral flake of that night-filled mountain, in itself forms a world. The struggle itself toward the heights is enough to fill a man's heart. One must imagine Sisyphus happy.

# NOTE

1. From the point of view of the relative value of truth. On the other hand, from the point of view of virile behavior, this scholar's fragility may well make us smile.

# CHAPTER 10

# KURT BAIER

## *The Meaning of Life*

Tolstoy, in his autobiographical work, "A Confession," reports how, when he was fifty and at the height of his literary success, he came to be obsessed by the fear that life was meaningless.

> At first I experienced moments of perplexity and arrest of life, as though I did not know what to do or how to live; and I felt lost and became dejected. But this passed, and I went on living as before. Then these moments of per-plexity began to recur oftener and oftener, and always in the same form. They were always expressed by the questions: What is it for? What does it lead to? At first it seemed to me that these were aimless and irrelevant questions. I thought that it was all well known, and that if I should ever wish to deal with the solution it would not cost me much effort; just at present I had no time for it, but when I wanted to, I should be able to find the answer. The questions however began to repeat themselves frequently, and to demand replies more and more insistently; and like drops of ink always falling on one place they ran together into one black blot.[1]

A Christian living in the Middle Ages would not have felt any serious doubts about Tolstoy's questions. To him it would have seemed quite certain that life had a meaning and quite clear what it was. The medieval Christian world picture assigned to man a highly significant, indeed the central part in the grand scheme of things. The universe was made for the express purpose of providing a stage on which to enact a drama starring Man in the title role.

To be exact, the world was created by God in the year 4004 B.C. Man was the last and the crown of this creation, made in the likeness of God, placed in the Garden of Eden on earth, the fixed centre of the universe, round which

Inaugural Lecture delivered at the Canberra University College, 1957. Copyright © 1957 by Kurt Baier. Used by permission of the author.

revolved the nine heavens of the sun, the moon, the planets and the fixed stars, producing as they revolved in their orbits the heavenly harmony of the spheres. And this gigantic universe was created for the enjoyment of man, who was originally put in control of it. Pain and death were unknown in paradise. But this state of bliss was not to last. Adam and Eve ate of the forbidden tree of knowledge, and life on this earth turned into a death-march through a vale of tears. Then, with the birth of Jesus, new hope came into the world. After He had died on the cross, it became at least possible to wash away with the purifying water of baptism some of the effects of Original Sin and to achieve salvation. That is to say, on condition of obedience to the law of God, man could now enter heaven and regain the state of everlasting, deathless bliss, from which he had been excluded because of the sin of Adam and Eve.

To the medieval Christian the meaning of human life was therefore perfectly clear. The stretch on earth is only a short interlude, a temporary incarceration of the soul in the prison of the body, a brief trial and test, fated to end in death, the release from pain and suffering. What really matters, is the life after the death of the body. One's existence acquires meaning not by gaining what this life can offer but by saving one's immortal soul from death and eternal torture, by gaining eternal life and everlasting bliss.

The scientific world picture which has found ever more general acceptance from the beginning of the modern era onwards is in profound conflict with all this. At first, the Christian conception of the world was discovered to be erroneous in various important details. The Copernican theory showed up the earth as merely one of several planets revolving round the sun, and the sun itself was later seen to be merely one of many fixed stars each of which is itself the nucleus of a solar system similar to our own. Man, instead of occupying the centre of creation, proved to be merely the inhabitant of a celestial body no different from millions of others. Furthermore, geological investigations revealed that the universe was not created a few thousand years ago, but was probably millions of years old.

Disagreements over details of the world picture, however, are only superficial aspects of a much deeper conflict. The appropriateness of the whole Christian outlook is at issue. For Christianity, the world must be regarded as the "creation" of a kind of Superman, a person possessing all the human excellences to an infinite degree and none of the human weaknesses, Who has made man in His image, a feeble, mortal, foolish copy of Himself. In creating the universe, God acts as a sort of playwright-cum-legislator-cum-judge-cum-executioner. In the capacity of playwright, He creates the historical world process, including man. He erects the stage and writes, in outline, the plot. He creates the *dramatis personae* and watches over them with the eye partly of a father, partly of the law. While on stage, the actors are free to extemporise, but if they infringe the divine commandments, they are later dealt with by their creator in His capacity of judge and executioner.

Within such a framework, the Christian attitudes towards the world are natural and sound: it is natural and sound to think that all is arranged for the best even if appearances belie it; to resign oneself cheerfully to one's lot; to be filled with awe and veneration in regard to anything and everything that happens; to want to fall on one's knees and worship and praise the Lord. These are wholly fitting attitudes within the framework of the world view just outlined. And this world view must have seemed wholly sound and acceptable because it offered the best explanation which was then available of all the observed phenomena of nature.

As the natural sciences developed, however, more and more things in the universe came to be explained without the assumption of a supernatural creator. Science, moreover, could explain them better, that is, more accurately and more reliably. The Christian hypothesis of a supernatural maker, whatever other needs it was capable of satisfying, was at any rate no longer indispensable for the purpose of explaining the existence or occurrence of anything. In fact, scientific explanations do not seem to leave any room for this hypothesis. The scientific approach demands that we look for a natural explanation of anything and everything. The scientific way of looking at and explaining things has yielded an immensely greater measure of understanding of, and control over, the universe than any other way. And when one looks at the world in this scientific way, there seems to be no room for a personal relationship between human beings and a supernatural perfect being ruling and guiding men. Hence many scientists and educated men have come to feel that the Christian attitudes towards the world and human existence are inappropriate. They have become convinced that the universe and human existence in it are without a purpose and therefore devoid of meaning.[2]

## 1. THE EXPLANATION OF THE UNIVERSE

Such beliefs are disheartening and unplausible. It is natural to keep looking for the error that must have crept into our arguments. And if an error has crept in, then it is most likely to have crept in with science. For before the rise of science, people did not entertain such melancholy beliefs, while the scientific world picture seems literally to force them on us.

There is one argument which seems to offer the desired way out. It runs somewhat as follows. Science and religion are not really in conflict. They are, on the contrary, mutually complementary, each doing an entirely different job. Science gives provisional, if precise, explanations of small parts of the universe, religion gives final and over-all, if comparatively vague, explanations of the universe as a whole. The objectionable conclusion, that human existence is devoid of meaning, follows only if we use scientific explanations where they do not apply, namely, where total explanations of the whole universe are concerned.[3]

After all, the argument continues, the scientific world picture is the inevitable outcome of rigid adherence to scientific method and explanation, but scientific, that is, causal explanations from their very nature are incapable of producing real illumination. They can at best tell us *how* things are or have come about, but never *why*. They are incapable of making the universe intelligible, comprehensible, meaningful to us. They represent the universe as meaningless, not because it *is* meaningless, but because scientific explanations are not designed to yield answers to investigations into the why and wherefore, into the meaning, purpose, or point of things. Scientific explanations (this argument continues) began, harmlessly enough, as partial and provisional explanations of the movement of material bodies, in particular the planets, within the general framework of the medieval world picture. Newton thought of the universe as a clock made, originally wound up, and occasionally set right by God. His laws of motion only revealed the ways in which the heavenly machinery worked. Explaining the movement of the planets by these laws was analogous to explaining the machinery of a watch. Such explanations showed *how* the thing worked, but not *what it was for* or *why* it existed. Just as the explanation of how a watch works can help our understanding of the watch only if, in addition, we assume that there is a watchmaker who has designed it for a purpose, made it, and wound it up, so the Newtonian explanation of the solar system helps our understanding of it only on the similar assumption that there is some divine artificer who has designed and made this heavenly clockwork for some purpose, has wound it up, and perhaps even occasionally sets it right, when it is out of order.

Socrates, in the "Phaedo," complained that only explanations of a thing showing the good or purpose for which it existed could offer a *real* explanation of it. He rejected the kind of explanation we now call "causal" as no more than mentioning "that without which a cause could not be a cause," that is, as merely a necessary condition, but not the *real* cause, the real explanation.[4] In other words, Socrates held that *all* things can be explained in two different ways: either by mentioning merely a necessary condition, or by giving the *real* cause. The former is not an elucidation of the explicandum, not really a help in understanding it, in grasping its "why" and "wherefore."

This Socratic view, however, is wrong. It is not the case that there are two kinds of explanation for everything, one partial, preliminary, and not really clarifying, the other full, final, and illuminating. The truth is that these two kinds of explanation are equally explanatory, equally illuminating, and equally full and final, but that they are appropriate for different kinds of explicanda.

When in an uninhabited forest we find what looks like houses, paved streets, temples, cooking utensils, and the like, it is no great risk to say that these things are the ruins of a deserted city, that is to say, of something man-made. In such a case, the appropriate explanation is teleological, that is, in terms of the purposes of the builders of that city. On the other hand, when a comet approaches the earth, it is similarly a safe bet that, unlike the city in the forest, it was not manufactured by intelligent creatures and that, therefore, a teleological explanation would be out of place, whereas a causal one is suitable.

It is easy to see that in some cases causal, and in others teleological, explanations are appropriate. A small satellite circling the earth may or may not have been made by man. We may never know which is the true explanation, but either hypothesis is equally explanatory. It would be wrong to say that only a teleological explanation can *really* explain it. Either explanation would yield complete clarity although, of course, only one can be true. Teleological explanation is only one of several that are possible.

It may indeed be strictly correct to say that the question *"Why* is there a satellite circling the earth?" can only be answered by a teleological explanation. It may be true that "Why?" questions can really be used properly only in order to elicit *someone's reasons for* doing something. If this is so, it would explain our dissatisfaction with causal answers to "Why?" questions. But even if it is so, it does not show that "Why is the satellite there?" *must be answered by a teleological explanation.* It shows only that either it must be so answered or it must not be asked. The question "Why have you stopped beating your wife?" can be answered only by a teleological explanation, but if you have never beaten her, it is an improper question. Similarly, if the satellite is not man-made, "Why is there a satellite?" is improper since it implies an origin it did not have. Natural science can indeed only tell us *how* things in nature have come about and not *why,* but this is so not because something else can tell us the *why* and *wherefore,* but because there is none.

There is, however, another point which has not yet been answered. The objection just stated was that causal explanations did not even set out to answer the crucial question. We ask the question "Why?" but science returns an answer to the question "How?" It might now be conceded that this is no ground for a complaint, but perhaps it will instead be said that causal explanations do not give complete or full answers even to that latter question. In causal explanations, it will be objected, the existence of one thing is explained by reference to its cause, but this involves asking for the cause of that cause, and so on, ad infinitum. There is no resting place which is not as much in need of explanation as what has already been explained. Nothing at all is ever fully and completely explained by this sort of explanation.

Leibniz has made this point very persuasively. "Let us suppose a book of the elements of geometry to have been eternal, one copy always having been taken down from an earlier one; it is evident that, even though a reason can be given for the present book out of a past one, nevertheless, out of any number of books, taken in order, going backwards, we shall never come upon *a full* reason; though we might well always wonder why there should have been such books from all time—why there were books at all, and why they were written in this manner. What is true of books is true also of the different states of the world; for what follows is in some way copied from what precedes . . . And so, however far you go back to earlier states, you will never find in those states *a full reason* why there should be any world rather than none, and why it should be such as it is."[5]

However, a moment's reflection will show that if any type of explanation is merely preliminary and provisional, it is teleological explanation, since it presupposes a background which itself stands in need of explanation. If I account for the existence of the man-made satellite by saying that it was made by some scientists for a certain purpose, then such an explanation can clarify the existence of the satellite only if I assume that there existed materials out of which the satellite was made, and scientists who made it for some purpose. It therefore does not matter what type of explanation we give, whether causal or teleological: either type, any type of explanation, will imply the existence of something by reference to which the explicandum can be explained. And this in turn must be accounted for in the same way, and so on for ever.

But is not God a necessary being? Do we not escape the infinite regress as soon as we reach God? It is often maintained that, unlike ordinary intelligent beings, God is eternal and necessary; hence His existence, unlike theirs, is not in need of explanation. For what is it that creates the vicious regress just mentioned? It is that, if we accept the principle of sufficient reason (that there must be an explanation for the existence of anything and everything the existence of which is not logically necessary, but merely contingent),[6] the existence of all the things referred to in any explanation requires itself to be explained. If, however, God is a logically necessary being, then His existence requires no explanation. Hence the vicious regress comes to an end with God.

Now, it need not be denied that God is a necessary being in some sense of that expression. In one of these senses, I, for instance, am a necessary being: it is impossible that I should not exist, because it is self-refuting to say "I do not exist." The same is true of the English language and of the universe. It is self-refuting to say "There is no such thing as the English language" because this sentence is in the English language, or "There is no such thing as the universe" because whatever there is, *is* the universe. It is impossible that these things should not in fact exist since it is impossible that we should be mistaken in thinking that they exist. For what possible occurrence could even throw doubt on our being right on these matters, let alone show that we are wrong? I, the English language, and the universe, are necessary beings, simply in the sense in which all is necessarily true which has been *proved* to be true. The occurrence of utterances such as "I exist," "The English language exists" and "The universe exists" is in itself sufficient proof of their truth. These remarks are therefore necessarily true, hence the things asserted to exist are necessary things.

But this sort of necessity will not satisfy the principle of sufficient reason, because it is only hypothetical or consequential necessity.[7] *Given that* someone says "I exist," then it is logically impossible that *he* should not exist. Given the evidence we have, the English language and the universe most certainly do exist. But there is no necessity about the evidence. On the principle of sufficient reason, we must explain the existence of the evidence, for its existence is not logically necessary.

In other words, the only sense of "necessary being" capable of terminating the vicious regress is "logically necessary being," but it is no longer seriously in dispute that the notion of a logically necessary being is self-contradictory.[8] Whatever can be conceived of as existing can equally be conceived of as not existing.

However, even if per impossible, there were such a thing as a logically necessary being, we could still not make out a case for the superiority of teleological over causal explanation. The existence of the universe cannot be explained in accordance with the familiar model of manufacture by a craftsman. For that model presupposes the existence of materials out of which the product is fashioned. God, on the other hand, must create the materials as well. Moreover, although we have a simple model of "creation out of nothing," for composers create tunes out of nothing, yet this is a great difference between creating *something to be sung*, and making the sounds which are a singing of it, or producing the piano on which to play it. Let us, however, waive all these objections and admit, for argument's sake, that creation out of nothing is conceivable. Surely, even so, no one can claim that it is the kind of explanation which yields the clearest and fullest understanding. Surely, to round off scientific explanations of the origin of the universe with creation out of nothing, does not add anything to our *understanding*. There may be merit of some sort in this way of speaking, but whatever it is, it is not greater clarity or explanatory power.[9]

What then, does all this amount to? Merely to the claim that scientific explanations are no worse than any other. All that has been shown is that all explanations suffer from the same defect: all involve a vicious infinite regress. In other words, no type of human explanation can help us to unravel the ultimate, unanswerable mystery. Christian ways of looking at things may not be able to render the world any more lucid than science can, but at least they do not pretend that there are no impenetrable mysteries. On the contrary, they point out untiringly that the claims of science to be able to elucidate everything are hollow. They remind us that science is not merely limited to the exploration of a tiny corner of the universe but that, however far out probing instruments may eventually reach, we can never even approach the answers to the last questions: "Why is there a world at all rather than nothing?" and "Why is the world such as it is and not different?" Here our finite human intellect bumps against its own boundary walls.

Is it true that scientific explanations involve an infinite vicious regress? Are scientific explanations really only provisional and incomplete? The crucial point will be this. Do *all* contingent truths call for explanation? Is the principle of sufficient reason sound? Can scientific explanations never come to a definite end? It will be seen that with a clear grasp of the nature and purpose of explanation we can answer these questions.[10]

Explaining something to someone is making him understand it. This involves bringing together in his mind two things, a model which is accepted as already simple and clear, and that which is to be explained, the explicandum, which is not so. Understanding the explicandum is seeing that it belongs to a range of things which could legitimately have been expected by anyone familiar with the model and with certain facts.

There are, however, two fundamentally different positions which a person may occupy relative to some explicandum. He may not be familiar with any model capable of leading him to expect the phenomenon to be explained. Most of us, for instance, are in that position in relation to the phenomena occurring in a good seance. With regard to other things people will differ. Someone who can play chess, already understands chess, already has such a model. Someone who has never seen a game of chess has not. He sees the moves on the board but he cannot understand, cannot follow, cannot make sense of what is happening. Explaining the game to him is giving him an explanation, is making him understand. He can understand or follow chess moves only if he can see them as conforming to a model of a chess game. In order to acquire such a model, he will, of course, need to know the constitutive rules of chess, that is, the permissible moves. But that is not all. He must know that a normal game of chess is a competition (not all games are) between two people, each trying to win, and he must know what it is to win at chess: to manoeuvre the opponent's king into a position of check-mate. Finally, he must acquire some knowledge of what is and what is not conducive to winning: the tactical rules or canons of the game.

A person who has been given such an explanation and who has mastered it—which may take quite a long time—has now reached understanding, in the sense of the ability to follow each move. A person cannot in that sense understand merely one single move of chess and no other. If he does not understand any other moves, we must say that he has not yet mastered the explanation, that he does not really understand the single move either. If he has mastered the explanation, then he understands all those moves which he can see as being in accordance with the model of the game inculcated in him during the explanation.

However, even though a person who has mastered such an explanation will understand many, perhaps most, moves of any game of chess he cares to watch, he will not necessarily understand them all, as some moves of a player may not be in accordance with his model of the game. White, let us say, at his fifteenth move, exposes his queen to capture by Black's knight. Though in accordance with the constitutive rules of the game, this move is nevertheless perplexing and calls for explanation, because it is not conducive to the achievement by White of what must be assumed to be his aim: to win the game. The queen is a much more valuable piece than the knight against which he is offering to exchange.

An onlooker who has mastered chess may fail to understand this move, be perplexed by it, and wish for an explanation. Of course he may fail to be perplexed, for if he is a very inexperienced player he may not *see* the disadvantageousness of the move. But there is such a need whether anyone sees it or not. The move *calls for* explanation because to anyone who knows the game it must appear to be incompatible with the model which we have learnt during the explanation of the game, and by reference to which we all explain and understand normal games.

However, the required explanation of White's fifteenth move is of a very different kind. What is needed now is not the acquisition of an explanatory model, but the removal of the real or apparent incompatibility between the player's move and the model of explanation he has already acquired. In such a case the perplexity can be removed only on the assumption that the incompatibility between the model and the game is merely apparent. As our model includes a presumed aim of both players, there are the following three possibilities: (a) White has made a mistake: he has over-looked the threat to his queen. In that case, the explanation is that White thought his move conducive to his end, but it was not. (b) Black has made a mistake: White set a trap for him. In that case, the explanation is that Black thought White's move was not conducive to White's end, but it was. (c) White is not pursuing the end which any chess player may be presumed to pursue: he is not trying to win his game. In that case, the explanation is that White has made a move which he knows is not conducive to the end of winning his game because, let us say, he wishes to please Black who is his boss.

Let us now set out the differences and similarities between the two types of understanding involved in these two kinds of explanation. I shall call the first kind "model"—understanding and explaining, respectively, because both involve the use of a model by reference to which understanding and explaining is effected. The second kind I shall call "unvexing," because the need for this type of explanation and understanding arises only when there is a perplexity arising out of the incompatibility of the model and the facts to be explained.

The first point is that unvexing presupposes model-understanding, but not vice versa. A person can neither have nor fail to have unvexing-understanding of White's fifteenth move at chess, if he does not already have model-understanding of chess. Obviously, if I don't know how to play chess, I shall fail to have model-understanding of White's fifteenth move. But I can neither fail to have nor, of course, can I have unvexing-understanding of it, for I cannot be perplexed by it. I merely fail to have model-understanding of this move as, indeed, of any other move of chess. On the other hand, I may well have model-understanding of chess without having unvexing-understanding of every move. That is to say, I may well know how to play chess without understanding White's fifteenth move. A person cannot fail to have unvexing-understanding of the move unless he is vexed or perplexed by it, hence he cannot even fail to have unvexing-understanding unless he already has model-understanding. It is not true that one either understands or fails to understand. On certain occasions, one neither understands nor fails to understand.

The second point is that there are certain things which cannot call for unvexing-explanations. No one can for instance call for an unvexing-explanation of White's first move, which is Pawn to King's Four. For no one can be perplexed or vexed by this move. Either a person knows how to play chess or he does not. If he does, then he must understand this move, for if he does not understand it, he has not yet mastered the game. And if he does not know how to play chess, then he cannot yet have, or fail to have, unvexing-understanding, he cannot therefore need an unvexing-explanation. Intellectual problems do not arise out of ignorance, but out of insufficient knowledge. An ignoramus is puzzled by very little. Once a student can see problems, he is already well into the subject.

The third point is that model-understanding implies being able, without further thought, to have model-understanding of a good many other things, unvexing-understanding does not. A person who knows chess and therefore has model-understanding of it, must understand a good many chess moves, in fact all except those that call for unvexing-explanations. If he claims that he can understand White's first move, but no others, then he is either lying or deceiving himself or he really does not understand any move. On the other hand, a person who, after an unvexing-explanation, understands White's fifteenth move, need not be able, without further explanation, to understand Black's or any other further move which calls for unvexing-explanation.

What is true of explaining deliberate and highly stylized human behaviour such as playing a game of chess is also true of explaining natural phenomena. For what is characteristic of natural phenomena, that they recur in essentially the same way, that they are, so to speak, repeatable, is also true of chess games, as it is not of games of tennis or cricket. There is only one important difference: man himself has invented and laid down the rules of chess, as he has not invented or laid down the "rules or laws governing the behaviour of things." This difference between chess and phenomena is important, for it adds another way to the three already mentioned,[11] in which a perplexity can be removed by an unvexing-explanation, namely, by abandoning the original explanatory model. This is, of course, not possible in the case of games of chess, because the model for chess is not a "construction" on the basis of the already existing phenomena of chess, but an invention. The person who first thought up the model of chess could not have been mistaken. The person who first thought of a model explaining some phenomenon could have been mistaken.

Consider an example. We may think that the following phenomena belong together: the horizon seems to recede however far we walk towards it; we seem to be able to see further the higher the mountain we climb; the sun and moon seem every day to fall into the sea on one side but to come back from behind the mountains on the other side without being any the worse for it. We may explain these phenomena by two alternative models: (a) that the earth is a large disc; (b) that it is a large sphere. However, to a believer in the first theory there arises the following perplexity: how is it that when we travel long enough towards the horizon in any one direction, we do eventually come back to our starting point without ever coming to the edge of the earth? We may at first attempt to "save" the model by saying that there is only an apparent contradiction. We may say either that the model does not require us to come to an edge, for it may be possible only to walk round and round on the flat surface. Or we may say that the person must have walked over the edge without noticing it, or perhaps that the travellers are all lying. Alternatively, the fact that our model is "constructed" and not invented or laid down enables us to say, what we could not do in the case of chess, that the model is inadequate or unsuitable. We can choose another model which fits all the facts, for instance, that the earth is round. Of course, then we have to give an unvexing-explanation for why it *looks* flat, but we are able to do that.

We can now return to our original question, "Are scientific explanations true and full explanations or do they involve an infinite regress, leaving them for ever incomplete?"

Our distinction between model- and unvexing-explanations will help here. It is obvious that only those things which are perplexing *call for* and *can be given* unvexing-explanations. We have already seen that in disposing of one perplexity, we do not necessarily raise another. On the contrary, unvexing-explanations truly and completely explain what they set out to explain, namely, how something is possible which, on our explanatory model, seemed to be impossible. There can therefore be no infinite regress here. Unvexing-explanations are real and complete explanations.

Can there be an infinite regress, then, in the case of model-explanations? Take the following example. European children are puzzled by the fact that their antipodean counterparts do not drop into empty space. This perplexity can be removed by substituting for their explanatory model another one. The European children imagine that throughout space there is an all-pervasive force operating in the same direction as the force that pulls them to the ground. We must, in our revised model, substitute for this force another acting everywhere in the direction of the centre of the earth. Having thus removed their perplexity by giving them an adequate model, we can, however, go on to ask *why* there should be such a force as the force of gravity, why bodies should "naturally," in the absence of forces acting on them, behave in the way stated in Newton's laws. And we might be able to give such an explanation. We might for instance construct a model of space which would exhibit as derivable from it what in Newton's theory are "brute facts." Here we would have a case of the brute facts of one theory being explained within the framework of another, more general theory. And it is a sound methodological principle that we should continue to look for more and more general theories.

Note two points, however. The first is that we must distinguish, as we have seen, between *the possibility* and *the necessity* of giving an explanation. Particular occurrences can be explained by being exhibited as instances of regularities, and regularities can be explained by being exhibited as instances of more general regularities. Such explanations make things clearer. They organize the material before us. They introduce order where previously there was disorder. But absence of this sort of explanation (model-explanation) does not leave us with a puzzle or perplexity, an intellectual restlessness or cramp. The unexplained things are not unintelligible, incomprehensible, or irrational. Some things, on the other hand, call for, require, demand an explanation. As long as we are without such an explanation, we are perplexed, puzzled, intellectually perturbed. We need an unvexing-explanation.

Now, it must be admitted that we may be able to construct a more general theory, from which, let us say, Newton's theory can be derived. This would further clarify the phenomena of motion and would be intellectually satisfying. But failure to do so would not leave us with an intellectual cramp.

The facts stated in Newton's theory do not require, or stand in need of, unvexing-explanations. They could do so only if we already had another theory or model with which Newton's theory was incompatible. They could not do so, by themselves, prior to the establishment of such another model.

The second point is that there is an objective limit to which such explanations tend, and beyond which they are pointless. There is a very good reason for wishing to explain a less general by a more general theory. Usually, such a unification goes hand in hand with greater precision in measuring the phenomena which both theories explain. Moreover, the more general theory, because of its greater generality, can explain a wider range of phenomena including not only phenomena already explained by some other theories but also newly discovered phenomena, which the less general theory cannot explain. Now, the ideal limit to which such expansions of theories tend is an all-embracing theory which unifies all theories and explains all phenomena. Of course, such a limit can never be reached, since new phenomena are constantly discovered. Nevertheless, theories may be tending towards it. It will be remembered that the contention made against scientific theories was that there is no such limit because they involve an infinite regress. On that view, which I reject, there is no conceivable point at which scientific theories could be said to have explained the whole universe. On the view I am defending, there is such a limit, and it is the limit towards which scientific theories are actually tending. I claim that the nearer we come to this limit, the closer we are to a full and complete explanation of everything. For if we were to reach the limit, then though we could, of course, be left with a model which is itself unexplained and could be yet further explained by derivation from another model, there would be no need for, and no point in, such a further explanation. There would be no need for it, because any clearly defined model permitting us to expect the phenomena it is designed to explain offers full and complete explanations of these phenomena, however narrow the range. And while, at lower levels of generality, there is a good reason for providing more general models, since they further simplify, systematize, and organize the phenomena, this, which is the only reason for building more general theories, no longer applies once we reach the ideal limit of an all-embracing explanation.

It might be said that there is another reason for using different models: that they might enable us to discover new phenomena. Theories are not only instruments of explanation, but also of discovery. With this I agree, but it is irrelevant to my point: that *the needs of explanation* do not require us to go on for ever deriving one explanatory model from another.

It must be admitted, then, that in the case of model-explanations there is a regress, but it is neither vicious nor infinite. It is not vicious because, in order to explain a group of explicanda, a model-explanation *need* not itself be derived from another more general one. It gives a perfectly full and consistent explanation by itself. And the regress is not infinite, for there is a natural limit, an all-embracing model, which can explain all phenomena, beyond which it would be pointless to derive model-explanations from yet others.

What about our most serious question, "Why is there anything at all?" Sometimes, when we think about how one thing has developed out of another and that one out of a third, and so on back throughout all time, we are driven to ask the same question about the universe as a whole. We want to add up all things and refer to them by the name, "the world," and we want to know why the world exists and why there is not nothing instead. In such moments, the world seems to us a kind of bubble floating on an ocean of nothingness. Why should such flotsam be adrift in empty space? Surely, its emergence from the hyaline billows of nothingness is more mysterious even than Aphrodite's emergence from the sea. Wittgenstein expressed in these words the mystification we all feel: "Not *how* the world is, is the mystical, but *that* it is. The contemplation of the world *sub specie aeterni* is the contemplation of it as a limited whole. The feeling of the world as a limited whole is the mystical feeling."[12]

Professor J. J. C. Smart expresses his own mystification in these moving words:

> That anything should exist at all does seem to me a matter for the deepest awe. But whether other people feel this sort of awe, and whether they or I ought to is another question. I think we ought to. If so, the question arises: If "Why should anything exist at all?" cannot be interpreted after the manner of the cosmological argument, that is, as an absurd request for the non-sensical postulation of a logically necessary being, what sort of question is it? What sort of question is this question "Why should anything exist at all?" All I can say is that I do not yet know.[13]

It is undeniable that the magnitude and perhaps the very existence of the universe is awe-inspiring. It is probably true that it gives many people "the mystical feeling." It is also undeniable that our awe, our mystical feeling, aroused by contemplating the vastness of the world, is justified, in the same sense in which our fear is justified when we realize we are in danger. There is no more appropriate object for our awe or for the mystical feeling than the magnitude and perhaps the existence of the universe, just as there is no more appropriate object for our fear than a situation of personal peril. However, it does not follow from this that it is a good thing to cultivate, or indulge in, awe or mystical feelings, any more than it is necessarily a good thing to cultivate, or indulge in, fear in the presence of danger.

In any case, whether or not we ought to have or are justified in having a mystical feeling or a feeling of awe when contemplating the universe, having such a feeling is not the same as asking a meaningful question, although having it may well *incline us* to utter certain forms of words. Our question "Why is there anything at all?" may be no more than the expression of our feeling of awe or mystification, and not a meaningful question at all. Just as the feeling of fear may naturally but illegitimately give rise to the question "What sin have I committed?" so the feeling of awe or mystification may naturally but illegitimately lead to the question "Why is there anything at all?" What we have to discover, then, is whether this question makes sense or is meaningless.

Yes, of course, it will be said, it makes perfectly good sense. There is an undeniable fact and it calls for explanation. The fact is that the universe exists. In the light of our experience, there can be no possible doubt that something or other exists, and the claim that the universe exists commits us to no more than that. And surely this calls for explanation, because the universe must have originated somehow. Everything has an origin and the universe is no exception. Since the universe is the totality of things, it must have originated out of nothing. If it had originated out of something, even something as small as one single hydrogen atom, what has so originated could not be the whole universe, but only the universe minus the atom. And then the atom itself would call for explanation, for it too must have had an origin, and it must be *an origin out of nothing*. And how can anything originate out of nothing? Surely that calls for explanation.

However, let us be quite clear what is to be explained. There are two facts here, not one. The first is that the universe exists, which is undeniable. The second is that the universe must have originated out of nothing, and that is not undeniable. It is true that, *if it has originated at all*, then it must have originated out of nothing, or else it is not the universe that has originated. But need it have originated? Could it not have existed for ever?[14] It might be argued that nothing exists for ever, that everything has originated out of something else. That may well be true, but it is perfectly compatible with the fact that the universe is everlasting. We may well be able to trace the origin of any thing to the time when, by some transformation, it has developed out of some other thing, and yet it may be the case that no thing has its origin in nothing, and the universe has existed for ever. For even if every *thing* has a beginning and an end, the total of mass and energy may well remain constant.

Moreover, the hypothesis that the universe originated out of nothing is, empirically speaking, completely empty. Suppose, for argument's sake, that the annihilation of an object without remainder is conceivable. It would still not be possible for any hypothetical observer to ascertain whether space was empty or not. Let us suppose that *within the range of observation of our observer* one object after another is annihilated without remainder and that only one is left. Our observer could not then tell whether in remote parts of the universe, beyond his range of observation, objects are coming into being or passing out of existence. What, moreover, are we to say of the observer himself? Is he to count for nothing? Must we not postulate him away as well, if the universe is to have arisen out of nothing?

Let us, however, ignore all these difficulties and assume that the universe really has originated out of nothing. Even that does not prove that the universe has not existed for ever. If the universe can conceivably develop out of nothing, then it can conceivably vanish without remainder. And it can arise out of nothing again and subside into nothingness once more, and so on ad infinitum. Of course, "again" and "once more" are not quite the right words. The concept of time hardly applies to such universes. It does not make sense to ask whether one of them is earlier or later than, or perhaps simultaneous with, the other because we cannot ask whether they occupy the same or different spaces. Being separated from one another by "nothing," they are not separated from one another by "anything." We cannot therefore make any statements about their mutual spatio-temporal relations. It is impossible to distinguish between one long continuous universe and two universes separated by nothing. How, for instance, can we tell whether the universe including ourselves is not frequently annihilated and "again" reconstituted just as it was?

Let us now waive these difficulties as well. Let us suppose for a moment that we understand what is meant by saying that the universe originated out of nothing and that this has happened only once. Let us accept this as a fact. Does this fact call for explanation?

It does not call for an unvexing-explanation. That would be called for only if there were a perplexity due to the incompatibility of an accepted model with some fact. In our case, the fact to be explained is the origination of the universe out of nothing, hence there could not be such a perplexity, for we need not employ a model incompatible with this. If we had a model incompatible with our "fact," then that would be the wrong model and we would simply have to substitute another for it. The model we employ to explain the origin of the universe out of nothing could not be based on the similar origins of other things for, of course, there is nothing else with a similar origin.

All the same, it seems very surprising that something should have come out of nothing. It is contrary to the principle that every thing has an origin, that is, has developed out of something else. It must be admitted that there is this incompatibility. However, it does not arise because a well-established model does not square with an undeniable fact; it arises because a well-established model does not square with *an assumption* of which it is hard even to make sense and for which there is no evidence whatsoever. In fact, the only reason we have for making this assumption, is a simple logical howler: that because every thing has an origin, the universe must have an origin, too, except, that, being the universe, it must have originated out of nothing. This is a howler, because it conceives of the universe as a big thing, whereas in fact it is the totality of things, that is, not a thing. That every thing has an origin does not entail that the totality of things has an origin. On the contrary, it strongly suggests that it has not. For to say that every thing has an origin implies that any given thing must have developed out of something else which in turn, being a thing, must have developed out of something else, and so forth. If we assume that every thing has an origin, we need not, indeed it is hard to see how we can, assume that the totality of things has an origin as well. There is therefore no perplexity, because we need not and should not assume that the universe has originated out of nothing.

If, however, in spite of all that has been said just now, someone still wishes to assume, contrary to all reason, that the universe has originated out of nothing, there would still be no perplexity, for then he would simply have to give up the principle which is incompatible with this assumption, namely, that no thing can originate out of nothing. After all, this principle *could* allow for exceptions. We have no proof that it does not. Again, there is no perplexity, because no incompatibility between our assumption and an inescapable principle.

But, it might be asked, do we not need a model-explanation of our supposed fact? The answer is No. We do not need such an explanation, for there could not possibly be a model for this origin other than this origin itself. We cannot say that origination out of nothing is like birth, or emergence, or evolution, or anything else we know for it is not like anything we know. In all these cases, there is *something* out of which the new thing has originated.

To sum up. The question, "Why is there anything at all?" looks like a perfectly sensible question modelled on "Why does *this* exist?" or "How has *this* originated?" It looks like a question about the origin of a thing. However, it is not such a question, for the universe is not a thing, but the totality of things. There is therefore no reason to assume that the universe has an origin. The very assumption that it has is fraught with contradictions and absurdities. If, nevertheless, it were true that the universe has originated out of nothing, then this would not call either for an unvexing or a model-explanation. It would not call for the latter, because there could be no model of it taken from another part of our experience, since there is nothing analogous in our experience to origination out of nothing. It would not call for the former, because there can be no perplexity due to the incompatibility of a well-established model and an undeniable fact, since there is no undeniable fact and no well-established model. If, on the other hand, as is more probable, the universe has not originated at all, but is eternal, then the question why or how it has originated simply does not arise. There can then be no question about why anything at all exists, for it could not mean how or why the universe had originated, since ex hypothesi it has no origin. And what else could it mean?

Lastly, we must bear in mind that the hypothesis that the universe was made by God out of nothing only brings us back to the question who made God or how God originated. And if we do not find it repugnant to say that God is eternal, we cannot find it repugnant to say that the universe is eternal. The only difference is that we know for certain that the universe exists, while we have the greatest difficulty in even making sense of the claim that God exists.

To sum up. According to the argument examined, we must reject the scientific world picture because it is the outcome of scientific types of explanation which do not really and fully explain the world around us, but only tell us *how* things have come about, not *why*, and can give no answer to the ultimate question, why there is anything at all rather than nothing. Against this, I have argued that scientific explanations are real and full, just like the explanations of everyday life and of the traditional religions. They differ from those latter only in that they are more precise and more easily disprovable by the observation of facts.

My main points dealt with the question why scientific explanations were thought to be merely provisional and partial. The first main reason is the misunderstanding of the difference between teleological and causal explanations. It is first, and rightly, maintained that teleological explanations are answers to "Why?" questions, while causal explanations are answers to "How?" questions. It is further, and wrongly, maintained that, in order to obtain real and full explanations of anything, one must answer both "Why?" and "How?" questions. In other words, it is thought that all matters can and must be explained by both teleological and causal types of explanation. Causal explanations, it is believed, are merely provisional and partial, waiting to be completed by teleological explanations. Until a teleological explanation has been given, so the story goes, we have not *really* understood the explicandum. However, I have shown that both types are equally real and full explanations. The difference between them is merely that they are appropriate to different types of explicanda.

It should, moreover, be borne in mind that teleological explanations are not, in any sense, unscientific. They are rightly rejected in the natural sciences, not however because they are unscientific, but because no intelligences or purposes are found to be involved there. On the other hand, teleological explanations are very much in place in psychology, for we find intelligence and purpose involved in a good deal of human behaviour. It is not only not unscientific to give teleological explanations of deliberate human behaviour, but it would be quite unscientific to exclude them.

The second reason why scientific explanations are thought to be merely provisional and partial, is that they are believed to involve a vicious infinite regress. Two misconceptions have led to this important error. The first is the general misunderstanding of the nature of explanation, and in particular the failure to distinguish between the two types which I have called model- and unvexing-explanations, respectively. If one does not draw this distinction, it is natural to conclude that scientific explanations lead to a vicious infinite regress. For while it is true of those perplexing matters which are elucidated by unvexing-explanations that they are incomprehensible and cry out for explanation, it is not true that after an unvexing-explanation has been given, this itself is again capable, let alone in need of, a yet further explanation of the same kind. Conversely, while it is true that model-explanations of regularities can themselves be further explained by more general model-explanations, it is not true that, in the absence of such more general explanations, the less general are incomplete, hang in the air, so to speak, leaving the explicandum incomprehensible and crying out for explanation. The distinction between the two types of explanation shows us that an explicandum is either perplexing and incomprehensible, in which case an explanation of it *is necessary* for clarification and, when given, *complete*, or it is a regularity capable of being subsumed under a model, in which case a further explanation *is possible* and often profitable, but *not necessary* for clarification.

The second misconception responsible for the belief in a vicious infinite regress is the misrepresentation of scientific explanation *as essentially causal*. It has generally been held that, in a scientific explanation, the explicandum is the effect of some event, the cause, temporally prior to the explicandum.

Combined with the principle of sufficient reason (the principle that anything is in need of explanation which might conceivably have been different from what it is), this error generates the nightmare of determinism. Since any event might have been different from what it was, acceptance of this principle has the consequence that *every* event must have a reason or explanation. But if the reason is itself an event *prior in time,* then every reason must have a reason preceding it, and so the infinite regress of explanation is necessarily tied to the time scale stretching infinitely back into the endless past. It is, however, obvious from our account that science is not primarily concerned with the forging of such causal chains. The primary object of the natural sciences is not historical at all. Natural science claims to reveal, not the beginnings of things, but their underlying reality. It does not dig up the past, it digs down into the structure of things existing here and now. Some scientists do allow themselves to speculate, and rather precariously at that, about origins. But their hard work is done on the structure of what exists now. In particular those explanations which are themselves further explained are not explanations linking event to event in a gapless chain reaching back to creation day, but generalisations of theories tending towards a unified theory.

## 2. THE PURPOSE OF MAN'S EXISTENCE

Our conclusion in the previous section has been that science is in principle able to give complete and real explanations of every occurrence and thing in the universe. This has two important corollaries: (i) Acceptance of the scientific world picture cannot be *one's reason for* the belief that the universe is unintelligible and therefore meaningless, though coming to accept it, after having been taught the Christian world picture, may well have been, in the case of many individuals, *the only or the main cause* of their belief that the universe and human existence are meaningless. (ii) It is not in accordance with reason to reject this pessimistic belief on the grounds that scientific explanations are only provisional and incomplete and must be supplemented by religious ones.

In fact, it might be argued that the more clearly we understand the explanations given by science, the more we are driven to the conclusion that human life has no purpose and therefore no meaning. The science of astronomy teaches us that our earth was not specially created about 6,000 years ago, but evolved out of hot nebulae which previously had whirled aimlessly through space for countless ages. As they cooled, the sun and the planets formed. On one of these planets at a certain time the circumstances were propitious and life developed. But conditions will not remain favourable to life. When our solar system grows old, the sun will cool, our planet will be covered with ice, and all living creatures will eventually perish. Another theory has it that the sun will explode and that the heat generated will be so great that all organic life on earth will be destroyed. That is the comparatively short history and prospect of life on earth. Altogether it amounts to very little when compared with the endless history of the inanimate universe.

Biology teaches us that the species man was not specially created but is merely, in a long chain of evolutionary changes of forms of life, the last link, made in the likeness not of God but of nothing so much as an ape. The rest of the universe, whether animate or inanimate, instead of serving the ends of man, is at best indifferent, at worst savagely hostile. Evolution to whose operation the emergence of man is due is a ceaseless battle among members of different species, one species being gobbled up by another, only the fittest surviving. Far from being the gentlest and most highly moral, man is simply the creature best fitted to survive, the most efficient if not the most rapacious and insatiable killer. And in this unplanned, fortuitous, monstrous, savage world man is madly trying to snatch a few brief moments of joy, in the short intervals during which he is free from pain, sickness, persecution, war or famine until, finally, his life is snuffed out in death. Science has helped us to know and understand this world, but what purpose or meaning can it find in it?

Complaints such as these do not mean quite the same to everybody, but one thing, I think, they mean to most people: science shows life to be meaningless, because life is without purpose. The medieval world picture provided life with a purpose, hence medieval Christians could believe that life had a meaning. The scientific account of the world takes away life's purpose and with it its meaning.

There are, however, two quite different senses of "purpose." Which one is meant? Has science deprived human life of purpose in both senses? And if not, is it a harmless sense, in which human existence has been robbed of purpose? Could human existence still have meaning if it did not have a purpose in that sense?

What are the two senses? In the first and basic sense, purpose is normally attributed only to persons or their behaviour as in "Did you have a purpose in leaving the ignition on?" In the second sense, purpose is normally attributed only to things, as in "What is the purpose of that gadget you installed in the workshop?" The two uses are intimately connected. We cannot attribute a purpose to a thing without implying that someone did something, in the doing of which he had some purpose, namely, to bring about the thing with the purpose. Of course, *his* purpose is not identical with *its* purpose. In hiring labourers and engineers and buying materials and a site for a factory and the like, the entrepreneur's purpose, let us say, is to manufacture cars, but the purpose of cars is to serve as a means of transportation.

There are many things that a man may do, such as buying and selling, hiring labourers, ploughing, felling trees, and the like, which it is foolish, pointless, silly, perhaps crazy, to do if one has no purpose in doing them. A man who does these things without a purpose is engaging in inane, futile pursuits. Lives crammed full with such activities devoid of purpose are pointless, futile, worthless. Such lives may indeed be dismissed as meaningless. But it should also be perfectly clear that acceptance of the scientific world picture does not force us to regard our lives as being without a purpose in this sense. Science has not only not robbed us of any purpose which we had before, but it has furnished us with enormously greater power to achieve these purposes. Instead of praying for rain or a good harvest or offspring, we now use ice pellets, artificial manure, or artificial insemination.

By contrast, having or not having a purpose, in the other sense, is value neutral. We do not think more or less highly of a thing for having or not having a purpose. "Having a purpose," in this sense, confers no kudos, "being purposeless" carries no stigma. A row of trees growing near a farm may or may not have a purpose: it may or may not be a windbreak, may or may not have been planted or deliberately left standing there in order to prevent the wind from sweeping across the fields. We do not in any way disparage the trees if we say they have no purpose, but have just grown that way. They are as beautiful, made of as good wood, as valuable, as if they had a purpose. And, of course, they break the wind just as well. The same is true of living creatures. We do not disparage a dog when we say that it has no purpose, is not a sheep dog or a watch dog or a rabbiting dog, but just a dog that hangs around the house and is fed by us.

Man is in a different category, however. To attribute to a human being a purpose in that sense is not neutral, let alone complimentary: it is offensive. It is degrading for a man to be regarded as merely serving a purpose. If, at a garden party, I ask a man in livery, "What is your purpose?" I am insulting him. I might as well have asked, "What are you *for?*" Such questions reduce him to the level of a gadget, a domestic animal, or perhaps a slave. I imply that *we* allot to *him* the tasks, the goals, the aims which he is to pursue; that *his* wishes and desires and aspirations and purposes are to count for little or nothing. We are treating him, in Kant's phrase, merely as a means to our ends, not as an end in himself.

The Christian and the scientific world pictures do indeed differ fundamentally on this point. The latter robs man of a purpose in this sense. It sees him as a being with no purpose allotted to him by anyone but himself. It robs him of any goal, purpose, or destiny appointed for him by any outside agency. The Christian world picture, on the other hand, sees man as a creature, a divine artefact, something halfway between a robot (manufactured) and an animal (alive), a homunculus, or perhaps Frankenstein, made in God's laboratory, with a purpose or task assigned him by his Maker.

However, lack of purpose in this sense does not in any way detract from the meaningfulness of life. I suspect that many who reject the scientific outlook because it involves the loss of purpose of life, and therefore meaning, are guilty of a confusion between the two senses of "purpose" just distinguished. They confusedly think that if the scientific world picture is true, then their lives must be futile because that picture implies that man has no purpose given him from without. But this is muddled thinking, for, as has already been shown, pointlessness, is implied only by purposelessness in the other sense, which is not at all implied by the scientific picture of the world. These people mistakenly conclude that there can be no purpose *in* life because there is no purpose *of* life; that *men* cannot themselves adopt and achieve purposes because *man*, unlike a robot or a watch dog, is not a creature with a purpose.[15]

However, not all people taking this view are guilty of the above confusion. Some really hanker after a purpose of life in this sense. To some people the greatest attraction of the medieval world picture is the belief in an omnipotent, omniscient, and all-good Father, the view of themselves as His children who worship Him, of their proper attitude to what befalls them as submission, humility, resignation in His will, and what is often described as the "creaturely feeling."[16] All these are attitudes and feelings appropriate to a being that stands to another in the same sort of relation, though of course on a higher plane, in which a helpless child stands to his progenitor. Many regard the scientific picture of the world as cold, unsympathetic, unhomely, frightening, because it does not provide for any appropriate object of this creaturely attitude. There is nothing and no one in the world, as science depicts it, in which we can have faith or trust, on whose guidance we can rely, to whom we can turn for consolation, whom we can worship or submit to— except other human beings. This may be felt as a keen disappointment, because it shows that the meaning of life cannot lie in submission to His will, in acceptance of whatever may come, and in worship. But it does not imply that life can have *no* meaning. It merely implies that it must have a different meaning from that which it was thought to have. Just as it is a great shock for a child to find that he must stand on his own feet, that his father and mother no longer provide for him, so a person who has lost his faith in God must reconcile himself to the idea that he has to stand on his own feet, alone in the world except for whatever friends he may succeed in making.

But is not this to miss the point of the Christian teaching? Surely, Christianity can tell us the meaning of life because it tells us the grand and noble end for which God has created the universe and man. No human life, however pointless it may seem, is meaningless because in being part of God's plan, every life is assured of significance.

This point is well taken. It brings to light a distinction of some importance: we call a person's life meaningful not only if it is worthwhile, but also if he has helped in the realization of some plan or purpose transcending his own concerns. A person who knows he must soon die a painful death, can give significance to the remainder of his doomed life by, say, allowing certain experiments to be performed on him which will be useful in the fight against cancer. In a similar way, only on a much more elevated plane, every man, however humble or plagued by suffering, is guaranteed significance by the knowledge that he is participating in God's purpose.

What, then, on the Christian view, is the grand and noble end for which God has created the world and man in it? We can immediately dismiss that still popular opinion that the smallness of our intellect prevents us from stating meaningfully God's design in all its imposing grandeur.[17] This view cannot possibly be a satisfactory answer to our question about the purpose of life. It is, rather, a confession of the impossibility of giving one. If anyone thinks that this "answer" can remove the sting from the impression of meaninglessness and insignificance in our lives, he cannot have been stung very hard.

If, then, we turn to those who are willing to state God's purpose in so many words, we encounter two insuperable difficulties. The first is to find a purpose grand and noble enough to explain and justify the great amount of undeserved suffering in this world. We are inevitably filled by a sense of bathos when we read statements such as this: "... history is the scene of a divine purpose, in which the whole history is included, and Jesus of Nazareth is the centre of that purpose, both as revelation and as achievement, as the fulfilment of all that was past, and the promise of all that was to come. . . . If God is God, and if He made all these things, why did He do it? . . . God created a universe, bounded by the categories of time, space, matter, and causality, because He desired to enjoy for ever the society of a fellowship of finite and redeemed spirits which have made to His love the response of free and voluntary love and service."[18] Surely this cannot be right? Could a God be called omniscient, omnipotent, *and* all-good who, for the sake of satisfying his desire to be loved and served, imposes (or has to impose) on his creatures the amount of undeserved suffering we find in the world?

There is, however, a much more serious difficulty still: God's purpose in making the universe must be stated in terms of a dramatic story many of whose key incidents symbolize religious conceptions and practices which we no longer find morally acceptable: the imposition of a taboo on the fruits of a certain tree, the sin and guilt incurred by Adam and Eve by violating the taboo, the wrath of God,[19] the curse of Adam and Eve and all their progeny, the expulsion from Paradise, the Atonement by Christ's bloody sacrifice on the cross which makes available by way of the sacraments God's Grace by which alone men can be saved (thereby, incidentally, establishing the valuable power of priests to forgive sins and thus alone make possible a man's entry to heaven),[20] Judgment Day on which the sheep are separated from the goats and the latter condemned to eternal torment in hellfire.

Obviously it is much more difficult to formulate a purpose for creating the universe and man that will justify the enormous amount of undeserved suffering which we find around us, if that story has to be fitted in as well. For now we have to explain not only why an omnipotent, omniscient, and all-good God should create such a universe and such a man, but also why, foreseeing every move of the feeble, weak-willed, ignorant, and covetous creature to be created, He should nevertheless have created him and, having done so, should be incensed and outraged by man's sin, and why He should deem it necessary to sacrifice His own son on the cross to atone for this sin which was, after all, only a disobedience of one of his commands, and why this atonement and consequent redemption could not have been followed by man's return to Paradise—particularly of those innocent children who had not yet sinned—and why, on Judgment Day, this merciful God should condemn some to eternal torment.[21] It is not surprising that in the face of these and other difficulties, we find, again and again, a return to the first view: that God's purpose cannot meaningfully be stated.

It will perhaps be objected that no Christian to-day believes in the dramatic history of the world as I have presented it. But this is not so. It is the official doctrine of the Roman Catholic, the Greek Orthodox, and a large section of the Anglican Church.[22] Nor does Protestantism substantially alter this picture. In fact, by insisting on "Justification by Faith Alone" and by rejecting the ritualistic, magical character of the medieval Catholic interpretation of certain elements in the Christian religion, such as indulgences, the sacraments, and prayer, while at the same time insisting on the necessity of grace, Protestantism undermined the moral element in medieval Christianity expressed in the Catholics' emphasis on personal merit.[23] Protestantism, by harking back to St. Augustine, who clearly realized the incompatibility of grace and personal merit,[24] opened the way for Calvin's doctrine of Predestination (the intellectual parent of that form of rigid determinism which is usually blamed on science) and Salvation or Condemnation from all eternity.[25] Since Roman Catholics, Lutherans, Calvinists, Presbyterians and Baptists officially subscribe to the views just outlined, one can justifiably claim that the overwhelming majority of professing Christians hold or ought to hold them.

It might still be objected that the best and most modern views are wholly different. I have not the necessary knowledge to pronounce on the accuracy of this claim. It may well be true that the best and most modern views are such as Professor Braithwaite's who maintains that Christianity is, roughly speaking, "morality plus stories," where the stories are intended merely to make the strict moral teaching both more easily understandable and more palatable.[26] Or it may be that one or the other of the modern views on the nature and importance of the dramatic story told in the sacred Scriptures is the best. My reply is that even if it is true, it does not prove what I wish to disprove, that one can extract a sensible answer to our question, "What is the meaning of life?" from the kind of story subscribed to by the overwhelming majority of Christians, who would, moreover, reject any such modernist interpretation at least as indignantly as the scientific account. Moreover, though such views can perhaps avoid some of the worst absurdities of the traditional story, they are hardly in a much better position to state the purpose for which God has created the universe and man in it, because they cannot overcome the difficulty of finding a purpose grand and noble enough to justify the enormous amount of undeserved suffering in the world.

Let us, however, for argument's sake, waive all these objections. There remains one fundamental hurdle which no form of Christianity can overcome: the fact that it demands of man a morally repugnant attitude towards the universe. It is now very widely held[27] that the basic element of the Christian religion is an attitude of worship towards a being supremely worthy of being worshipped and that it is religious feelings and experiences which apprise their owner of such a being and which inspire in him the knowledge or the feeling of complete dependence, awe, worship, mystery, and self-abasement. There is, in other words, a bi-polarity (the famous "I-Thou relationship") in which the object, "the wholly-other," is exalted whereas the subject is abased to the limit. Rudolf Otto has called this the "creature-feeling"[28] and he quotes as an expression of it, Abraham's words when venturing to plead for the men of Sodom: "Behold now, I have taken upon me to speak unto the Lord, which am but dust and ashes" (Genesis XVIII.27). Christianity thus demands of men an attitude inconsistent with one of the presuppositions of morality: that man is not wholly dependent on something else, that man has free will, that man is in principle capable of responsibility. We have seen that the concept of grace is the Christian attempt to reconcile the claim of total dependence and the claim of individual responsibility (partial independence), and it is obvious that such attempts must fail. We may dismiss certain doctrines, such as the doctrine of original sin or the doctrine of eternal hellfire or the doctrine that there can be no salvation outside the Church as extravagant and peripheral, but we cannot reject the doctrine of total dependence without rejecting the characteristically Christian attitude as such.

## 3. THE MEANING OF LIFE

Perhaps some of you will have felt that I have been shirking the real problem. To many people the crux of the matter seems as follows. How can there be any meaning in our life if it ends in death? What meaning can there be in it that our inevitable death does not destroy? How can our existence be meaningful if there is no after-life in which perfect justice is meted out? How can life have any meaning if all it holds out to us are a few miserable earthly pleasures and even these to be enjoyed only rarely and for such a piteously short time?

I believe this is the point which exercises most people most deeply. Kirilov, in Dostoevsky's novel, *The Possessed*, claims, just before committing suicide, that as soon as we realize that there is no God, we cannot live any longer, we must put an end to our lives. One of the reasons which he gives is that when we discover that there is no paradise, we have nothing to live for.

"... there was a day on earth, and in the middle of the earth were three crosses. One on the cross had such faith that He said to another, 'To-day thou shalt be with me in paradise.' The day came to an end, both died, and they went, but they found neither paradise nor resurrection. The saying did not come true. Listen: that man was the highest of all on earth. . . . There has never been any one like Him before or since, and never will be. . . . And if that is so, if the laws of Nature did not spare even *Him,* and made even Him live in the midst of lies and die for a lie, then the whole planet is a lie and is based on a lie and a stupid mockery. So the very laws of the planet are a lie and a farce of the devil. What, then, is there to live for?"[29] And Tolstoy, too, was nearly driven to suicide when he came to doubt the existence of God and an after-life.[30] And this is true of many.

What, then, is it that inclines us to think that if life is to have a meaning, there would be an after-life? It is this. The Christian world view contains the following three propositions. The first is that since the Fall, God's curse of Adam and Eve, and the expulsion from Paradise, life on earth for mankind has not been worth while, but a vale of tears, one long chain of misery, suffering, unhappiness, and injustice. The second is that a perfect after-life is awaiting us after the death of the body. The third is that we can enter this perfect life only on certain conditions, among which is also the condition of enduring our earthly existence to its bitter end. In this way, our earthly existence which, in itself, would not (at least for many people if not all) be worth living, acquires meaning and significance: only if we endure it, can we gain admission to the realm of the blessed.

It might be doubted whether this view is still held to-day. However, there can be no doubt that even to-day we all imbibe a good deal of this view with our earliest education. In sermons, the contrast between the perfect life of the blessed and our life of sorrow and drudgery is frequently driven home and we hear it again and again that Christianity has a message of hope and consolation for all those "who are weary and heavy laden."[31]

It is not surprising, then, that when the implications of the scientific world picture begin to sink in, when we come to have doubts about the existence of God and another life, we are bitterly disappointed. For if there is no afterlife, then all we are left is our earthly life which we have come to regard as a necessary evil, the painful fee of admission to the land of eternal bliss. But if there is no eternal bliss to come and if this hell on earth is all, why hang on till the horrible end?

Our disappointment therefore arises out of these two propositions, that the earthly life is not worth living, and that there is another perfect life of eternal happiness and joy which we may enter upon if we satisfy certain conditions. We can regard our lives as meaningful, if we believe both. We cannot regard them as meaningful if we believe merely the first and not the second. It seems to me inevitable that people who are taught something of the history of science, will have serious doubts about the second. If they cannot overcome these, as many will be unable to do, then they must either accept the sad view that their life is meaningless or they must abandon the first proposition: that this earthly life is not worth living. They must find the meaning of their life in this earthly existence. But is this possible?

A moment's examination will show us that the Christian evaluation of our earthly life as worthless, which we accept in our moments of pessimism and dissatisfaction, is not one that we normally accept. Consider only the question of murder and suicide. On the Christian view, other things being equal, the most kindly thing to do would be for every one of us to kill as many of our friends and dear ones as still have the misfortune to be alive, and then to commit suicide without delay, for every moment spent in this life is wasted. On the Christian view, God has not made it that easy for us. He has forbidden us to hasten others or ourselves into the next life. Our bodies are his private property and must be allowed to wear themselves out in the way decided by Him, however painful and horrible that may be. We are, as it were, driving a burning car. There is only one way out, to jump clear and let it hurtle to destruction. But the owner of the car has forbidden it on pain of eternal tortures worse than burning. And so we do better to burn to death inside.

On this view, murder is a less serious wrong than suicide. For murder can always be confessed and repented and therefore forgiven, suicide cannot—unless we allow the ingenious way out chosen by the heroine of Graham Greene's play, *The Living Room*, who swallows a slow but deadly poison and, while awaiting its taking effect, repents having taken it. Murder, on the other hand, is not so serious because, in the first place, it need not rob the victim of anything but the last lap of his march in the vale of tears, and, in the second place, it can always be forgiven. Hamlet, it will be remembered, refrains from killing his uncle during the latter's prayers because, as a true Christian, he believes that killing his uncle at that point, when the latter has purified his soul by repentance, would merely be doing him a good turn, for murder at such a time would simply despatch him to undeserved and everlasting happiness.

These views strike us as odd, to say the least. They are the logical consequence of the official medieval evaluation of this our earthly existence. If this life is not worth living, then taking it is not robbing the person concerned of much. The only thing wrong with it is the damage to God's property, which is the same both in the case of murder and suicide. We do not take this view at all. Our view, on the contrary, is that murder is the most serious wrong because it consists in taking away from some one else against his will his most precious possession, his life. For this reason, when a person suffering from an incurable disease asks to be killed, the mercy killing of such a person is regarded as a much less serious crime than murder because, in such a case, the killer is not robbing the other of a good against his will. Suicide is not regarded as a real crime at all, for we take the view that a person can do with his own possessions what he likes.

However, from the fact that these are our normal opinions, we can infer nothing about their truth. After all, we could easily be mistaken. Whether life is or is not worthwhile, is a value judgment. Perhaps all this is merely a matter of opinion or taste. Perhaps no objective answer can be given. Fortunately, we need not enter deeply into these difficult and controversial questions. It is quite easy to show that the medieval evaluation of earthly life is based on a misguided procedure.

Let us remind ourselves briefly of how we arrive at our value judgments. When we determine the merits of students, meals, tennis players, bulls, or bathing belles, we do so on the basis of some criteria and some standard or norm. Criteria and standards notoriously vary from field to field and even from case to case. But that does not mean that we have *no* idea about what are the appropriate criteria or standards to use. It would not be fitting to apply the criteria for judging bulls to the judgment of students or bathing belles. They score on quite different points. And even where the same criteria are appropriate as in the judgment of students enrolled in different schools and universities, the standards will vary from one institution to another. Pupils who would only just pass in one, would perhaps obtain honours in another. The higher the standard applied, the lower the marks, that is, the merit conceded to the candidate.

The same procedure is applicable also in the evaluation of a life. We examine it on the basis of certain criteria and standards. The medieval Christian view uses the criteria of the ordinary man: a life is judged by what the person concerned can get out of it: the balance of happiness over unhappiness, pleasure over pain, bliss over suffering. Our earthly life is judged not worthwhile because it contains much unhappiness, pain, and suffering, little happiness, pleasure, and bliss. The next life is judged worthwhile because it provides eternal bliss and no suffering.

Armed with these criteria, we can compare the life of this man and that, and judge which is more worthwhile, which has a greater balance of bliss over suffering. But criteria alone enable us merely to make comparative judgments of value, not absolute ones. We can say which is more and which is less worthwhile, but we cannot say which is worthwhile and which is not. In order to determine the latter, we must introduce a standard. But what standard ought we to choose?

Ordinarily, the standard we employ is the average of the kind. We call a man and a tree tall if they are well above the average of their kind. We do not say that Jones is a short man because he is shorter than a tree. We do not judge a boy a bad student because his answer to a question in the Leaving Examination is much worse than that given in reply to the same question by a young man sitting for his finals for the Bachelor's degree.

The same principles must apply to judging lives. When we ask whether a given life was or was not worthwhile, then we must take into consideration the range of worthwhileness which ordinary lives normally cover. Our end poles of the scale must be the best possible and the worst possible life that one finds. A good and worthwhile life is one that is well above average. A bad one is one well below.

The Christian evaluation of earthly lives is misguided because it adopts a quite unjustifiably high standard. Christianity singles out the major shortcomings of our earthly existence: there is not enough happiness; there is too much suffering; the good and bad points are quite unequally and unfairly distributed; the underprivileged and underendowed do not get adequate compensation; it lasts only a short time. It then quite accurately depicts the perfect or ideal life as that which does not have any of these shortcomings. Its next step is to promise the believer that he will be able to enjoy this perfect life later on. And then it adopts as its standard of judgment the perfect life, dismissing as inadequate anything that falls short of it. Having dismissed earthly life as miserable, it further damns it by characterizing most of the pleasures of which earthly existence allows as bestial, gross, vile, and sinful, or alternatively as not really pleasurable.

This procedure is as illegitimate as if I were to refuse to call anything tall unless it is infinitely tall, or anything beautiful unless it is perfectly flawless, or any one strong unless he is omnipotent. Even if it were true that there is available to us an after-life which is flawless and perfect, it would still not be legitimate to judge earthly lives by this standard. We do not fail every candidate who is not an Einstein. And if we do not believe in an after-life, we must of course use ordinary earthly standards.

I have so far only spoken of the worthwhileness, only of what a person can get out of a life. There are other kinds of appraisal. Clearly, we evaluate people's lives not merely from the point of view of what they yield to the persons that lead them, but also from that of other men on whom these lives have impinged. We judge a life more significant if the person has contributed to the happiness of others, whether directly by what he did for others, or by the plans, discoveries, inventions, and work he performed. Many lives that hold little in the way of pleasure or happiness for its owner are highly significant and valuable, deserve admiration and respect on account of the contributions made.

It is now quite clear that death is simply irrelevant. If life can be worthwhile at all, then it can be so even though it be short. And if it is not worthwhile at all, then an eternity of it is simply a nightmare. It may be sad that we have to leave this beautiful world, but it is so only if and because it is beautiful. And it is no less beautiful for coming to an end. I rather suspect that an eternity of it might make us less appreciative, and in the end it would be tedious.

It will perhaps be objected now that I have not really demonstrated that life has a meaning, but merely that it can be worthwhile or have value. It must be admitted that there is a perfectly natural interpretation of the question, "What is the meaning of life?" on which my view actually proves that life has no meaning. I mean the interpretation discussed in Section 2 of this lecture, where I attempted to show that, if we accept the explanations of natural science, we cannot believe that living organisms have appeared on earth in accordance with the deliberate plan of some intelligent being. Hence, on this view, life cannot be said to have a purpose, in the sense in which man-made things have a purpose. Hence it cannot be said to have a meaning or significance in that sense.

However, this conclusion is innocuous. People are disconcerted by the thought that *life as such* has no meaning in that sense only because they very naturally think it entails that no individual life can have meaning either. They naturally assume that *this* life or *that* can have meaning only if *life as such* has meaning. But it should by now be clear that your life and mine may or may not have meaning (in one sense) even if life as such has none (in the other). Of course, it follows from this that your life may have meaning while mine has not. The Christian view guarantees a meaning (in one sense) to every life, the scientific view does not (in any sense). By relating the question of the meaningfulness of life to the particular circumstances of an individual's existence, the scientific view leaves it an open question whether an individual's life has meaning or not. It is, however, clear that the latter is the important sense of "having a meaning." Christians, too, must feel that their life is wasted and meaningless if they have not achieved salvation. To know that even such lost lives have a meaning in another sense is no consolation to them: What matters is not that life should have a guaranteed meaning, whatever happens here or here-after, but that, by luck (Grace) or the right temperament and attitude (Faith) or a judicious life (Works) a person should make the most of his life.

"But here lies the rub," it will be said. "Surely, it makes all the difference whether there is an after-life. This is where morality comes in." It would be a mistake to believe that. Morality is not the meting out of punishment and reward. To be moral is to refrain from doing to others what, if they followed reason, they would not do to themselves, and to do for others what, if they followed reason, they would want to have done. It is, roughly speaking, to recognize that others, too, have a right to a worthwhile life. Being moral does not make one's own life worthwhile, it helps others to make theirs so.

# 4. CONCLUSION

I have tried to establish three points: (i) that scientific explanations render their explicanda as intelligible as pre-scientific explanations; they differ from the latter only in that, having testable implications and being more precisely formulated, their truth or falsity can be determined with a high degree of probability; (ii) that science does not rob human life of purpose, in the only sense that matters, but, on the contrary, renders many more of our purposes capable of realization; (iii) that common sense, the Christian world view, and the scientific approach agree on the criteria but differ on the standard to be employed in the evaluation of human lives; judging human lives by the standards of perfection, as Christians do, is unjustified; if we abandon this excessively high standard and replace it by an everyday one, we have no longer any reason for dismissing earthly existence as not worthwhile.

On the basis of these three points I have attempted to explain why so many people come to the conclusion that human existence is meaningless and to show that this conclusion is false. In my opinion, this pessimism rests on a combination of two beliefs, both partly true and partly false: the belief that the meaningfulness of life depends on the satisfaction of at least three conditions, and the belief that this universe satisfies none of them. The conditions are, first, that the universe is intelligible, second, that life has a purpose, and third, that all men's hopes and desires can ultimately be satisfied. It seemed to medieval Christians and it seems to many Christians today that Christianity offers a picture of the world which can meet these conditions. To many Christians and non-Christians alike it seems that the scientific world picture is incompatible with that of Christianity, therefore with the view that these three conditions are met, therefore with the view that life has a meaning. Hence they feel that they are confronted by the dilemma of accepting either a world picture incompatible with the discoveries of science or the view that life is meaningless.

I have attempted to show that the dilemma is unreal because life can be meaningful even if not all of these conditions are met. My main conclusion, therefore, is that acceptance of the scientific world picture provides no reason for saying that life is meaningless, but on the contrary every reason for saying that there are many lives which are meaningful and significant. My subsidiary conclusion is that one of the reasons frequently offered for retaining the Christian world picture, namely, that its acceptance gives us a guarantee of a meaning for human existence, is unsound. We can see that our lives can have a meaning even if we abandon it and adopt the scientific world picture instead. I have, moreover, mentioned several reasons for rejecting the Christian world picture: (i) the biblical explanations of the details of our universe are often simply false; (ii) the so-called explanations of the whole universe are incomprehensible or absurd; (iii) Christianity's low evaluation of earthly existence (which is the main cause of the belief in the meaninglessness of life) rests on the use of an unjustifiably high standard of judgment.

# NOTES

1. Count Leo Tolstoy, "A Confession," reprinted in *A Confession, The Gospel in Brief, and What I Believe*, No. 229, The World's Classics (London: Geoffrey Cumberlege, 1940).

2. See, e.g., Edwyn Bevan, *Christianity*, pp. 211–227. See also H. J. Paton, *The Modern Predicament* (London: George Allen and Unwin Ltd., 1955), pp. 103–116, 374.

3. See for instance, L. E. Elliott-Binns, *The Development of English Theology in the Later Nineteenth Century* (London: Longmans, Green & Co., 1952), pp. 30–33.

4. See "Phaedo" (*Five Dialogues* by Plato, Everyman's Library No. 456), para. 99, p. 189.

5. "On the Ultimate Origination of Things" (*The Philosophical Writings of Leibniz*, Everyman's Library No. 905), p. 32.

6. See "Monadology" (*The Philosophical Writings of Leibniz*, Everyman's Library No. 905), para. 32–38, pp. 8–10.

7. To borrow the useful term coined by Professor D. A. T. Gasking of Melbourne University.

8. See, e.g., J. J. C. Smart, "The Existence of God," reprinted in *New Essays in Philosophical Theology*, ed. by A. Flew and A. MacIntyre (London: S.C.M. Press, 1957), pp. 35–39.

9. That creation out of nothing is not a clarificatory notion becomes obvious when we learn that "in the philosophical sense" it does not imply creation at a particular time. The universe could be regarded as a creation out of nothing even if it had no beginning. See, e.g., E. Gilson, *The Christian Philosophy of St. Thomas Aquinas* (London: Victor Gollancz Ltd. 1957), pp. 147–155 and E. L. Mascall, *Via Media* (London: Longmans, Green & Co., 1956), pp. 28 ff.

10. In what follows I have drawn heavily on the work of Ryle and Toulmin. See for instance G. Ryle, *The Concept of Mind* (London: Hutchinson's University Library, 1949), pp. 56–60 etc. and his article, "If, So, and Because," in *Philosophical Analysis* by Max Black, and S. E. Toulmin, *Introduction to the Philosophy of Science* (London: Hutchinson's University Library, 1953).

11. See above, p. 109 points (a)–(c).

12. L. Wittgenstein, *Tractatus Logico-Philosophicus* (London: Routledge & Kegan Paul Ltd., 1922), Sect. 6.44–6.45.

13. Op. cit. p. 46. See also Rudolf Otto, *The Idea of the Holy* (London: Geoffrey Cumberlege, 1952), esp. pp. 9–29.

14. Contemporary theologians would admit that it cannot be proved that the universe must have had a beginning. They would admit that we know it only through revelation. (See footnote No. 9.) I take it more or less for granted that Kant's attempted proof of the Thesis in his First Antinomy of Reason [Immanuel Kant's *Critique of Pure Reason*, trans. by Norman Kemp Smith (London: Macmillan and Co. Ltd., 1950), pp. 396–402] is invalid. It rests on a premise which is false: that the completion of the infinite series of succession of states, which must have preceded the present state if the world has had no beginning, is logically impossible. We can persuade ourselves to think that this infinite series is logically impossible if we insist that it is a series which must, literally, be *completed*. For the verb "to complete," as normally used, implies an activity which, in turn, implies an agent who must have *begun* the activity at some time. If an infinite series is a whole that must be *completed* then, indeed, the world must have had a beginning. But that is precisely the question at issue. If we say, as Kant does at first, "that an eternity has elapsed," we do not feel the same impossibility. It is only when we take seriously the words "synthesis" and "completion," both of which suggest or imply "work" or "activity" and therefore "beginning," that it seems necessary that an infinity of successive states cannot have elapsed. [See also R. Crawshay-Williams, *Methods and Criteria of Reasoning* (London: Routledge & Kegan Paul, 1957), App. iv.]

15. See, e.g., "Is Life Worth Living?" B.B.C. Talk by the Rev. John Sutherland Bonnell in *Asking Them Questions*, Third Series, ed. by R. S. Wright (London: Geoffrey Cumberlege, 1950).

16. See, e.g., Rudolf Otto, *The Idea of the Holy*, pp. 9–11. See also C. A. Campbell, *On Selfhood and Godhood* (London: George Allen & Unwin Ltd., 1957), p. 246, and H. J. Paton, *The Modern Predicament*, pp. 69–71.

17. For a discussion of this issue, see the eighteenth century controversy between Deists and Theists, for instance, in Sir Leslie Stephen's *History of English Thought in the Eighteenth Century* (London: Smith, Elder & Co., 1902), pp. 112–119 and pp. 134–163. See also the attacks by Toland and Tindal on "the mysterious" in *Christianity not Mysterious and Christianity as Old as the Creation, or the Gospel a Republication of the Religion of Nature*, resp., parts of which are reprinted in Henry Bettenson's *Doctrines of the Christian Church*, pp. 426–431. For modern views maintaining that mysteriousness is an essential element in religion, see Rudolf Otto, *The Idea of the Holy*, esp. pp. 25–40, and most recently M. B. Foster, *Mystery and Philosophy* (London: S.C.M. Press, 1957), esp. Chs. IV. and VI. For the view that statements about God must be nonsensical or absurd, see, e.g., H. J. Paton, op. cit. pp. 119–120, 367–369. See also "Theology and Falsification" in *New Essays in Philosophical Theology*, ed. by A. Flew and A. MacIntyre (London: S.C.M. Press, 1955), pp. 96–131; also N. McPherson, "Religion as the Inexpressible," ibid., esp. pp. 137–143.

18. Stephen Neill, *Christian Faith To-day* (London: Penguin Books, 1955), pp. 240–241.

19. It is difficult to feel the magnitude of this first sin unless one takes seriously the words "Behold, the man has eaten of the fruit of the tree of knowledge of good and evil, and is become as one of us; and now, may he not put forth his hand, and take also of the tree of life, and eat, and live for ever?" Genesis iii, 22.

20. See in this connection the pastoral letter of 2nd February, 1905, by Johannes Katschtaler, Prince Bishop of Salzburg on the honour due to priests, contained in *Quellen zur Geschichte des Papsttums*, by Mirbt, pp. 497–499, translated and reprinted

in *The Protestant Tradition,* by J. S. Whale (Cambridge: University Press, 1955), pp. 259–262.

21. How impossible it is to make sense of this story has been demonstrated beyond any doubt by Tolstoy in his famous "Conclusion of A Criticism of Dogmatic Theology," reprinted in *A Confession, The Gospel in Brief, and What I Believe.*

22. See "The Nicene Creed," "The Tridentine Profession of Faith," "The Syllabus of Errors," reprinted in *Documents of the Christian Church,* pp. 34, 373, and 380 resp.

23. See, e.g., J. S. Whale, *The Protestant Tradition,* Ch. IV., esp. pp. 48–56.

24. See ibid., pp. 61 ff.

25. See "The Confession of Augsburg" esp. Articles II., IV., XVIII., XIX., XX.; "Christianae Religionis Institutio," "The Westminster Confession of Faith," esp. Articles III., VI., IX., X., XI., XVI., XVII.; "The Baptist Confession of Faith," esp. Articles III., XXI., XXIII., reprinted in *Documents of the Christian Church,* pp. 294 ff., 298 ff., 344 ff., 349 ff.

26. See, e.g., his *An Empiricist's View of the Nature of Religious Belief* (Eddington Memorial Lecture).

27. See, e.g., the two series of Gifford Lectures most recently published: *The Modern Predicament* by H. J. Paton (London: George Allen & Unwin Ltd., 1955), pp. 69 ff., and *On Selfhood and Godhood* by C. A. Campbell (London: George Allen & Unwin Ltd., 1957), pp. 231–250.

28. Rudolf Otto, *The Idea of the Holy,* p. 9.

29. Fyodor Dostoyevsky, *The Devils* (London: The Penguin Classics, 1953), pp. 613–614.

30. Leo Tolstoy, *A Confession, The Gospel in Brief, and What I Believe,* The World's Classics, p. 24.

31. See, for instance, J. S. Whale, *Christian Doctrine,* pp. 171, 176–178, etc. See also Stephen Neill, *Christian Faith To-day,* p. 241.

CHAPTER 11

# PAUL EDWARDS

# *The Meaning and Value of Life*

To the questions "Is human life ever worthwhile?" and "Does (or can) human life have any meaning?" many religious thinkers have offered affirmative answers with the proviso that these answers would not be justified unless two of the basic propositions of most Western religions were true—that human life is part of a divinely ordained cosmic scheme and that after death at least some human beings will be rewarded with eternal bliss. Thus, commenting on Bertrand Russell's statement that not only must each individual human life come to an end but that life in general will eventually die out, C. H. D. Clark contrasts this "doctrine of despair" with the beauty of the Christian scheme. "If we are asked to believe that all our striving is without final consequence," then "life is meaningless and it scarcely matters how we live if all will end in the dust of death." According to Christianity, on the other hand, "each action has vital significance." Clark assures us that "God's grand design is life eternal for those who walk in the steps of Christ. Here is the one grand incentive to good living. . . . As life is seen to have purpose and meaning, men find release from despair and the fear of death" (*Christianity and Bertrand Russell*, p. 30). In a similar vein, the Jewish existentialist Emil Fackenheim claims that "whatever meaning life acquires" is derived from the encounter between God and man. The meaning thus conferred upon human life "cannot be understood in terms of some finite human purpose, supposedly more ultimate than the meeting itself. For what could be more ultimate than the Presence of God?" It is true that God is not always "near," but "times of Divine farness" are by no means devoid of meaning. "Times of Divine nearness do not light up themselves alone. Their meaning extends over all of life." There is a "dialectic between Divine nearness and Divine farness," and it points to "an eschatological future in which it is overcome" ("Judaism and the Meaning of Life").

Among unbelievers not a few maintain that life can be worthwhile and have meaning in some humanly important sense even if the religious world view is rejected. Others, however, agree with the religious theorists that our two questions must be given negative answers if there is no God and if death means personal annihilation. Having rejected the claims of religion, they therefore conclude that life is not worthwhile and that it is devoid of meaning. These writers, to whom we shall refer here as "pessimists," do not present their judgments as being merely expressions of certain moods or feelings but as conclusions that are in some sense objectively warranted. They offer reasons for their conclusions and imply that anybody reaching a contradictory conclusion is mistaken or irrational. Most pessimists do not make any clear separation between the statements that life is not worthwhile and that life is without meaning. They usually speak of the "futility" or the "vanity" of life, and presumably they mean by this both that life is not worth living and that it has no meaning. For the time being we, too, shall treat these statements as if they were equivalent. However, later we shall see that in certain contexts it becomes important to distinguish between them.

Our main concern in this article will be to appraise pessimism as just defined. We shall not discuss either the question whether life is part of a divinely ordained plan or the question whether we survive our bodily death. Our question will be whether the pessimistic conclusions are justified if belief in God and immortality are rejected.

## SCHOPENHAUER'S ARGUMENTS

Let us begin with a study of the arguments offered by the pessimists, remembering that many of these are indirectly endorsed by religious apologists. The most systematic and probably the most influential, though in fact not the gloomiest, of the pessimists was Schopenhauer. The world, he wrote, is something which ought not to exist: the truth is that "we have not to rejoice but rather to mourn at the existence of the world; that its non-existence would be preferable to its existence; that it is something which ought not to be." It is absurd to speak of life as a gift, as so many philosophers and thoughtless people have done. "It is evident that everyone would have declined such a gift if he could have seen it and tested it beforehand." To those who assure us that life is only a lesson, we are entitled to reply: "For this very reason I wish I had been left in the peace of the all-sufficient nothing, where I would have no need of lessons or of anything else" (*The World as Will and Idea*, Vol. III, p. 390).

Schopenhauer offers numerous arguments for his conclusion. Some of these are purely metaphysical and are based on his particular system. Others, however, are of a more empirical character and are logically independent of his brand of metaphysical voluntarism. Happiness, according to Schopenhauer, is unobtainable for the vast majority of mankind. "Everything in life shows that earthly happiness is destined to be frustrated or recognized as illusion." People either fail to achieve the ends they are striving for or else they do achieve them only to find them grossly disappointing. But as soon as a man discovers that a particular goal was not really worth pursuing, his eye is set on a new one and the same illusory quest begins all over again. Happiness, accordingly, always lies in the future or in the past, and "the present may be compared to a small dark cloud which the wind drives over the sunny plain: before and behind it all is bright, only it itself always casts a shadow. The present is therefore always insufficient; but the future is uncertain, and the past is irrevocable" (ibid., p. 383). Men in general, except for those sufficiently rational to become totally resigned, are constantly deluded—"now by hope, now by what was hoped for." They are taken in by "the enchantment of distance," which shows them "paradises." These paradises, however, vanish like "optical illusions when we have allowed ourselves to be mocked by them." The "fearful envy" excited in most men by the thought that somebody else is genuinely happy shows how unhappy they really are, whatever they pretend to others or to themselves. It is only "because they feel themselves unhappy" that "men cannot endure the sight of one whom they imagine happy."

On occasions Schopenhauer is ready to concede that some few human beings really do achieve "comparative" happiness, but this is not of any great consequence. For aside from being "rare exceptions," these happy people are really like "decoy birds"—they represent a possibility which must exist in order to lure the rest of mankind into a false sense of hope. Moreover, happiness, insofar as it exists at all, is a purely "negative" reality. We do not become aware of the greatest blessings of life—health, youth, and freedom—until we have lost them. What is called pleasure or satisfaction is merely the absence of craving or pain. But craving and pain are positive. As for the few happy days of our life—if there are any—we notice them only "after they have given place to unhappy ones."

Schopenhauer not infrequently lapsed from his doctrine of the "negative" nature of happiness and pleasure into the more common view that their status is just as "positive" as that of unhappiness and pain. But he had additional arguments which do not in any way depend on the theory that happiness and pleasure are negative. Perhaps the most important of these is the argument from the "perishableness" of all good things and the ultimate extinction of all our hopes and achievements in death. All our pleasures and joys "disappear in our hands, and we afterwards ask astonished where they have gone." Moreover, a joy which no longer exists does not "count"—it counts as little as if it had never been experienced at all:

> That which *has been* exists no more; it exists as little as that which has *never* been. But of everything that exists you may say, in the next moment, that it has been. Hence something of great importance in our past is inferior to something of little importance in our present, in that the latter is a *reality,* and related to the former as something to nothing. ("The Vanity of Existence," in *The Will to Live,* p. 229)

Some people have inferred from this that the enjoyment of the present should be "the supreme object of life." This is fallacious; for "that which in the next moment exists no more, and vanishes utterly, like a dream, can never be worth a serious effort."

The final "judgment of nature" is destruction by death. This is "the last proof" that life is a "false path," that all man's wishing is "a perversity," and that "nothing at all is worth our striving, our efforts and struggles." The conclusion is inescapable: "All good things are vanity, the world in all its ends bankrupt, and life a business which does not cover its expenses" (*The World as Will and Idea*, Vol. III, p. 383).

## THE POINTLESSNESS OF IT ALL

Some of Schopenhauer's arguments can probably be dismissed as the fantasies of a lonely and embittered man who was filled with contempt for mankind and who was singularly incapable of either love or friendship. His own misery, it may be plausibly said, made Schopenhauer overestimate the unhappiness of human beings. It is frequently, but not universally, true that what is hoped for is found disappointing when it is attained, and while "fearful envy" of other people's successes is common enough, real sympathy and generosity are not quite so rare as Schopenhauer made them out to be. Furthermore, his doctrine that pleasure is negative while pain is positive, insofar as one can attach any clear meaning to it, seems glaringly false. To this it should be added, however, that some of Schopenhauer's arguments are far from idiosyncratic and that substantially the same conclusions have been endorsed by men who were neither lonely nor embittered and who did not, as far as one can judge, lack the gift of love or friendship.

### Darrow

Clarence Darrow, one of the most compassionate men who ever lived, also concluded that life was an "awful joke." Like Schopenhauer, Darrow offered as one of his reasons the apparent aimlessness of all that happens. "This weary old world goes on, begetting, with birth and with living and with death," he remarked in his moving plea for the boy-murderers Loeb and Leopold, "and all of it is blind from the beginning to the end" (*Clarence Darrow—Attorney for the Damned*, A. Weinberg, ed., New York, 1957). Elsewhere he wrote: "Life is like a ship on the sea, tossed by every wave and by every wind; a ship headed for no port and no harbor, with no rudder, no compass, no pilot; simply floating for a time, then lost in the waves" ("Is Life Worth Living?," p. 43). In addition to the aimlessness of life and the universe, there is the fact of death. "I love my friends," wrote Darrow, "but they all must come to a tragic end." Death is more terrible the more one is attached to things in the world. Life, he concludes, is "not worth while," and he adds (somewhat inconsistently, in view of what he had said earlier) that "it is an unpleasant interruption of nothing, and the best thing you can say of it is that it does not last long" ("Is the Human Race Getting Anywhere?," p. 53).

## Tolstoy

Tolstoy, unlike Darrow, eventually came to believe in Christianity, or at least in his own idiosyncratic version of Christianity, but for a number of years the only position for which he could see any rational justification was an extreme form of pessimism. During that period (and there is reason to believe that in spite of his later protestations to the contrary, his feelings on this subject never basically changed) Tolstoy was utterly overwhelmed by the thought of his death and the death of those he cared for and, generally, by the transitory nature of all human achievements. "Today or tomorrow," he wrote in "A Confession," "sickness and death will come to those I love or to me; nothing will remain but stench and worms. Sooner or later my affairs, whatever they may be, will be forgotten, and I shall not exist. Then why go on making any effort?" Tolstoy likened the fate of man to that of the traveler in the Eastern tale who, pursued by an enraged beast, seeks refuge in a dry well. At the bottom of the well he sees a dragon that has opened its jaws to swallow him. To escape the enraged beast above and the dragon below, he holds onto a twig that is growing in a crack in the well. As he looks around he notices that two mice are gnawing at the stem of the twig. He realizes that very soon the twig will snap and he will fall to his doom, but at the same time he sees some drops of honey on the leaves of the branch and reaches out with his tongue to lick them. "So I too clung to the twig of life, knowing that the dragon of death was inevitably awaiting me, ready to tear me to pieces. . . . I tried to lick the honey which formerly consoled me, but the honey no longer gave me pleasure. . . . I only saw the unescapable dragon and the mice, and I could not tear my gaze from them. And this is not a fable but the real unanswerable truth."

These considerations, according to Tolstoy, inevitably lead to the conclusion that life is a "stupid fraud," that no "reasonable meaning" can be given to a single action or to a whole life. To the questions "What is it for?" "What then?" "Why should I live?" the answer is "Nothing can come of it," "Nothing is worth doing," "Life is not worthwhile."

What ways out are available to a human being who finds himself in this "terrible position"? Judging by the conduct of the people he observed, Tolstoy relates that he could see only four possible "solutions." The first is the way of ignorance. People who adopt this solution (chiefly women and very young and very dull people) have simply not or not yet faced the questions that were tormenting him. Once a person has fully realized what death means, this solution is not available to him. The second way is that of "Epicureanism," which consists in admitting the "hopelessness of life" but seizing as many of life's pleasures as possible while they are within reach. It consists in "disregarding the dragon and the mice and licking the honey in the best way, especially if much of it is around." This, Tolstoy adds, is the solution adopted by the majority of the people belonging to his "circle," by which he presumably means the well-to-do intellectuals of his day. Tolstoy rejects this solution because the vast majority of human beings are not well-to-do and hence have little or no honey at their disposal and also because it is a matter of accident whether one is among those who have honey or those who have not. Moreover, Tolstoy observes, it requires a special "moral dullness," which he himself lacked, to enjoy the honey while knowing the truth about death and the deprivations of the great majority of men. The third solution is suicide. Tolstoy calls this the way of "strength and energy." It is chosen by a few "exceptionally strong and consistent people." After they realize that "it is better to be dead than to be alive, and that it is best of all not to exist," they promptly end the whole "stupid joke." The means for ending it are readily at hand for everybody, but most people are too cowardly or too irrational to avail themselves of them. Finally, there is the way of "weakness." This consists in seeing the dreadful truth and clinging to life nevertheless. People of this kind lack the strength to act rationally and Tolstoy adds that he belonged to this last category.

## Strengths of the Pessimist Position

Is it possible for somebody who shares the pessimists' rejection of religion to reach different conclusions without being plainly irrational? Whatever reply may be possible, any intelligent and realistic person would surely have to concede that there is much truth in the pessimists' claims. That few people achieve real and lasting happiness, that the joys of life (where there are any) pass away much too soon, that totally unpredictable events frequently upset the best intentions and wreck the noblest plans—this and much more along the same lines is surely undeniable. Although one should not dogmatize that there will be no significant improvements in the future, the fate of past revolutions, undertaken to rid man of some of his apparently avoidable suffering, does not inspire great hope. The thought of death, too, even in those who are not so overwhelmed by it as Tolstoy, can be quite unendurable. Moreover, to many who have reflected on the implications of physical theory it seems plain that because of the constant increase of entropy in the universe all life anywhere will eventually die out. Forebodings of this kind moved Bertrand Russell to write his famous essay "A Free Man's Worship," in which he concluded that "all the labors of the ages, all the devotion, all the inspiration, all the noonday brightness of human genius, are destined to extinction in the vast death of the solar system, and the whole temple of man's achievement must inevitably be buried beneath the debris of a universe in ruins." Similarly, Wilhelm Ostwald observed that "in the longest run the sum of all human endeavor has no recognizable significance." Although it is disputed whether physical theory really has such gloomy implications, it would perhaps be wisest to assume that the position endorsed by Russell and Ostwald is well-founded.

# COMPARATIVE VALUE JUDGMENTS
## ABOUT LIFE AND DEATH

Granting the strong points in the pessimists' claims, it is still possible to detect certain confusions and dubious inferences in their arguments. To begin with, there is a very obvious inconsistency in the way writers like Darrow and Tolstoy arrive at the conclusion that death is better than life. They begin by telling us that death is something terrible because it terminates the possibility of any of the experiences we value. From this they infer that nothing is really worth doing and that death is better than life. Ignoring for the moment the claim that in view of our inevitable death nothing is "worth doing," there very plainly seems to be an inconsistency in first judging death to be such a horrible evil and in asserting later on that death is better than life. Why was death originally judged to be an evil? Surely because it is the termination of life. And if something, $y$, is bad because it is the termination of something, $x$, this can be so only if $x$ is good or has positive value. If $x$ were not good, the termination of $x$ would not be bad. One cannot consistently have it both ways.

To this it may be answered that life did have positive value prior to one's realization of death but that once a person has become aware of the inevitability of his destruction life becomes unbearable and that this is the real issue. This point of view is well expressed in the following exchange between Cassius and Brutus in Shakespeare's *Julius Caesar* (III.i.102–105):

> CASSIUS.  Why he that cuts off twenty years of life
> Cuts off so many years of fearing death.
>
> BRUTUS.  Grant that, and then is death a benefit:
> So are we Caesar's friends that have abridged
> His time of fearing death.

There is a very simple reply to this argument. Granting that some people after once realizing their doom cannot banish the thought of it from their minds, so much so that it interferes with all their other activities, this is neither inevitable nor at all common. It is, on the contrary, in the opinion of all except some existentialists, morbid and pathological. The realization that one will die does not in the case of most people prevent them from engaging in activities which they regard as valuable or from enjoying the things they used to enjoy. To be told that one is not living "authentically" if one does not brood about death day and night is simply to be insulted gratuitously. A person who knows that his talents are not as great as he would wish or that he is not as handsome as he would have liked to be is not usually judged to live "inauthentically," but on the contrary to be sensible if he does not constantly brood about his limitations and shortcomings and uses whatever talents he does possess to maximum advantage.

There is another and more basic objection to the claim that death is better than life. This objection applies equally to the claim that while death is better than life it would be better still not to have been born in the first place and to the judgment that life is better than death. It should be remembered that we are here concerned with such pronouncements when they are intended not merely as the expression of certain moods but as statements which are in some sense true or objectively warranted. It may be argued that a value comparison—any judgment to the effect that *A* is better or worse than *B* or as good as *B*—makes sense only if *both A* and *B* are, in the relevant respect, in principle open to inspection. If somebody says, for example, that Elizabeth Taylor is a better actress than Betty Grable, this seems quite intelligible. Or, again, if it is said that life for the Jews is better in the United States than it was in Germany under the Nazis, this also seems readily intelligible. In such cases the terms of the comparison are observable or at any rate describable. These conditions are fulfilled in some cases when value comparisons are made between life and death, but they are not fulfilled in the kind of case with which Tolstoy and the pessimists are concerned. If the conception of an afterlife is intelligible, then it would make sense for a believer or for somebody who has not made up his mind to say such things as "Death cannot be worse than this life" or "I wonder if it will be any better for me after I am dead." Achilles, in the *Iliad*, was not making a senseless comparison when he exclaimed that he would rather act

> . . . as a serf of another,
> A man of little possessions, with scanty means of
>     subsistence,
> Than rule as a ghostly monarch the ghosts of all
>     the departed.

Again, the survivors can meaningfully say about a deceased individual "It is better (for the world) that he is dead" or the opposite. For the person himself, however, if there is no afterlife, death is not a possible object of observation or experience, and statements by him that his own life is better than, as good as, or worse than his own death, unless they are intended to be no more than expressions of certain wishes or moods, must be dismissed as senseless. At first sight the contention that in the circumstances under discussion value comparisons between life and death are senseless may seem implausible because of the widespread tendency to think of death as a shadowy kind of life—as sleep, rest, or some kind of homecoming. Such "descriptions" may be admirable as poetry or consolation, but taken literally they are simply false.

## IRRELEVANCE OF THE DISTANT FUTURE

These considerations do not, however, carry us very far. They do not show either that life is worth living or that it "has meaning." Before tackling these problems directly, something should perhaps be said about the curious and totally arbitrary preference of the future to the present, to which writers like

Tolstoy and Darrow are committed without realizing it. Darrow implies that life would not be "futile" if it were not an endless cycle of the same kind of activities and if instead it were like a journey toward a destination. Tolstoy clearly implies that life would be worthwhile, that some of our actions at least would have a "reasonable meaning," if the present life were followed by eternal bliss. Presumably, what would make life no longer futile as far as Darrow is concerned is some feature of the destination, not merely the fact that it is a destination; and what would make life worthwhile in Tolstoy's opinion is not merely the eternity of the next life but the "bliss" which it would confer—eternal misery and torture would hardly do. About the bliss in the next life, if there is such a next life, Tolstoy shows no inclination to ask "What for?" or "So what?" But if bliss in the next life is not in need of any further justification, why should any bliss that there might be in the present life need justification?

## The Logic of Value Judgments

Many of the pessimists appear to be confused about the logic of value judgments. It makes sense for a person to ask about something "Is it really worthwhile?" or "Is it really worth the trouble?" if he does not regard it as intrinsically valuable or if he is weighing it against another good with which it may be in conflict. It does not make sense to ask such a question about something he regards as valuable in its own right and where there is no conflict with the attainment of any other good. (This observation, it should be noted, is quite independent of what view one takes of the logical status of intrinsic value judgments.) A person driving to the beach on a crowded Sunday, may, upon finally getting there, reflect on whether the trip was really worthwhile. Or, after undertaking a series of medical treatments, somebody may ask whether it was worth the time and the money involved. Such questions make sense because the discomforts of a car ride and the time and money spent on medical treatments are not usually judged to be valuable for their own sake. Again, a woman who has given up a career as a physician in order to raise a family may ask herself whether it was worthwhile, and in this case the question would make sense not because she regards the raising of a family as no more than a means, but because she is weighing it against another good. However, if somebody is very happy, for any number of reasons—because he is in love, because he won the Nobel prize, because his child recovered from a serious illness—and if this happiness does not prevent him from doing or experiencing anything else he regards as valuable, it would not occur to him to ask "Is it worthwhile?" Indeed, this question would be incomprehensible to him, just as Tolstoy himself would presumably not have known what to make of the question had it been raised about the bliss in the hereafter.

It is worth recalling here that we live not in the distant future but in the present and also, in a sense, in the relatively near future. To bring the subject down to earth, let us consider some everyday occurrences: A man with a toothache goes to a dentist, and the dentist helps him so that the toothache disappears. A man is falsely accused of a crime and is faced with the possibility of a severe sentence as well as with the loss of his reputation; with the help of a devoted attorney his innocence is established, and he is acquitted. It is true that a hundred years later all of the participants in these events will be dead and none of them will *then* be able to enjoy the fruits of any of the efforts involved. But this most emphatically does not imply that the dentist's efforts were not worthwhile or that the attorney's work was not worth doing. To bring in considerations of what will or will not happen in the remote future is, in such and many other though certainly not in all human situations, totally irrelevant. Not only is the finality of death irrelevant here; equally irrelevant are the facts, if they are facts, that life is an endless cycle of the same kind of activities and that the history of the universe is not a drama with a happy ending.

This is, incidentally, also the answer to religious apologists like C. H. D. Clark who maintain that all striving is pointless if it is "without final consequence" and that "it scarcely matters how we live if all will end in the dust of death." Striving is not pointless if it achieves what it is intended to achieve even if it is without *final* consequence, and it matters a great deal how we live if we have certain standards and goals, although we cannot avoid "the dust of death."

## The Vanished Past

In asserting the worthlessness of life Schopenhauer remarked that "what has been exists as little as what has never been" and that "something of great importance now past is inferior to something of little importance now present." Several comments are in order here. To begin with, if Schopenhauer is right, it must work both ways: if only the present counts, then past sorrows no less than past pleasures do not "count." Furthermore, the question whether "something of great importance now past is inferior to something of little importance now present" is not, as Schopenhauer supposed, a straightforward question of fact but rather one of valuation, and different answers, none of which can be said to be mistaken, will be given by different people according to their circumstances and interests. Viktor Frankl, the founder of "logotherapy," has compared the pessimist to a man who observes, with fear and sadness, how his wall calendar grows thinner and thinner as he removes a sheet from it every day. The kind of person whom Frankl admires, on the other hand, "files each successive leaf neatly away with its predecessors" and reflects "with pride and joy" on all the richness represented by the leaves removed from the calendar. Such a person will not in old age envy the young. "'No, thank you,' he will think. 'Instead of possibilities, I have realities in my past'" (*Man's Search for Meaning*, pp. 192–193). This passage is quoted not because it contains any great wisdom but because it illustrates that we are concerned here not with judgments of fact but with value judgments and that Schopenhauer's is not the only one that is possible. Nevertheless, his remarks are, perhaps, a healthy antidote to the cheap consolation and the attempts to cover up deep and inevitable misery that are the stock in trade of a great deal of popular psychology. Although Schopenhauer's judgments about the inferior value of the past cannot be treated as objectively true propositions, they express only too well what a great many human beings are bound to feel on certain occasions. To a man dying of cancer it is small consolation to reflect that there was a time when he was happy and flourishing; and while there are undoubtedly some old people who do not envy the young, it may be suspected that more often the kind of talk advocated by the prophets of positive thinking is a mask for envy and a defense against exceedingly painful feelings of regret and helplessness in the face of aging and death and the now-unalterable past.

## THE MEANINGS OF THE "MEANING OF LIFE"

Let us now turn to the question whether, given the rejection of belief in God and immortality, life can nevertheless have any "meaning" or "significance." Kurt Baier has called attention to two very different senses in which people use these expressions and to the confusions that result when they are not kept apart. Sometimes when a person asks whether life has any meaning, what he wants to know is whether there is a superhuman intelligence that fashioned human beings along with other objects in the world to serve some end— whether their role is perhaps analogous to the part of an instrument (or its player) in a symphony. People who ask whether history has a meaning often use the word in the same sense. When Macbeth exclaimed that life "is a tale / Told by an idiot, full of sound and fury, / Signifying nothing," he was answering this cosmic question in the negative. His point evidently was not that human life is part of a scheme designed by a superhuman idiot but that it is not part of any design. Similarly, when Fred Hoyle, in his book *The Nature of the Universe* (rev. ed., New York, 1960), turns to what he calls "the deeper issues" and remarks that we find ourselves in a "dreadful situation" in which there is "scarcely a clue as to whether our existence has any real significance," he is using the word "significance" in this cosmic sense.

On the other hand, when we ask whether a *particular* person's life has or had any meaning, we are usually concerned not with cosmic issues but with the question whether certain purposes are to be found *in* his life. Thus, most of us would say without hesitation that a person's life had meaning if we knew that he devoted himself to a cause (such as the spread of Christianity or communism or the reform of mental institutions), or we would at least be ready to say that it "acquired meaning" once he became sufficiently attached to his cause. Whether we approve of what they did or not, most of us would be ready to admit—to take some random examples—that Dorothea Dix, Pasteur, Lenin, Margaret Sanger, Anthony Comstock, and Winston Churchill led meaningful lives. We seem to mean two things in characterizing such lives as meaningful: we assert, first, that the life in question had some dominant, over-all goal or goals which gave direction to a great many of the individual's actions and, second, that these actions and possibly others not immediately related to the overriding goal were performed with a special zest that was not present before the person became attached to his goal or that would not have been present if there had been no such goal in his life. It is not necessary, however, that a person should be devoted to a cause, in the sense just indicated, before we call his life meaningful. It is sufficient that he should have some attachments that are not too shallow. This last expression is of course rather vague, but so is the use of the word "meaning" when applied to human lives. Since the depth or shallowness of an attachment is a matter of degree, it makes perfectly good sense to speak of degrees of meaning in this context. Thus, C. G. Jung writes that in the lives of his patients there never was "sufficient meaning" (*Memories, Dreams, Reflections*, New York and Toronto, 1963, p. 140). There is nothing odd in such a locution, and there is equally nothing odd in saying about a man who has made a partial recovery from a deep depression that there is now again "some" meaning in his life.

Although frequently when people say about somebody that his life has or had meaning, they evidently regard this as a good thing, this is not invariably the case. One might express this point in the following way: saying that attachment to a certain goal has made a man's life meaningful is *not* tantamount to saying that the acts to which the goal has given direction are of positive value. A man might himself observe—and there would be nothing logically odd about it—"As long as I was a convinced Nazi (or communist or Christian or whatever) my life had meaning, my acts had a zest with which I have not been able to invest them since, and yet most of my actions were extremely harmful." Even while fully devoted to his cause or goal the person need not, and frequently does not, regard it as *intrinsically* valuable. If challenged he will usually justify the attachment to his goal by reference to more fundamental value judgments. Thus, somebody devoted to communism or to medical research or to the dissemination of birth-control information will in all likelihood justify his devotion in terms of the production of happiness and the reduction of suffering, and somebody devoted to Christianity will probably justify his devotion by reference to the will of God.

Let us refer to the first of the two senses we have been discussing as the "cosmic" sense and to the second as the "terrestrial" sense. (These are by no means the only senses in which philosophers and others have used the word "meaning" when they have spoken of the meaning or meaninglessness of life, but for our purposes it is sufficient to take account of these two senses.) Now if the theory of cosmic design is rejected it immediately follows that human life has no meaning in the first or cosmic sense. It does not follow in the least, however, that a particular human life is meaningless in the second, or terrestrial, sense. This conclusion has been very clearly summarized by Baier: "Your life or mine may or may not have meaning (in one sense)," he writes, "even if life as such has none (in the other). . . . The Christian view guarantees a meaning (in one sense) to every life, the scientific view [what we have simply been calling the unbeliever's position] does not in any sense" (*The Meaning of Life*, p. 28). In the terrestrial sense it will be an open question whether an individual's life has meaning or not, to be decided by the particular circumstances of his existence. It may indeed be the case that once a person comes to believe that life has no meaning in the cosmic sense his attachment to terrestrial goals will be undermined to such an extent that his life will cease to be meaningful in the other sense as well. However, it seems very plain that this is by no means what invariably happens, and even if it did invariably happen the meaninglessness of a given person's life in the terrestrial sense would not *logically* follow from the fact, if it is a fact, that life is meaningless in the cosmic sense.

This is perhaps the place to add a few words of protest against the rhetorical exaggerations of certain theological writers. Fackenheim's statement, quoted earlier, that "whatever meaning life acquires, it derives from the encounter between God and man" is typical of many theological pronouncements. Statements of this kind are objectionable on several grounds. Let us assume that there is a God and that meetings between God and certain human beings do take place; let us also grant that activities commanded by God in these meetings "acquire meaning" by being or becoming means to the end of pleasing or obeying God. Granting all this, it does not follow that obedience of God is the only possible unifying goal. It would be preposterous to maintain that the lives of *all* unbelievers have been lacking in such goals and almost as preposterous to maintain that the lives of believers never contain unifying goals other than obedience of God. There have been devout men who were also attached to the advance of science, to the practice of medicine, or to social reform and who regarded these ends as worth pursuing independently of any divine commandments. Furthermore, there is really no good reason to grant that the life of a particular person becomes meaningful in the terrestrial sense just because human life in general has meaning in the cosmic sense. If a superhuman being has a plan in which I am included, this fact will make (or help to make) my life meaningful in the terrestrial sense only if I know the plan and approve of it and of my place in it, so that working toward the realization of the plan gives direction to my actions.

## IS HUMAN LIFE EVER WORTHWHILE?

Let us now turn to the question of whether life is ever worth living. This also appears to be denied by the pessimists when they speak of the vanity or the futility of human life. We shall see that in a sense it cannot be established that the pessimists are "mistaken," but it is also quite easy to show that in at least two senses which seem to be of importance to many people, human lives frequently are worth living. To this end, let us consider under what circumstances a person is likely to raise the question "Is my life (still) worthwhile?" and what is liable to provoke somebody into making a statement like "My life has ceased to be worth living." We saw in an earlier section that when we say of certain acts, such as the efforts of a dentist or a lawyer, that they were worthwhile we are claiming that they achieved certain goals. Something similar seems to be involved when we say that a person's life is (still) worthwhile or worth living. We seem to be making two assertions: first, that the person has some goals (other than merely to be dead or to have his pains eased) which do not seem to him to be trivial and, second, that there is some genuine possibility that he will attain these goals. These observations are confirmed by various systematic studies of people who contemplated suicide, of others who unsuccessfully attempted suicide, and of situations in which people did commit suicide. When the subjects of these studies declared that their lives were no longer worth living they generally meant either that there was nothing left in their lives about which they seriously cared or that there was no real likelihood of attaining any of the goals that mattered to them. It should be noted that in this sense an individual may well be mistaken in his assertion that his life is or is not worthwhile any longer: he may, for example, mistake a temporary indisposition for a more permanent loss of interest, or, more likely, he may falsely estimate his chances of achieving the ends he wishes to attain.

## Different Senses of "Worthwhile"

According to the account given so far, one is saying much the same thing in declaring a life to be worthwhile and in asserting that it has meaning in the "terrestrial" sense of the word. There is, however, an interesting difference. When we say that a person's life has meaning (in the terrestrial sense) we are not committed to the claim that the goal or goals to which he is devoted have any positive value. (This is a slight oversimplification, assuming greater uniformity in the use of "meaning of life" than actually exists, but it will not seriously affect any of the controversial issues discussed here.) The question "As long as his life was dedicated to the spread of communism it had meaning *to him*, but was it really meaningful?" seems to be senseless. We are inclined to say, "If his life had meaning to him, then it had meaning—that's all there is to it." We are not inclined (or we are much less inclined) to say something of this kind when we speak of the worth of a person's life. We might say—for example, of someone like Eichmann—"While he was carrying out the extermination program, his life *seemed* worthwhile to him, but since his goal was so horrible, his life *was not* worthwhile." One might perhaps distinguish between a "subjective" and an "objective" sense of "worthwhile." In the subjective sense, saying that a person's life is worthwhile simply means that he is attached to some goals which he does not consider trivial and that these goals are attainable for him. In declaring that somebody's life is worthwhile in the objective sense, one is saying that he is attached to certain goals which are both attainable and of positive value.

It may be held that unless one accepts some kind of rationalist or intuitionist view of fundamental value judgments one would have to conclude that in the objective sense of "worthwhile" no human life (and indeed no human action) could ever be shown to be worthwhile. There is no need to enter here into a discussion of any controversial questions about the logical status of fundamental value judgments. But it may be pointed out that somebody who favors a subjectivist or emotivist account can quite consistently allow for the distinction between ends that only seem to have positive value and those that really do. To mention just one way in which this could be done: one may distinguish between ends that would be approved by rational and sympathetic human beings and those that do not carry such an endorsement. One may then argue that when we condemn such a life as Eichmann's as not being worthwhile we mean not that the ends to which he devoted himself possess some non-natural characteristic of badness but that no rational or sympathetic person would approve of them.

## The Pessimists' Special Standards

The unexciting conclusion of this discussion is that some human lives are at certain times not worthwhile in either of the two senses we have distinguished, that some are worthwhile in the subjective but not in the objective sense, some in the objective but not in the subjective sense, and some are worthwhile in both senses. The unexcitingness of this conclusion is not a reason for rejecting it, but some readers may question whether it meets the challenge of the pessimists. The pessimist, it may be countered, surely does not deny the plain fact that human beings are on occasions attached to goals which do not seem to them trivial, and it is also not essential to his position to deny (and most pessimists do not in fact deny) that these goals are sometimes attainable. The pessimist may even allow that in a superficial ("immediate") sense the goals which people try to achieve are of positive value, but he would add that because our lives are not followed by eternal bliss they are not "really" or "ultimately" worthwhile. If this is so, then the situation may be characterized by saying that the ordinary man and the pessimist do not mean the same by "worthwhile," or that they do mean the same in that both use it as a positive value expression but that their standards are different: the standards of the pessimist are very much more demanding than those of most ordinary people.

Anybody who agrees that death is final will have to concede that the pessimist is not mistaken in his contention that judged by *his* standards, life is never worthwhile. However, the pessimist is mistaken if he concludes, as frequently happens, that life is not worthwhile by ordinary standards because it is not worthwhile by his standards. Furthermore, setting aside the objection mentioned earlier (that there is something arbitrary about maintaining that eternal bliss makes life worthwhile but not allowing this role to bliss in the present life), one may justifiably ask why one should abandon ordinary standards in favor of those of the pessimist. Ordinarily, when somebody changes standards (for example, when a school raises or lowers its standards of admission) such a change can be supported by reasons. But how can the pessimist justify his special standards? It should be pointed out here that our ordinary standards do something for us which the pessimist's standards do not: they guide our choices, and as long as we live we can hardly help making choices. It is true that in one type of situation the pessimist's standards also afford guidance—namely, in deciding whether to go on living. It is notorious, however, that whether or not they are, by their own standards, rational in this, most pessimists do not commit suicide. They are then faced with much the same choices as other people. In these situations their own demanding standards are of no use, and in fact they avail themselves of the ordinary standards. Schopenhauer, for example, believed that if he had hidden his antireligious views he would have had no difficulty in obtaining an academic appointment and other worldly honors. He may have been mistaken in this belief, but in any event his actions indicate that he regarded intellectual honesty as worthwhile in a sense in which worldly honors were not. Again, when Darrow had the choice between continuing as counsel for the Chicago and North Western Railway and taking on the defense of Eugene V. Debs and his harassed and persecuted American Railway Union, he did not hesitate to choose the latter, apparently regarding it as worthwhile to go to the assistance of the suppressed and not worthwhile to aid the suppressor. In other words, although no human action is worthwhile, some human actions and presumably some human lives are less unworthwhile than others.

## IS THE UNIVERSE BETTER WITH HUMAN LIFE THAN WITHOUT IT?

We have not—at least not explicitly—discussed the claims of Schopenhauer, Eduard von Hartmann, and other pessimists that the nonexistence of the world would be better than its existence, by which they mean that a world without human life would be better than one with it.

### Arguments of a Phenomenologist

Some writers do not think that life can be shown to have meaning in any philosophically significant sense unless an affirmative answer to this question can be justified. Thus, in his booklet *Der Sinn unseres Daseins* the German phenomenologist Hans Reiner distinguishes between the everyday question about what he calls the "need-conditioned" meaning of life, which arises only for a person who is already in existence and has certain needs and desires, and the question about the meaning of human life in general. The latter question arises in concrete form when a responsible person is faced with the *Zeugungsproblem*—the question whether he should bring a child into the world. Reiner allows that a person's life has meaning in the former or "merely subjective" sense as long as his ordinary goals (chiefly his desire for happiness) are attained. This, however, does not mean that his life has an "objective" or "existential" (*seinshaft*) meaning—a significance or meaning which "attaches to life as such" and which, unlike the need-conditioned meaning, cannot be destroyed by any accident of fate. The philosopher, according to Reiner, is primarily concerned with the question of whether life has meaning in this objective or existential sense. "Our search for the meaning of our life," Reiner writes, "is identical with the search for a logically compelling reason (*einen einsichtigen Grund*) why it is better for us to exist than not to exist" (*Der Sinn unseres Daseins*, p. 27). Again, the real question is "whether it is better that mankind should exist than that there should be a world without any human life" (ibid., p. 31). It may be questioned whether this is what anybody normally means when he asks whether life has any meaning, but Reiner certainly addresses himself to one of the questions raised by Schopenhauer and other pessimists that ought to be discussed here.

Reiner believes that he can provide a "logically compelling reason" why a world with human life is better than one without it. He begins by pointing out that men differ from animals by being, among other things, "moral individuals." To be a moral individual is to be part of the human community and to be actively concerned in the life of other human beings. It is indeed undeniable that people frequently fail to bring about the ends of morally inspired acts or wishes, but phenomenological analysis discloses that "the real moral value and meaning" of an act does not depend on the attainment of the "external goal." As Kant correctly pointed out, the decisive factor is "the good will," the moral intent or attitude. It is here that we find the existential meaning of life: "Since that which is morally good contains its meaning and value within itself, it follows that it is intrinsically worthwhile. The existence of what is morally good is therefore better than its nonexistence" (ibid., pp. 54–55). But the existence of what is morally good is essentially connected with the existence of free moral individuals, and hence it follows that the existence of human beings as moral agents is better than their nonexistence.

Unlike happiness, which constitutes the meaning of life in the everyday or need-conditioned sense, the morally good does not depend on the accidents of life. It is not within a person's power to be happy, but it is "essentially" (*grundsätzlich*) in everybody's power to do what is good. Furthermore, while all happiness is subjective and transitory, leaving behind it no more than a "melancholy echo," the good has eternal value. Nobody would dream of honoring and respecting a person for his happiness or prosperity. On the other hand, we honor every good deed and the expression of every moral attitude, even if it took place in a distant land and among a foreign people. If we discover a good act or a good attitude in an enemy we nevertheless respect it and cannot help deriving a certain satisfaction from its existence. The same is true of good deeds carried out in ages long past. In all this the essentially timeless nature of morality becomes evident. Good deeds cease to exist as historical events only; their value, on the other hand, has eternal reality and is collected as an indestructible "fund." This may be a metaphysical statement, but it is not a piece of "metaphysical speculation." It simply makes explicit what the experience of the morally good discloses to phenomenological analysis (ibid., pp. 55–57).

## Replies to Reiner

There is a great deal in this presentation with which one could take issue. If one is not misled by the image of the ever-growing, indestructible "fund," one may wonder, for example, what could be meant by claiming that the value of a good deed is "eternal," other than that most human beings tend to approve of such an action regardless of when or where it took place. However, we are here concerned primarily with the question whether Reiner has met the challenge of the pessimists, and it seems clear that he has not. A pessimist like Schopenhauer or Darrow might provisionally grant the correctness of Reiner's phenomenological analysis of morality but still offer the following rejoinder: The inevitable misery of all or nearly all human beings is so great that even if in the course of their lives they have a chance to preserve their inner moral natures or their good will, the continued torture to which their lives condemn them would not be justified. Given the pessimist's estimate of human life, this is surely not an unreasonable rejoinder. Even without relying on the pessimist's description of human life, somebody while accepting Reiner's phenomenological analysis might reach the opposite conclusion. He might, for example, share the quietist strain of Schopenhauer's teachings and object to the whole hustle and bustle of life, concluding that the "peace of the all-sufficient nothing"—or, more literally, a universe without human life—was better in spite of the fact that moral deeds could not then be performed. Since he admits the "facts" of morality on which Reiner bases his case but considers the peace of the all-sufficient nothing more valuable than morality, it is not easy to see how an appeal to the latter would show him to be mistaken. What phenomenological analysis has not disclosed, to Reiner or, as far as is known, to anybody else, is that doing good is the only or necessarily the greatest value.

## Why the Pessimist Cannot Be Answered

The conclusion suggests itself that the pessimist cannot here be refuted, not because what he says is true or even because we do not know who is right and who is wrong but because the question whether a universe with human life is better than one without it does not have any clear meaning unless it is interpreted as a request for a statement of personal preference. The situation seems to be somewhat similar to what we found in the case of the question "Is my life better than my death?" when asked in certain circumstances. In some contexts indeed when we talk about human life in general, the word "better" has a reasonably clear meaning. Thus, if it is maintained that life for the human race will be better than it is now after cancer and mental illness have been conquered, or that human life will be better (or worse) after religion has disappeared, we understand fairly well what is meant, what facts would decide the issue either way. However, we do not really know what would count as evidence for or against the statement "The existence of human life as such is better than its nonexistence." Sometimes it is claimed that the question has a fairly clear meaning, namely, whether happiness outweighs unhappiness. Thus, von Hartmann supports his answer that the nonexistence of human life is better than its existence, that in fact an inanimate world would be better than one with life, with the argument that as we descend the scale of civilization and "sensitivity," we reach ever lower levels of misery. "The individuals of the lower and poorer classes and of ruder nations," he writes, "are happier than those of the elevated and wealthier classes and of civilized nations, not indeed because they are poorer and have to endure more want and privations, but because they are coarser and duller" (*Philosophy of the Unconscious*, Vol. III, p. 76). The "brutes," similarly, are "happier (i.e., less miserable)" than man, because "the excess of pain which an animal has to bear is less than that which a man has to bear." The same principle holds within the world of animals and plants:

> How much more painful is the life of the more finely-feeling horse compared with that of the obtuse pig, or with that of the proverbially happy fish in the water, its nervous system being of a grade so far inferior! As the life of a fish is more enviable than that of a horse, so is the life of an oyster than that of a fish, and the life of a plant than that of an oyster. (ibid.)

The conclusion is inevitable: the best or least undesirable form of existence is reached when, finally, we "descend beneath the threshold of consciousness"; for only there do we "see individual pain entirely disappear" (*Philosophy of the Unconscious*, Vol. III, pp. 76–77). Schopenhauer, also, addressing himself directly to the "*Zeugungsproblem*," reaches a negative answer on the ground that unhappiness usually or necessarily outweighs happiness. "Could the human race continue to exist," he asks (in *Parerga und Paralipomena*, Vol. II, pp. 321–322), if "the generative act were . . . an affair of pure rational reflection? Would not rather everyone have so much compassion for the coming generation as to prefer to spare it the burden of existence, or at least be unwilling to take on himself the responsibility of imposing such a burden in cold blood?" In these passages Schopenhauer and von Hartmann assume that in the question "Is a world with human life better than one without human life?" the word "better" must be construed in a hedonistic or utilitarian sense—and the same is true of several other philosophers who do not adopt their pessimistic answer. However, while one may *stipulate* such a sense for "better" in this context, it is clear that this is *not* what is meant prior to the stipulation. Spinoza, for example, taught that the most miserable form of existence is preferable to nonexistence. Perhaps few who have directly observed the worst agonies and tortures that may be the lot of human beings or of animals would subscribe to this judgment, but Spinoza can hardly be accused of a self-contradictory error. Again, Nietzsche's philosophy is usually and quite accurately described as an affirmation of life, but Nietzsche was very careful not to play down the horrors of much of life. While he did not endorse Schopenhauer's value judgments, he thought that, by and large, Schopenhauer had not been far wrong in his description of the miseries of the human scene. In effect Nietzsche maintained that even though unhappiness is more prevalent than happiness, the existence of life is nevertheless better than its nonexistence, and this surely is not a self-contradiction.

It is important to point out what does not follow from the admission that in a nonarbitrary sense of "better," the existence of the human race cannot be shown to be better than its nonexistence: It does not follow that I or anybody else cannot or should not prefer the continued existence of the human race to its nonexistence or my own life to my death, and it does not follow that I or anybody else cannot or should not enjoy himself or that I or anybody else is "irrational" in any of these preferences. It is also impossible to prove that in some nonarbitrary sense of "better," coffee with cream is better than black coffee, but it does not follow that I cannot or should not prefer or enjoy it or that I am irrational in doing so. There is perhaps something a trifle absurd and obsessive in the need for a "proof" that the existence of life is better than its nonexistence. It resembles the demand to have it "established by argument" that love is better than hate.

Perhaps it would be helpful to summarize the main conclusions reached in this essay:

(1) In certain familiar senses of "meaning," which are not usually regarded as trivial, an action or a human life can have meaning quite independently of whether there is a God or whether we shall live forever.

(2) Writers like Tolstoy, who, because of the horror that death inspires, conclude that death is better than life, are plainly inconsistent. Moreover, the whole question of whether my life is better than my death, unless it is a question about my preference, seems to be devoid of sense.

(3) Those who argue that no human action can be worthwhile because we all must eventually die ignore what may be called the "short-term context" of much of our lives.

(4) Some human lives are worthwhile in one or both of the two senses in which "worthwhile" is commonly used, when people raise the question of whether a given person's life is worthwhile. The pessimists who judge human life by more demanding standards are not mistaken when they deny that by *their* standards no human life is ever worthwhile. However, they are guilty of a fallacious inference if they conclude that for this reason no human life can be worthwhile by the usual standards. Nor is it clear why anybody should embrace their standards in the place of those commonly adopted.

(5) It appears that the pessimists cannot be answered if in order to answer them one has to be able to prove that in some nonarbitrary sense of the word "better," the existence of life is better than its nonexistence. But this admission does not have any of the gloomy consequences which it is sometimes believed to entail.

CHAPTER 12          R I C H A R D   T A Y L O R

# The Meaning of Life

The question whether life has any meaning is difficult to interpret, and the more one concentrates his critical faculty on it the more it seems to elude him, or to evaporate as any intelligible question. One wants to turn it aside, as a source of embarrassment, as something that, if it cannot be abolished, should at least be decently covered. And yet I think any reflective person recognizes that the question it raises is important, and that it ought to have a significant answer.

If the idea of meaningfulness is difficult to grasp in this context, so that we are unsure what sort of thing would amount to answering the question, the idea of meaninglessness is perhaps less so. If, then, we can bring before our minds a clear image of meaningless existence, then perhaps we can take a step toward coping with our original question by seeing to what extent our lives, as we actually find them, resemble that image, and draw such lessons as we are able to from the comparison.

## MEANINGLESS EXISTENCE

A perfect image of meaninglessness, of the kind we are seeking, is found in the ancient myth of Sisyphus. Sisyphus, it will be remembered, betrayed divine secrets to mortals, and for this he was condemned by the gods to roll a stone to the top of a hill, the stone then immediately to roll back down, again to be pushed to the top by Sisyphus, to roll down once more, and so on again and again, *forever*. Now in this we have the picture of meaningless, pointless toil, of a meaningless existence that is absolutely *never* redeemed. It is not even redeemed by a death that, if it were to accomplish nothing more, would at least bring this idiotic cycle to a close. If we were invited to imagine Sisyphus struggling for awhile and accomplishing nothing, perhaps eventually falling from exhaustion, so that we might suppose him then eventually turning to something having some sort of promise, then the meaninglessness of that chapter of his life would not be so stark. It would be a dark and dreadful dream, from which he eventually awakens to sunlight and reality. But he does not awaken, for there is nothing for him to awaken to. His repetitive toil is his life and reality, and it goes on forever, and it is without any meaning whatever. Nothing ever comes of what he is doing, except simply, more of the same. Not by one step, nor by a thousand, nor by ten thousand does he even expiate by the smallest token the sin against the gods that led him into this fate. Nothing comes of it, nothing at all.

This ancient myth has always enchanted men, for countless meanings can be read into it. Some of the ancients apparently thought it symbolized the perpetual rising and setting of the sun, and others the repetitious crashing of the waves upon the shore. Probably the commonest interpretation is that it symbolizes man's eternal struggle and unquenchable spirit, his determination always to try once more in the face of overwhelming discouragement. This interpretation is further supported by that version of the myth according to which Sisyphus was commanded to roll the stone *over* the hill, so that it would finally roll down the other side, but was never quite able to make it.

I am not concerned with rendering or defending any interpretation of this myth, however. I have cited it only for the one element it does unmistakably contain, namely, that of a repetitious, cyclic activity that never comes to anything. We could contrive other images of this that would serve just as well, and no myth-makers are needed to supply the materials of it. Thus, we can imagine two persons transporting a stone—or even a precious gem, it does not matter—back and forth, relay style. One carries it to a near or distant point where it is received by the other; it is returned to its starting point, there to be recovered by the first, and the process is repeated over and over. Except in this relay nothing counts as winning, and nothing brings the contest to any close, each step only leads to a repetition of itself. Or we can imagine two groups of prisoners, one of them engaged in digging a prodigious hole in the ground that is no sooner finished than it is filled in again by the other group, the latter then digging a new hole that is at once filled in by the first group, and so on and on endlessly.

Now what stands out in all such pictures as oppressive and dejecting is not that the beings who enact these roles suffer any torture or pain, for it need not be assumed that they do. Nor is it that their labors are great, for they are no greater than the labors commonly undertaken by most men most of the time. According to the original myth, the stone is so large that Sisyphus never quite gets it to the top and must groan under every step, so that his enormous labor is all for nought. But this is not what appalls. It is not that his great struggle comes to nothing, but that his existence itself is without meaning. Even if we suppose, for example, that the stone is but a pebble that can be carried effortlessly, or that the holes dug by the prisoners are but small ones, not the slightest meaning is introduced into their lives. The stone that Sisyphus moves to the top of the hill, whether we think of it as large or small, still rolls back every time, and the process is repeated forever. Nothing comes of it, and the work is simply pointless. That is the element of the myth that I wish to capture.

Again, it is not the fact that the labors of Sisyphus continue forever that deprives them of meaning. It is, rather, the implication of this: that they come to nothing. The image would not be changed by our supposing him to push a different stone up every time, each to roll down again. But if we supposed that these stones, instead of rolling back to their places as if they had never been moved, were assembled at the top of the hill and there incorporated, say, in a beautiful and enduring temple, then the aspect of meaninglessness would disappear. His labors would then have a point, something would come of them all, and although one could perhaps still say it was not worth it, one could not say that the life of Sisyphus was devoid of meaning altogether. Meaningfulness would at least have made an appearance, and we could see what it was.

That point will need remembering. But in the meantime, let us note another way in which the image of meaninglessness can be altered by making only a very slight change. Let us suppose that the gods, while condemning Sisyphus to the fate just described, at the same time, as an afterthought, waxed perversely merciful by implanting in him a strange and irrational impulse; namely, a compulsive impulse to roll stones. We may if we like, to make this more graphic, suppose they accomplish this by implanting in him some substance that has this effect on his character and drives. I call this perverse, because from our point of view there is clearly no reason why anyone should have a persistent and insatiable desire to do something so pointless as that. Nevertheless, suppose that is Sisyphus' condition. He has but one obsession, which is to roll stones, and it is an obsession that is only for the moment appeased by his rolling them—he no sooner gets a stone rolled to the top of the hill than he is restless to roll up another.

Now it can be seen why this little afterthought of the gods, which I called perverse, was also in fact merciful. For they have by this device managed to give Sisyphus precisely what he wants—by making him want precisely what they inflict on him. However it may appear to us, Sisyphus' fate now does not appear to him as a condemnation, but the very reverse. His one desire in life is to roll stones, and he is absolutely guaranteed its endless fulfillment. Where otherwise he might profoundly have wished surcease, and even welcomed the quiet of death to release him from endless boredom and meaninglessness, his life is now filled with mission and meaning, and he seems to himself to have been given an entry to heaven. Nor need he even fear death, for the gods have promised him an endless opportunity to indulge his single purpose, without concern or frustration. He will be able to roll stones *forever*.

What we need to mark most carefully at this point is that the picture with which we began has not really been changed in the least by adding this supposition. Exactly the same things happen as before. The only change is in Sisyphus' view of them. The picture before was the image of meaningless activity and existence. It was created precisely to be an image of that. It has not lost that meaninglessness, it has now gained not the least shred of meaningfulness. The stones still roll back as before, each phase of Sisyphus' life still exactly resembles all the others, the task is never completed, nothing comes of it, no temple ever begins to rise, and all this cycle of the same pointless thing over and over goes on forever in this picture as in the other. The *only* thing that has happened is this: Sisyphus has been reconciled to it, and indeed more, he has been led to embrace it. Not, however, by reason or persuasion, but by nothing more rational than the potency of a new substance in his veins.

## THE MEANINGLESSNESS OF LIFE

I believe the foregoing provides a fairly clear content to the idea of meaning-lessness and, through it, some hint of what meaningfulness, in this sense, might be. Meaninglessness is essentially endless pointlessness, and mean-ingfulness is therefore the opposite. Activity, and even long, drawn out and repetitive activity, has a meaning if it has some significant culmination, some more or less lasting end that can be considered to have been the direction and purpose of the activity. But the descriptions so far also provide something else; namely, the suggestion of how an existence that is objectively meaning-less, in this sense, can nevertheless acquire a meaning for him whose exis-tence it is.

Now let us ask: Which of these pictures does life in fact resemble? And let us not begin with our own lives, for here both our prejudices and wishes are great, but with the life in general that we share with the rest of creation. We shall find, I think, that it all has a certain pattern, and that this pattern is by now easily recognized.

We can begin anywhere, only saving human existence for our last con-sideration. We can, for example, begin with any animal. It does not matter where we begin, because the result is going to be exactly the same.

Thus, for example, there are caves in New Zealand, deep and dark, whose floors are quiet pools and whose walls and ceilings are covered with soft light. As one gazes in wonder in the stillness of these caves it seems that the Creator has reproduced there in microcosm the heavens themselves, until one scarcely remembers the enclosing presence of the walls. As one looks more closely, however, the scene is explained. Each dot of light identifies an ugly worm, whose luminous tail is meant to attract insects from the sur-rounding darkness. As from time to time one of these insects draws near it becomes entangled in a sticky thread lowered by the worm, and is eaten. This goes on month after month, the blind worm lying there in the barren stillness waiting to entrap an occasional bit of nourishment that will only sustain it to another bit of nourishment until. . . . Until what? What great thing awaits all this long and repetitive effort and makes it worthwhile? Really nothing. The larva just transforms itself finally to a tiny winged adult that lacks even mouth parts to feed and lives only a day or two. These adults, as soon as they have mated and laid eggs, are themselves caught in the threads and are devoured by the cannibalist worms, often without having ventured into the day, the only point to their existence having now been fulfilled. This has been going on for millions of years, and to no end other than that the same meaningless cycle may continue for another millions of years.

All living things present essentially the same spectacle. The larva of a certain cicada burrows in the darkness of the earth for seventeen years, through season after season, to emerge finally into the daylight for a brief flight, lay its eggs, and die—this all to repeat itself during the next seventeen years, and so on to eternity. We have already noted, in another connection, the struggles of fish, made only that others may do the same after them and that this cycle, having no other point than itself, may never cease. Some birds span an entire side of the globe each year and then return, only to insure that others may follow the same incredibly long path again and again. One is led to wonder what the point of it all is, with what great triumph this ceaseless effort, repeating itself through millions of years, might finally culminate, and why it should go on and on for so long, accomplishing nothing, getting nowhere. But then one realizes that there is no point to it at all, that it really culminates in nothing, that each of these cycles, so filled with toil, is to be followed only by more of the same. The point of any living thing's life is, evidently, nothing but life itself.

This life of the world thus presents itself to our eyes as a vast machine, feeding on itself, running on and on forever to nothing. And we are part of that life. To be sure, we are not just the same, but the differences are not so great as we like to think; many are merely invented, and none really cancels the kind of meaninglessness that we found in Sisyphus and that we find all around, wherever anything lives. We are conscious of our activity. Our goals, whether in any significant sense we choose them or not, are things of which we are at least partly aware and can therefore in some sense appraise. More significantly, perhaps, men have a history, as other animals do not, such that each generation does not precisely resemble all those before. Still, if we can in imagination disengage our wills from our lives and disregard the deep interest each man has in his own existence, we shall find that they do not so little resemble the existence of Sisyphus. We toil after goals, most of them—indeed every single one of them—of transitory significance and, having gained one of them, we immediately set forth for the next, as if that one had never been, with this next one being essentially more of the same. Look at a busy street any day, and observe the throng going hither and thither. To what? Some office or shop, where the same things will be done today as were done yesterday, and are done now so they may be repeated tomorrow. And if we think that, unlike Sisyphus, these labors do have a point, that they culminate in something lasting and, independently of our own deep interests in them, very worthwhile, then we simply have not considered the thing closely enough. Most such effort is directed only to the establishment and perpetuation of home and family; that is, to the begetting of others who will follow in our steps to do more of the same. Each man's life thus resembles one of Sisyphus' climbs to the summit of his hill, and each day of it one of his steps; the difference is that whereas Sisyphus himself returns to push the stone up again, we leave this to our children. We at one point imagined that the labors of Sisyphus finally culminated in the creation of a temple, but for this to make any difference it had to be a temple that would at least endure, adding beauty to the world for the remainder of time. Our achievements, even though they are often beautiful, are mostly bubbles; and those that do last, like the sand-swept pyramids, soon become mere curiosities while around them the rest of mankind continues its perpetual toting of rocks, only to see them roll down. Nations are built upon the bones of their founders and pioneers, but only to decay and crumble before long, their rubble then becoming the foundation for others directed to exactly the same fate. The picture of Sisyphus is the picture of existence of the individual man, great or unknown, of nations, of the race of men, and of the very life of the world.

On a country road one sometimes comes upon the ruined hulks of a house and once extensive buildings, all in collapse and spread over with weeds. A curious eye can in imagination reconstruct from what is left a once warm and thriving life, filled with purpose. There was the hearth, where a family once talked, sang, and made plans; there were the rooms, where people loved, and babes were born to a rejoicing mother; there are the musty remains of a sofa, infested with bugs, once bought at a dear price to enhance an ever-growing comfort, beauty, and warmth. Every small piece of junk fills the mind with what once, not long ago, was utterly real, with children's voices, plans made, and enterprises embarked upon. That is how these stones of Sisyphus were rolled up, and that is how they became incorporated into a beautiful temple, and that temple is what now lies before you. Meanwhile other buildings, institutions, nations, and civilizations spring up all around, only to share the same fate before long. And if the question "What for?" is now asked, the answer is clear: so that just this may go on forever.

The two pictures—of Sisyphus and of our own lives, if we look at them from a distance—are in outline the same and convey to the mind the same image. It is not surprising, then, that men invent ways of denying it, their religions proclaiming a heaven that does not crumble, their hymnals and prayer books declaring a significance to life of which our eyes provide no hint whatever.[1] Even our philosophies portray some permanent and lasting good at which all may aim, from the changeless forms invented by Plato to the beatific vision of St. Thomas and the ideals of permanence contrived by the moderns. When these fail to convince, then earthly ideals such as universal justice and brotherhood are conjured up to take their places and give meaning to man's seemingly endless pilgrimage, some final state that will be ushered in when the last obstacle is removed and the last stone pushed to the hilltop. No one believes, of course, that any such state will be final, or even wants it to be in case it means that human existence would then cease to be a struggle; but in the meantime such ideas serve a very real need.

# THE MEANING OF LIFE

We noted that Sisyphus' existence would have meaning if there were some point to his labors, if his efforts ever culminated in something that was not just an occasion for fresh labors of the same kind. But that is precisely the meaning it lacks. And human existence resembles his in that respect. Men do achieve things—they scale their towers and raise their stones to their hill-tops—but every such accomplishment fades, providing only an occasion for renewed labors of the same kind.

But here we need to note something else that has been mentioned, but its significance not explored, and that is the state of mind and feeling with which such labors are undertaken. We noted that if Sisyphus had a keen and unap-peasable desire to be doing just what he found himself doing, then, although his life would in no way be changed, it would nevertheless have a meaning for him. It would be an irrational one, no doubt, because the desire itself would be only the product of the substance in his veins, and not any that rea-son could discover, but a meaning nevertheless.

And would it not, in fact, be a meaning incomparably better than the other? For let us examine again the first kind of meaning it could have. Let us suppose that, without having any interest in rolling stones, as such, and find-ing this, in fact, a galling toil, Sisyphus did nevertheless have a deep interest in raising a temple, one that would be beautiful and lasting. And let us sup-pose he succeeded in this, that after ages of dreadful toil, all directed at this final result, he did at last complete his temple, such that now he could say his work was done, and he could rest and forever enjoy the result. Now what? What picture now presents itself to our minds? It is precisely the picture of infinite boredom! Of Sisyphus doing nothing ever again, but contemplating what he has already wrought and can no longer add anything to, and con-templating it for an eternity! Now in this picture we have a meaning for Sisy-phus' existence, a point for his prodigious labor, because we have put it there; yet, at the same time, that which is really worthwhile seems to have slipped away entirely. Where before we were presented with the nightmare of eternal and pointless activity, we are now confronted with the hell of its eternal absence.

Our second picture, then, wherein we imagined Sisyphus to have had inflicted on him the irrational desire to be doing just what he found himself doing, should not have been dismissed so abruptly. The meaning that picture lacked was no meaning that he or anyone could crave, and the strange mean-ing it had was perhaps just what we were seeking.

At this point, then, we can reintroduce what has been until now, it is hoped, resolutely pushed aside in an effort to view our lives and human exis-tence with objectivity; namely, our own wills, our deep interest in what we find ourselves doing. If we do this we find that our lives do indeed still resemble that of Sisyphus, but that the meaningfulness they thus lack is pre-cisely the meaningfulness of infinite boredom. At the same time, the strange meaningfulness they possess is that of the inner compulsion to be doing just what we were put here to do, and to go on doing it forever. This is the nearest we may hope to get to heaven, but the redeeming side of that fact is that we do thereby avoid a genuine hell.

If the builders of a great and flourishing ancient civilization could somehow return now to see archaeologists unearthing the trivial remnants of what they had once accomplished with such effort—see the fragments of pots and vases, a few broken statues, and such tokens of another age and greatness—they could indeed ask themselves what the point of it all was, if this is all it finally came to. Yet, it did not seem so to them then, for it was just the building, and not what was finally built, that gave their life meaning. Similarly, if the builders of the ruined home and farm that I described a short while ago could be brought back to see what is left, they would have the same feelings. What we construct in our imaginations as we look over these decayed and rusting pieces would reconstruct itself in their very memories, and certainly with unspeakable sadness. The piece of a sled at our feet would revive in them a warm Christmas. And what rich memories would there be in the broken crib? And the weed-covered remains of a fence would reproduce the scene of a great herd of livestock, so laboriously built up over so many years. What was it all worth, if this is the final result? Yet, again, it did not seem so to them through those many years of struggle and toil, and they did not imagine they were building a Gibraltar. The things to which they bent their backs day after day, realizing one by one their ephemeral plans, were precisely the things in which their wills were deeply involved, precisely the things in which their interests lay, and there was no need then to ask questions. There is no more need of them now—the day was sufficient to itself, and so was the life.

This is surely the way to look at all of life—at one's own life, and each day and moment it contains; of the life of a nation; of the species; of the life of the world; and of everything that breathes. Even the glow worms I described, whose cycles of existence over the millions of years seem so pointless when looked at by us, will seem entirely different to us if we can somehow try to view their existence from within. Their endless activity, which gets nowhere, is just what it is their will to pursue. This is its whole justification and meaning. Nor would it be any salvation to the birds who span the globe every year, back and forth, to have a home made for them in a cage with plenty of food and protection, so that they would not have to migrate any more. It would be their condemnation, for it is the doing that counts for them, and not what they hope to win by it. Flying these prodigious distances, never ending, is what it is in their veins to do, exactly as it was in Sisyphus' veins to roll stones, without end, after the gods had waxed merciful and implanted this in him.

A human being no sooner draws his first breath than he responds to the will that is in him to live. He no more asks whether it will be worthwhile, or whether anything of significance will come of it, than the worms and the birds. The point of his living is simply to be living, in the manner that it is his nature to be living. He goes through his life building his castles, each of these beginning to fade into time as the next is begun; yet, it would be no salvation to rest from all this. It would be a condemnation, and one that would in no way be redeemed were he able to gaze upon the things he has done, even if these were beautiful and absolutely permanent, as they never are. What counts is that one should be able to begin a new task, a new castle, a new bubble. It counts only because it is there to be done and he has the will to do it. The same will be the life of his children, and of theirs; and if the philosopher is apt to see in this a pattern similar to the unending cycles of the existence of Sisyphus, and to despair, then it is indeed because the meaning and point he is seeking is not there—but mercifully so. The meaning of life is from within us, it is not bestowed from without, and it far exceeds in both its beauty and permanence any heaven of which men have ever dreamed or yearned for.

## NOTE

1. A popular Christian hymn, sung often at funerals and typical of many hymns, expresses this thought:

> Swift to its close ebbs out life's little day;
> Earth's joys grow dim, its glories pass away;
> Change and decay in all around I see:
> O thou who changest not, abide with me.

CHAPTER 13          T H O M A S   N A G E L

# The Absurd

Most people feel on occasion that life is absurd, and some feel it vividly and continually. Yet the reasons usually offered in defense of this conviction are patently inadequate: they *could* not really explain why life is absurd. Why then do they provide a natural expression for the sense that it is?

## I

Consider some examples. It is often remarked that nothing we do now will matter in a million years. But if that is true, then by the same token, nothing that will be the case in a million years matters now. In particular, it does not matter now that in a million years nothing we do now will matter. Moreover, even if what we did now *were* going to matter in a million years, how could that keep our present concerns from being absurd? If their mattering now is not enough to accomplish that, how would it help if they mattered a million years from now?

Whether what we do now will matter in a million years could make the crucial difference only if its mattering in a million years depended on its mattering, period. But then to deny that whatever happens now will matter in a million years is to beg the question against its mattering, period; for in that sense one cannot know that it will not matter in a million years whether (for example) someone now is happy or miserable, without knowing that it does not matter, period.

From *The Journal of Philosophy*, Vol. LXIII, No. 20, 1971. Used by permission of the journal and the author.

What we say to convey the absurdity of our lives often has to do with space or time: we are tiny specks in the infinite vastness of the universe; our lives are mere instants even on a geological time scale, let alone a cosmic one; we will all be dead any minute. But of course none of these evident facts can be what *makes* life absurd, if it is absurd. For suppose we lived forever; would not a life that is absurd if it lasts seventy years be infinitely absurd if it lasted through eternity? And if our lives are absurd given our present size, why would they be any less absurd if we filled the universe (either because we were larger or because the universe was smaller)? Reflection on our minuteness and brevity appears to be intimately connected with the sense that life is meaningless; but it is not clear what the connection is.

Another inadequate argument is that because we are going to die, all chains of justification must leave off in mid-air: one studies and works to earn money to pay for clothing, housing, entertainment, food, to sustain oneself from year to year, perhaps to support a family and pursue a career—but to what final end? All of it is an elaborate journey leading nowhere. (One will also have some effect on other people's lives, but that simply reproduces the problem, for they will die too.)

There are several replies to this argument. First, life does not consist of a sequence of activities each of which has as its purpose some later member of the sequence. Chains of justification come repeatedly to an end within life, and whether the process as a whole can be justified has no bearing on the finality of these end-points. No further justification is needed to make it reasonable to take aspirin for a headache, attend an exhibit of the work of a painter one admires, or stop a child from putting his hand on a hot stove. No larger context or further purpose is needed to prevent these acts from being pointless.

Even if someone wished to supply a further justification for pursuing all the things in life that are commonly regarded as self-justifying, that justification would have to end somewhere too. If *nothing* can justify unless it is justified in terms of something outside itself, which is also justified, then an infinite regress results, and no chain of justification can be complete. Moreover, if a finite chain of reasons cannot justify anything, what could be accomplished by an infinite chain, each link of which must be justified by something outside itself?

Since justifications must come to an end somewhere, nothing is gained by denying that they end where they appear to, within life—or by trying to subsume the multiple, often trivial ordinary justifications of action under a single, controlling life scheme. We can be satisfied more easily than that. In fact, through its misrepresentation of the process of justification, the argument makes a vacuous demand. It insists that the reasons available within life are incomplete, but suggests thereby that all reasons that come to an end are incomplete. This makes it impossible to supply any reasons at all.

The standard arguments for absurdity appear therefore to fail as arguments. Yet I believe they attempt to express something that is difficult to state, but fundamentally correct.

## II

In ordinary life a situation is absurd when it includes a conspicuous discrepancy between pretension or aspiration and reality: someone gives a complicated speech in support of a motion that has already been passed; a notorious criminal is made president of a major philanthropic foundation; you declare your love over the telephone to a recorded announcement; as you are being knighted, your pants fall down.

When a person finds himself in an absurd situation, he will usually attempt to change it, by modifying his aspirations, or by trying to bring reality into better accord with them, or by removing himself from the situation entirely. We are not always willing or able to extricate ourselves from a position whose absurdity has become clear to us. Nevertheless, it is usually possible to imagine some change that would remove the absurdity—whether or not we can or will implement it. The sense that life as a whole is absurd arises when we perceive, perhaps dimly, an inflated pretension or aspiration which is inseparable from the continuation of human life and which makes its absurdity inescapable, short of escape from life itself.

Many people's lives are absurd, temporarily or permanently, for conventional reasons having to do with their particular ambitions, circumstances, and personal relations. If there is a philosophical sense of absurdity, however, it must arise from the perception of something universal—some respect in which pretension and reality inevitably clash for us all. This condition is supplied, I shall argue, by the collision between the seriousness with which we take our lives and the perpetual possibility of regarding everything about which we are serious as arbitrary, or open to doubt.

We cannot live human lives without energy and attention, nor without making choices which show that we take some things more seriously than others. Yet we have always available a point of view outside the particular form of our lives, from which the seriousness appears gratuitous. These two inescapable viewpoints collide in us, and that is what makes life absurd. It is absurd because we ignore the doubts that we know cannot be settled, continuing to live with nearly undiminished seriousness in spite of them.

This analysis requires defense in two respects: first as regards the unavoidability of seriousness; second as regards the inescapability of doubt.

We take ourselves seriously whether we lead serious lives or not and whether we are concerned primarily with fame, pleasure, virtue, luxury, triumph, beauty, justice, knowledge, salvation, or mere survival. If we take other people seriously and devote ourselves to them, that only multiplies the problem. Human life is full of effort, plans, calculation, success and failure: we *pursue* our lives, with varying degrees of sloth and energy.

It would be different if we could not step back and reflect on the process, but were merely led from impulse to impulse without self-consciousness. But human beings do not act solely on impulse. They are prudent, they reflect, they weigh consequences, they ask whether what they are doing is worth while. Not only are their lives full of particular choices that hang together in larger activities with temporal structure: they also decide in the broadest terms what to pursue and what to avoid, what the priorities among their various aims should be, and what kind of people they want to be or become. Some men are faced with such choices by the large decisions they make from time to time; some merely by reflection on the course their lives are taking as the product of countless small decisions. They decide whom to marry, what profession to follow, whether to join the Country Club, or the Resistance; or they may just wonder why they go on being salesmen or academics or taxi drivers, and then stop thinking about it after a certain period of inconclusive reflection.

Although they may be motivated from act to act by those immediate needs with which life presents them, they allow the process to continue by adhering to the general system of habits and the form of life in which such motives have their place—or perhaps only by clinging to life itself. They spend enormous quantities of energy, risk, and calculation on the details. Think of how an ordinary individual sweats over his appearance, his health, his sex life, his emotional honesty, his social utility, his self-knowledge, the quality of his ties with family, colleagues, and friends, how well he does his job, whether he understands the world and what is going on in it. Leading a human life is a full-time occupation, to which everyone devotes decades of intense concern.

This fact is so obvious that it is hard to find it extraordinary and important. Each of us lives his own life—lives with himself twenty-four hours a day. What else is he supposed to do—live someone else's life? Yet humans have the special capacity to step back and survey themselves, and the lives to which they are committed, with that detached amazement which comes from watching an ant struggle up a heap of sand. Without developing the illusion that they are able to escape from their highly specific and idiosyncratic position, they can view it *sub specie aeternitatis*—and the view is at once sobering and comical.

The crucial backward step is not taken by asking for still another justification in the chain, and failing to get it. The objections to that line of attack have already been stated; justifications come to an end. But this is precisely what provides universal doubt with its object. We step back to find that the whole system of justification and criticism, which controls our choices and supports our claims to rationality, rests on responses and habits that we never question, that we should not know how to defend without circularity, and to which we shall continue to adhere even after they are called into question.

The things we do or want without reasons, and without requiring reasons—the things that define what is a reason for us and what is not—are the starting points of our skepticism. We see ourselves from outside, and all the contingency and specificity of our aims and pursuits become clear. Yet when we take this view and recognize what we do as arbitrary, it does not disengage us from life, and there lies our absurdity: not in the fact that such an external view can be taken of us, but in the fact that we ourselves can take it, without ceasing to be the persons whose ultimate concerns are so coolly regarded.

## III

One may try to escape the position by seeking broader ultimate concerns, from which it is impossible to step back—the idea being that absurdity results because what we take seriously is something small and insignificant and individual. Those seeking to supply their lives with meaning usually envision a role or function in something larger than themselves. They therefore seek fulfillment in service to society, the state, the revolution, the progress of history, the advance of science, or religion and the glory of God.

But a role in some larger enterprise cannot confer significance unless that enterprise is itself significant. And its significance must come back to what we can understand, or it will not even appear to give us what we are seeking. If we learned that we were being raised to provide food for other creatures fond of human flesh, who planned to turn us into cutlets before we got too stringy—even if we learned that the human race had been developed by animal breeders precisely for this purpose—that would still not give our lives meaning, for two reasons. First, we would still be in the dark as to the significance of the lives of those other beings; second, although we might acknowledge that this culinary role would make our lives meaningful to them, it is not clear how it would make them meaningful to us.

Admittedly, the usual form of service to a higher being is different from this. One is supposed to behold and partake of the glory of God, for example, in a way in which chickens do not share in the glory of coq au vin. The same is true of service to a state, a movement, or a revolution. People can come to feel, when they are part of something bigger, that it is part of them too. They worry less about what is peculiar to themselves, but identify enough with the larger enterprise to find their role in it fulfilling.

However, any such larger purpose can be put in doubt in the same way that the aims of an individual life can be, and for the same reasons. It is as legitimate to find ultimate justification there as to find it earlier, among the details of individual life. But this does not alter the fact that justifications come to an end when we are content to have them end—when we do not find it necessary to look any further. If we can step back from the purposes of individual life and doubt their point, we can step back also from the progress of human history, or of science, or the success of a society, or the kingdom, power, and glory of God,[1] and put all these things into question in the same way. What seems to us to confer meaning, justification, significance, does so in virtue of the fact that we need no more reasons after a certain point.

What makes doubt inescapable with regard to the limited aims of individual life also makes it inescapable with regard to any larger purpose that encourages the sense that life is meaningful. Once the fundamental doubt has begun, it cannot be laid to rest.

Camus maintains in *The Myth of Sisyphus* that the absurd arises because the world fails to meet our demands for meaning. This suggests that the world might satisfy those demands if it were different. But now we can see that this is not the case. There does not appear to be any conceivable world (containing us) about which unsettlable doubts could not arise. Consequently the absurdity of our situation derives not from a collision between our expectations and the world, but from a collision within ourselves.

## IV

It may be objected that the standpoint from which these doubts are supposed to be felt does not exist—that if we take the recommended backward step we will land on thin air, without any basis for judgment about the natural responses we are supposed to be surveying. If we retain our usual standards of what is important, then questions about the significance of what we are doing with our lives will be answerable in the usual way. But if we do not, then those questions can mean nothing to us, since there is no longer any content to the idea of what matters, and hence no content to the idea that nothing does.

But this objection misconceives the nature of the backward step. It is not supposed to give us an understanding of what is *really* important, so that we see by contrast that our lives are insignificant. We never, in the course of these reflections, abandon the ordinary standards that guide our lives. We merely observe them in operation, and recognize that if they are called into question we can justify them only by reference to themselves, uselessly. We adhere to them because of the way we are put together; what seems to us important or serious or valuable would not seem so if we were differently constituted.

In ordinary life, to be sure, we do not judge a situation absurd unless we have in mind some standards of seriousness, significance, or harmony with which the absurd can be contrasted. This contrast is not implied by the philosophical judgment of absurdity, and that might be thought to make the concept unsuitable for the expression of such judgments. This is not so, however, for the philosophical judgment depends on another contrast which makes it a natural extension from more ordinary cases. It departs from them only in contrasting the pretensions of life with a larger context in which *no* standards can be discovered, rather than with a context from which alternative, overriding standards may be applied.

## V

In this respect, as in others, philosophical perception of the absurd resembles epistemological skepticism. In both cases the final, philosophical doubt is not contrasted with any unchallenged certainties, though it is arrived at by extrapolation from examples of doubt within the system of evidence or justification, where a contrast with other certainties *is* implied. In both cases our limitedness joins with a capacity to transcend those limitations in thought (thus seeing them as limitations, and as inescapable).

Skepticism begins when we include ourselves in the world about which we claim knowledge. We notice that certain types of evidence convince us, that we are content to allow justifications of belief to come to an end at certain points, that we feel we know many things even without knowing or having grounds for believing the denial of others which, if true, would make what we claim to know false.

For example, I know that I am looking at a piece of paper, although I have no adequate grounds to claim I know that I am not dreaming; and if I am dreaming then I am not looking at a piece of paper. Here an ordinary conception of how appearance may diverge from reality is employed to show that we take our world largely for granted; the certainty that we are not dreaming cannot be justified except circularly, in terms of those very appearances which are being put in doubt. It is somewhat farfetched to suggest I may be dreaming; but the possibility is only illustrative. It reveals that our claim to knowledge depends on our not feeling it necessary to exclude certain incompatible alternatives, and the dreaming possibility or the total-hallucination possibility are just representatives for limitless possibilities most of which we cannot even conceive.[2]

Once we have taken the backward step to an abstract view of our whole system of beliefs, evidence, and justification, and seen that it works only, despite its pretensions, by taking the world largely for granted, we are *not* in a position to contrast all these appearances with an alternative reality. We cannot shed our ordinary responses, and if we could it would leave us with no means of conceiving a reality of any kind.

It is the same in the practical domain. We do not step outside our lives to a new vantage point from which we see what is really, objectively significant. We continue to take life largely for granted while seeing that all our decisions and certainties are possible only because there is a great deal we do not bother to rule out.

Both epistemological skepticism and a sense of the absurd can be reached via initial doubts posed within systems of evidence and justification that we accept, and can be stated without violence to our ordinary concepts. We can ask not only why we should believe there is a floor under us, but also why we should believe the evidence of our senses at all—and at some point the framable questions will have outlasted the answers. Similarly, we can ask not only why we should take aspirin, but why we should take trouble over our own comfort at all. The fact that we shall take the aspirin without waiting for an answer to this last question does not show that it is an unreal question. We shall also continue to believe there is a floor under us without waiting for an answer to the other question. In both cases it is this unsupported natural confidence that generates skeptical doubts; so it cannot be used to settle them.

Philosophical skepticism does not cause us to abandon our ordinary beliefs, but it lends them a peculiar flavor. After acknowledging that their truth is incompatible with possibilities that we have no grounds for believing do not obtain—apart from grounds in those very beliefs which we have called into question—we return to our familiar convictions with a certain irony and resignation. Unable to abandon the natural responses on which they depend, we take them back, like a spouse who has run off with someone else and then decided to return; but we regard them differently (not that the new attitude is necessarily inferior to the old, in either case).

The same situation obtains after we have put in question the seriousness with which we take our lives and human life in general and have looked at ourselves without presuppositions. We then return to our lives, as we must, but our seriousness is laced with irony. Not that irony enables us to escape the absurd. It is useless to mutter: "Life is meaningless; life is meaningless ..." as an accompaniment to everything we do. In continuing to live and work and strive, we take ourselves seriously in action no matter what we say.

What sustains us, in belief as in action, is not reason or justification, but something more basic than these—for we go on in the same way even after we are convinced that the reasons have given out.[3] If we tried to rely entirely on reason, and pressed it hard, our lives and beliefs would collapse—a form of madness that may actually occur if the inertial force of taking the world and life for granted is somehow lost. If we lose our grip on that, reason will not give it back to us.

## VI

In viewing ourselves from a perspective broader than we can occupy in the flesh, we become spectators of our own lives. We cannot do very much as pure spectators of our own lives, so we continue to lead them, and devote ourselves to what we are able at the same time to view as no more than a curiosity, like the ritual of an alien religion.

This explains why the sense of absurdity finds its natural expression in those bad arguments with which the discussion began. Reference to our small size and short lifespan and to the fact that all of mankind will eventually vanish without a trace are metaphors for the backward step which permits us to regard ourselves from without and to find the particular form of our lives curious and slightly surprising. By feigning a nebula's-eye view, we illustrate the capacity to see ourselves without presuppositions, as arbitrary, idiosyncratic, highly specific occupants of the world, one of countless possible forms of life.

Before turning to the question whether the absurdity of our lives is something to be regretted and if possible escaped, let me consider what would have to be given up in order to avoid it.

Why is the life of a mouse not absurd? The orbit of the moon is not absurd either, but that involves no strivings or aims at all. A mouse, however, has to work to stay alive. Yet he is not absurd, because he lacks the capacities for self-consciousness and self-transcendence that would enable him to see that he is only a mouse. If that *did* happen, his life would become absurd, since self-awareness would not make him cease to be a mouse and would not enable him to rise above his mousely strivings. Bringing his new-found self-consciousness with him, he would have to return to his meagre yet frantic life, full of doubts that he was unable to answer, but also full of purposes that he was unable to abandon.

Given that the transcendental step is natural to us humans, can we avoid absurdity by refusing to take that step and remaining entirely within our sublunar lives? Well, we cannot refuse consciously, for to do that we would have to be aware of the viewpoint we were refusing to adopt. The only way to avoid the relevant self-consciousness would be either never to attain it or to forget it—neither of which can be achieved by the will.

On the other hand, it is possible to expend effort on an attempt to destroy the other component of the absurd—abandoning one's earthly, individual, human life in order to identify as completely as possible with that universal viewpoint from which human life seems arbitrary and trivial. (This appears to be the ideal of certain Oriental religions.) If one succeeds, then one will not have to drag the superior awareness through a strenuous mundane life, and absurdity will be diminished.

However, insofar as this self-etiolation is the result of effort, will-power, asceticism, and so forth, it requires that one take oneself seriously as an individual—that one be willing to take considerable trouble to avoid being creaturely and absurd. Thus one may undermine the aim of unworldliness by pursuing it too vigorously. Still, if someone simply allowed his individual, animal nature to drift and respond to impulse, without making the pursuit of its needs a central conscious aim, then he might, at considerable dissociative cost, achieve a life that was less absurd than most. It would not be a meaningful life either, of course; but it would not involve the engagement of a transcendent awareness in the assiduous pursuit of mundane goals. And that is the main condition of absurdity—the dragooning of an unconvinced transcendent consciousness into the service of an immanent, limited enterprise like a human life.

## VII

The final escape is suicide; but before adopting any hasty solutions, it would be wise to consider carefully whether the absurdity of our existence truly presents us with a *problem,* to which some solution must be found—a way of dealing with prima facie disaster. That is certainly the attitude with which Camus approaches the issue, and it gains support from the fact that we are all eager to escape from absurd situations on a smaller scale.

Camus—not on uniformly good grounds—rejects suicide and the other solutions he regards as escapist. What he recommends is defiance or scorn.

We can salvage our dignity, he appears to believe, by shaking a fist at the world which is deaf to our pleas, and continuing to live in spite of it. This will not make our lives un-absurd, but it will lend them a certain nobility.[4]

This seems to me romantic and slightly self-pitying. Our absurdity warrants neither that much distress nor that much defiance. At the risk of falling into romanticism by a different route, I would argue that absurdity is one of the most human things about us: a manifestation of our most advanced and interesting characteristics. Like skepticism in epistemology, it is possible only because we possess a certain kind of insight—the capacity to transcend ourselves in thought.

If a sense of the absurd is a way of perceiving our true situation (even though the situation is not absurd until the perception arises), then what reason can we have to resent or escape it? Like the capacity for epistemological skepticism, it results from the ability to understand our human limitations. It need not be a matter for agony unless we make it so. Nor need it evoke a defiant contempt of fate that allows us to feel brave or proud. Such dramatics, even if carried on in private, betray a failure to appreciate the cosmic unimportance of the situation. If *sub specie aeternitatis* there is no reason to believe that anything matters, then that doesn't matter either, and we can approach our absurd lives with irony instead of heroism or despair.

## NOTES

1. Cf. Robert Nozick, "Teleology," *Mosaic,* xii, 1 (Spring 1971), 27/8.

2. I am aware that skepticism about the external world is widely thought to have been refuted, but I have remained convinced of its irrefutability since being exposed at Berkeley to Thompson Clarke's largely unpublished ideas on the subject.

3. As Hume says in a famous passage of the *Treatise:* "Most fortunately it happens, that since reason is incapable of dispelling these clouds, nature herself suffices to that purpose, and cures me of this philosophical melancholy and delirium, either by relaxing this bent of mind, or by some avocation, and lively impression of my senses, which obliterate all these chimeras. I dine, I play a game of backgammon, I converse, and am merry with my friends; and when after three or four hours' amusement, I would return to these speculations, they appear so cold, and strain'd, and ridiculous, that I cannot find in my heart to enter into them any farther" (Book 1 Part 4, Section 7; Selby-Bigge, p. 269).

4. "Sisyphus, proletarian of the gods, powerless and rebellious, knows the whole extent of his wretched condition: it is what he thinks of during his descent. The lucidity that was to constitute his torture at the same time crowns his victory. There is no fate that cannot be surmounted by scorn" (*The Myth of Sisyphus,* Vintage edition, p. 90).

# CHAPTER 14

# JOEL FEINBERG

## *Absurd Self-Fulfillment*

A recent author adds a twist to the ancient legend of Sisyphus, who was condemned by the gods to perpetual life spent pushing a large rock to the top of a hill from which it fell down the other side, once more to be pushed to the top, and so on forever. "Let us suppose," writes Richard Taylor, "that the gods, while condemning Sisyphus to the fate just described, at the same time, as an afterthought, waxed perversely merciful by implanting in him a strange and irrational impulse; namely, a compulsive impulse to roll stones . . . [e.g.] through implanting some substance in him that has this effect on his character and drives."[1] Such a modification would be merciful but also "perverse," Taylor maintains, "because from our point of view there is clearly no reason why anyone should have a persistent and insatiable desire to do something as pointless as that."[2]

Taylor's remodeled Sisyphus, meaningless as his activities may seem to us, at least can find his rock-pushing career *fulfilling*. Insofar as a powerful disposition to push rocks has been built into him, he is only doing what he is inclined by his nature to do when he pushes the rock, just as a dog fulfills his nature by chasing a rabbit, or a bird by building a nest. One can criticize Taylor, however, for his apparent confusion of self-fulfillment (doing what it is in one's nature to do) with compulsion. In Taylor's revision of the legend, a substance in Sisyphus's blood forces him to "want" to push stones, just as repeated injections of heroin into the veins of an unwilling prisoner would impose an addiction to heroin on him and make him "want" his subsequent fixes. The causal mechanism employed by the gods, however, need not be that crude, and we can imagine that they remake Sisyphus's nature in a more thoroughgoing way so that the disposition to push large objects, stemming from a reconstructed complex of glands and nerves and basic drives, becomes an integral part of Sisyphus's self rather than an alien element

Feinberg, Joel; *Freedom and Fulfillment.* © 1992 by Princeton University Press. Reprinted by permission of Princeton University Press.

restraining him. Let us add a twist to Taylor's twist then, and have the gods provide Sisyphus with a new nature rather than imposing an addiction on his old one. We can think of a rock-pushing Sisyphus as no more "addicted" to his characteristic activities than we are to walking upright or to speaking a language. Our new Sisyphus's activities, furthermore, are self-fulfilling, not simply because they satisfy his desires, nor simply because they involve his own willful acquiescence, but rather because they express some basic genetic disposition of his nature.

Taylor does not use the word "absurd" in describing Sisyphus's peculiar activities, but a whole tradition, one of whose most prominent recent members was Albert Camus,[3] finds that term eminently appropriate. The words Taylor uses are "meaningless," "pointless," and "endless." Perhaps endless repetitive cycles of pointless labor with no apparent purpose or result is only one species of absurdity, or perhaps pointlessness is only one among several grounds for judging an activity to be absurd. (The closely related but distinct characteristic of futility through purposeful but self-defeating actions may be another.) In either case, pointlessness and generic absurdity are not identical notions. But few would deny the synthetic judgment that there *is* an absurdity in pointless labors that will plainly come to nothing, Taylor isolates this absurdity by contrasting it with both painfulness and loneliness. It is not because Sisyphus's labors are arduous and body-bruising that they are absurd, for we can imagine that his rock is small and his labors undemanding. They would be no less pointless, and therefore no less absurd for that. Moreover, as Taylor suggests, we could give Sisyphus some partners so that the rock-moving activities are conducted by teams of two or more persons. That would reduce the loneliness of the enterprise but not its silliness. The essential absurdity of pointless activity is captured in a non-Sisyphean example that Taylor himself provides: "Two groups of prisoners, one of them engaged in digging a prodigious hole in the ground that is no sooner finished than it is filled in again by the other group, the latter then digging a new hole that is at once filled in by the first group and so on endlessly."[4]

Many philosophers have said that insofar as human existence is absurd there is a ground for certain negative attitudes—suicidal despair, detached cynicism, philosophical pessimism, Camus' haughty scorn or existential defiance. Other philosophers, addressing a somewhat different datum, have said that insofar as a given human life is self-fulfilled it is a good life, and provides a reason for certain positive attitudes toward the human condition—hope, satisfaction, acceptance, or reconciliation. Often the "optimists say that some lives, at least, are completely fulfilled and most lives fulfilled to some degree or other. There is no antecedent necessity that they all be fulfilled or that they all be unfulfilled; it all depends on skill or luck "Pessimists," on the other hand, claim that all lives are necessarily absurd (meaningless, pointless, futile), so their view is more sweeping. In any event, "absurdity" and "self-fulfillment" are quite different notions so that optimists and pessimists are not even talking about the same thing. Taylor suggests, quite plausibly, that life might be *both* absurd and at its best, sometimes, self-fulfilling. What are we to make of that combination of truths? What are the consequences for optimism and pessimism? What general attitudes are appropriate if it is accepted? These questions call for closer examination of the concepts of "absurdity" and "self-fulfillment" and how they might fit together, and some comments on the question of how we can judge the rational appropriateness of cosmic attitudes.

## ABSURDITY IN INDIVIDUAL LIVES

We should attend to the undeniable examples of absurdity *in* life before raising the subject of the absurdity *of* life. Since some elements in any life are absurd, we can focus our attention on these familiar occurrences and inquire what it is we are saying about them when we judge them to be absurd. Thomas Nagel provides some useful instances of absurd events that, since they are easy to respond to playfully, are irresistibly comic: "Someone gives a complicated speech in support of a motion that has already been passed; a notorious criminal is made president of a major philanthropic foundation; you declare your love over the telephone to a recorded announcement; as you are knighted your pants fall down."[5] Some of Nagel's examples are human actions that can be criticized as reasonable or unreasonable in relation to the actor's presumed motives and ends. Others are mere happenings leading directly to states of affairs that themselves can be thought of as irrational relative to some larger presumed purposes: The image of a great statesman or scientist standing bare-legged with his trousers around his ankles as the queen tries to award him his knighthood conflicts irrationally with the presumed purpose of the ceremony, which in part is to create a dignified and moving spectacle. *If* the pants-dropping incident had been deliberately chosen it would have been subject to the charge of irrationality, since it could have been anticipated to produce results that would defeat the larger purposes for which it was chosen. In this indirect way, even mere occurrences and unchosen states of affairs can be judged "irrational," and sometimes irrational to the point of absurdity. In addition to doings, activities, careers and lives, mere happenings and states of affairs, we also judge beliefs, hypotheses, convictions, desires, purposes, and even people to be absurd, and usually we can explain what this means in a fairly straightforward way by substituting the word "irrational" and locating the absurdity in question on a map of the various species of irrationality. On other occasions, as in the fallen pants example, a mere occurrence is related indirectly to irrationality by the showing that *if* it were thought, contrary to fact, to be somebody's deliberate doing, that doing would be patently irrational.

The paradigmatic type of irrationality is false or unwarranted belief. When something analogous to flagrant falsity or manifestly fallacious argument is a defect of such nonbeliefs as desires, purposes, instrumentalities, actions, and states of affairs, then they too can be characterized as irrational or unreasonable, although the word "absurd" seems to fit them more comfortably. *Webster's Collegiate Dictionary* tells us that when the intensifier *ab* was added to the Latin word *surdus* (dull, deaf, insensible), the result was a Latin word translatable as "not to be heard from," and the derivative English word meaning "laughingly inconsistent with what is judged as true or reasonable." "Falsehood" and "invalidity," then, arc not quite enough to explain absurdity. The absurd is what is *palpably* untrue or unreasonable, outlandishly and preposterously so, literally "unheard of" or not to be entertained. One element, then, that the various sorts of absurd things have in common is their extreme irrationality, whether that be the apparently knowing assertion of manifestly false propositions, or the apparently voluntary making of manifestly unreasonable decisions, or the apparently eager living of a manifestly pointless life.

A second element in all absurdity is implicit in the first, but deserves to be clearly stated on its own. Where there is absurdity there are always two things clashing or in disharmony, distinguishable entities that conflict with one another. This element is referred to variously as the "divorce,"[6] disparity, discrepancy, disproportion, or incongruity between discordant objects. In general, things that do not fit together—means discrepant with ends, premises incongruous with conclusions, ideals disharmonious with practice, pretensions in conflict with realities—arc found wherever there is absurdity. But having located the absurdity, we may attribute it either to the relation of disharmony itself, or exclusively to one, or to the other, of the discordant objects.

In some cases we adopt the point of view of the standard and "laugh down" at the incongruous object, as when we delight in the undignified fall of the pompously powerful. In other cases we take the opposite viewpoint, that of the comically discrepant object itself, and we laugh at the standard, as, for example, when we laugh at cute children masquerading as adults, or in a quite different example, we laugh at a cute risqué story and thus have some fun with the sexual conventions violated in the tale. Perhaps not all funny things are absurd, and surely not all absurd things are funny, but discordance is an element common to many comic and absurd things.

Another form of disparity is described in Nagel's astute account of absurdity,[7] namely, the clash or disharmony between various perspectives from which we form attitudes and make judgments. There is an unavoidable discrepancy between the natural subjective way of viewing ourselves—as precious in our own eyes, full of genuinely important projects, whole universes in ourselves, persons who "live only once" and have to make the most of the time allotted us—and various hypothetical judgments made from a more universal perspective: we are mere specks, or drops in the ocean, or one of the teeming hive, absolutely inessential to the grand scheme of things, no more lovable in ourselves than are any of the zillions of individual insects whose infinitesimally transitory lives are equally as unimportant in the long run as our own. Our subjective point of view is an expression of the "seriousness" with which all living beings must view their situations, a necessary expression of our biological natures. But the broader perspectives that yield a different and conflicting picture are available to any being with imagination and modest conceptual development. Judged from these perspectives, the human expenditures of effort and emotion in the pursuit of "important goals" are just so many posturings, and we mortals are absurd figures who strut and fret our hour upon the stage. The absurdity in the human condition, Nagel tells us, consists in a special kind of conspicuous discrepancy, that between unavoidable pretension or aspiration, on the one hand, and reality as perceived from a truer perspective on the other.

Not all of Nagel's examples of absurdity within human lives are equally plausible models for the alleged absurdity of human life as such. Applied to Sisyphus, at any rate, and to some actual Sisyphean lives, Nagel's "conspicuous discrepancy between pretension or aspiration and reality" seems less strikingly relevant than Taylor's conception of absurdity as ultimate futility and pointlessness. Careful reconsideration, however, will reveal that Taylor's "futility or pointlessness of activity" and Nagel's "discrepancy of perspectives for viewing oneself," while irreducibly distinct types of absurdity, are nonetheless equally proper examples of the absurd genus. Taylor's type of absurdity applies more naturally to the Sisyphean model for the human condition, but Nagel's conception provides another model of its own, equally challenging as a picture of the absurdity of human life as a whole, and equally familiar, as a recent *New Yorker* cartoon shows. Two small figures, recognizable as a well-dressed middle-class couple, are on the patio of their suburban home, while above them a full moon and vast panoply of stars glimmer and sparkle. The discrepancy between the human beings' inevitably extravagant sense of self-importance and their actual tiny role in the whole picture is indicated by the little man's comment to his little wife: "Why, no! Why should I feel small? I've just been put in charge of the whole Eastern region."[8]

Nagel's kind of absurdity is not necessarily involved in the Sisyphus story, but if it is added to the pointless labor that *is* involved, it adds a whole new dimension of absurdity to that already present. Moreover, Sisyphus's labors might be motivated by a genuinely sensible purpose, and thus be unabsurd in Taylor's sense, yet absurd anyway in a sense closer to Nagel's. Imagine, for example, that the gods have sentenced Sisyphus only to climb a large mountain and plant a small flag on the top. As soon as he succeeds in doing that, his penalty has been paid once and for all. It takes Sisyphus years (or centuries) to climb the mountain but then he finds that he has forgotten the flag. He returns to the base, recovers the flag, and spends another millennium or so climbing a peak only to discover that he is on the wrong mountain. And so on ad infinitum. Sisyphus's labors would not be pointless in that case since they would have a sensible aim, but how genuinely absurd his constant mistakes would be whether committed in pursuit of a purpose or not! Or suppose that the gods in the original legend had not only assigned Sisyphus his endless self-defeating labor, but had also required him, before each trip to the summit, to write "I am a bad boy" one hundred times on his rock. What an absurd comedown for the proud and once mighty Sisyphus! Now his labors are doubly absurd, both pointless and conflicting with his natural self-importance.

Moreover, to further accentuate the difference between Taylor's and Nagel's criteria, it can be noted that the traditional Sisyphus, before we began tampering with the legend, was *not* absurd by Nagel's criterion. He had no illusions or false pretensions, and his resigned "aspiration," although point-less, was perfectly realistic. If his plight, therefore, is to be taken as a model for the absurdity of the whole human enterprise, we shall have to expand Nagel's account of absurdity to include examples from within human life of the sort Taylor emphasized, for instance, the prisoners' digging and filling in of holes, or the ordering of intricately ornate wedding cakes and consuming of them before they are even wrapped, or in general giving with one hand and taking away with the other[9] contrary to all reason. Taylor's and Nagel's conceptions of absurdity, however, do share a generic character. They are two distinct species of absurdity but both can be subsumed, in their separate ways, under the "discrepancy" rubric. The discrepancy in Taylor's case is that between the kind of labor that is normally thought to be sheer drudgery and a purpose inadequate to justify it or to provide it with any reason what-soever. Ultimately, pointlessness is a kind of discrepancy, or massive dispro-portion, between means and ends. It must also be said, in fairness to Nagel, that his conception of absurdity *can* be applied to some Sisyphean individu-als. If in fact some of us are quite similar to Sisyphus, but we pretend to be otherwise, then we are absurd in Nagel's sense too.

A careful perusal of absurd elements within individual human lives will disclose still other models of absurdity in addition to Taylor's "pointless-ness" and Nagel's "unrealistic pretension and aspiration," and these addi-tional types of absurdity can also be treated as species of discrepancy, conflict, or disproportion. We must first follow up our earlier suggestion by distin-guishing pointlessness from futility. A pointless action or activity is one that has no intelligible purpose the achievement of which gives it value and explanation ("point" or "meaning"). Moreover, it is not the kind of activity that carries its own reward quite independently of any further purpose, but rather the sort of activity we normally think of as sheer drudgery (like rock-pushing). Since it does not possess value in itself, but rather, if anything, a kind of negative value, and it has no envisaged consequences for the sake of which it is undertaken, it is utterly valueless, or worse. A totally pointless activity will not only lack a conscious objective beyond itself; it will also lack any unforeseen actual consequences that could confer value back on it by a kind of fluke.

Some activities have a point, but are very little less absurd than totally pointless activities since their conscious objective is manifestly incapable of justifying the drudgery that is meant to achieve it. The intrinsic disvalue of the activity is an exorbitant (hence irrational) price to pay for so trivial a reward. Sisyphus's labors would not be totally pointless if his whole motive was to receive a piece of candy from the gods every century or so. His endless labors would hardly be any less absurd in that case, and the absurdity in question would be a manifest disproportion between means and end. Following W. D. Joske, we can call this species of absurdity *triviality*.[10] Obviously burdensome activities that are absurdly trivial are not much less absurd than burdensome activities that are wholly pointless.

Futile activities (still another species of absurdity) do have a point, and a reasonably proportionate one, but nonetheless are absurd because they are manifestly inefficacious means to the achievement of their nontrivial goals. If they had a chance to achieve the worthy objective that motivates them, they would not be absurd, but it is evident to us, the observers, or even in the worst case to the actors themselves, that continued participation in the intrinsically valueless activity will be fruitless, hence futile. The reasons for the absurd activity's instrumental inefficacy can be various. In the simplest cases, nature itself stands in the way and success is rendered impossible by laws of nature, as with efforts to high-jump ten feet off the ground, or by contingent individual incapacities, as when a dog repeatedly chases sea gulls on a beach with the presumed intention of catching one of them, but continually fails because of its lack of speed and other requisite physical skills, but never gives up making its absurd efforts. The most interesting class of futile activities, however, are those in which the instrumental inefficacies are the result of the self-defeating character of the actor's own techniques and strategies, especially when flagrant and manifest to any observer. The tale is told of a workman who opens his lunch pail every noon, examines his sandwiches, and comments; "Ugh, tuna fish again." Finally, after weeks of witnessing this ritual, a fellow worker asks, "Why don't you have your wife make you some other kind of sandwich?" to which the first worker replies, "Oh, I'm not married. I make my own lunches." The worker's constant failure could be charged to poor memory or some other cognitive failure, but to the observer who thinks of it as absurd, it is as if the actor deliberately takes steps every day to frustrate his own purposes.

In summary, purposeful activities can be placed on a spectrum of absurdity. At the one extreme are intrinsically worthless activities that are engaged in even though they have no vindicating purpose beyond themselves. These activities are totally pointless. Then come burdensome or disliked activities engaged in only because they are expected to produce some minor advantage for which the instrumental labors are massively disproportionate. These are absurdly trivial activities. They too constitute a whole section of the spectrum, becoming less and less absurd as their achieved goals reduce the disproportion of their means. Then come the inherently burdensome activities that do have a clearly vindicating purpose but are ill-designed to achieve them. These are absurdly futile activities when it would be plainly evident to an observer that they are hopelessly inefficacious. If there is a chance of success, the activity may be reasonable, hence unabsurd, even though in fact the vindicating objective is never achieved. To these absurdities, explained in term of means-ends disproportions, we must add Nagel's favorite types of absurdity, which are explained in terms of other poor fits, especially the failure of pretensions and aspirations to fit objective facts. In short, an absurd element within an individual life can fall within five or more categories. It can be pointless, trivial (instrumentally disproportionate), futile, unrealistically pretentious, or otherwise incongruous or a "poor fit," like actions that presuppose false or logically inconsistent beliefs.

## THE ALLEGED ABSURDITY OF HUMAN LIFE AS SUCH: SOME PHILOSOPHICAL INDICTMENTS

Taylor, Camus, and Nagel, each in his own way and each making his own special qualifications, looks with favor on the judgment that there is absurdity in the human condition as such. It will be useful here to discuss critically some of the reasons given by these philosophers. We can begin with Taylor who finds all human activity to be as pointless (in the long run) as that of Sisyphus. He uses the words "meaningless" and "pointless" instead of "absurd," and as we have seen, means by them "endless repetitive activity that comes to nothing." The endlessness, no doubt, is not essential to the meaninglessness. If Sisyphus pushed his rock continuously for four score and ten years only, before being mercifully killed by the gods, Taylor could and would judge his finite career as a rock-mover to be absurd, just as he judges the finite lives of men and mice to be absurd.

Meaninglessness for Taylor is mitigated but not cancelled by achievement, because achievements do not last. Some achievements, for example *Hamlet*, Beethoven's *Fifth Symphony*, and the Notre Dame cathedral, last longer than others, and might therefore qualify as less absurd than the transient and trivial triumphs in which most of us take what pride we can. But from any sufficiently broad point of view, long compared with the span of human lives or even the lives of nations and planets, but infinitely narrower than the perspective *sub specie aeternitatis*, the difference between the durability of Notre Dame and that of a pioneer's log cabin is utterly insignificant. All of our goals, Taylor says, are of "transitory significance," and "having gained one of them we immediately set forth for the next as if that one had never been, with this next one being essentially more of the same."[11] Unlike Sisyphus, however, most of us beget children and pass on our values, our modest achievements, and fresh opportunities to them. That fact does not impress Taylor, who replies that "Each man's life thus resembles one of Sisyphus's climbs to the summit of his hill and each day of it one of his steps; the difference is that whereas Sisyphus himself returns to push the stone up again, we leave this to our children."[12] The enterprise is thus collective, but it still comes to nothing in the end.

What could human existence conceivably be like if it were to escape this absurdity? This is a crucial question that all philosophical pessimists must answer if their sweeping judgments of universal absurdity are to be fully intelligible. For unless we know what contrasting situation is being ruled out we cannot be sure what a given assertion is "including in." Unless we know what *would* count as nonabsurdity, if there were such a thing, we have nothing to contrast absurdity with. If all conceivable universes are equally and necessarily absurd on their face, so that one cannot even describe what nonabsurd existence would be like, it is not very informative, to put it mildly, to affirm that this our actual universe is absurd. It is a test of the intelligiblity of a philosophical doctrine that it succeed in ruling out some contrasting state of affairs.

Taylor's doctrine fortunately seems to pass the test, more or less. He has us imagine that Sisyphus is permitted to push an assortment of stones to the top of his hill and combine them there into a beautiful and enduring temple. This would be to escape absurdity, Taylor says at first, for "activity . . . has a meaning if it has some significant culmination, some more or less lasting end that can be considered to have been the direction and purpose of the activity."[13] But soon he changes his mind. He does not wish to make meaningfulness a matter of "more or less," for then he would have to admit that some human activities and lives are to some degree, at least, meaningful, and comparisons of the relative meaningfulness of various individual lives would at least make sense. But that would be to vindicate rather than to destroy common sense on this question, and Taylor, his sights set high, quickly withdraws his concession by requiring that the temple must endure—not simply be "more or less lasting"—"adding beauty to the world for the remainder of time."[14] When we look at a meaningless life like that of the legendary Sisyphus or that of a drug-addicted teenage suicide, and compare it with one of the relatively meaningful human lives suggested by common sense, say that of Jefferson or Shakespeare, the differences at first are striking. But "if we look at them from a distance" (say from a point in time one hundred million years from now) they "are in outline the same and convey to the mind the same image"—pointless labor and emotion coming to nothing.[15] It is the temporal distance that make the difference. The view from remote distances in time reveals things as they truly are, whereas the detailed close-up picture is distorted and illusory.

Taylor makes another hypothetical supposition. Let us suppose that after a finite period of intense labor Sisyphus finishes a gloriously beautiful temple, and then is allowed by the gods to rest on his laurels and spend the rest of eternal time in admiring contemplation of his significant achievement. Now at last we seem to have an unchallengeable conception of nonabsurd existence, but Taylor quickly dashes our hopes. Eternal rest, he rightly claims, would be "infinite boredom," and that too would become in due time a kind of pointlessness or absurdity. Unfortunately, he does not consider other possibilities that would save his doctrine of universal absurdity from vacuity. For example, Sisyphus could be allowed to die after a brief rest period but before his proud satisfaction turns to boredom, while his temple is preserved forever by the gods, or Sisyphus could be permitted to live forever, alternating creative activity with replenishing periods of rest, while the gods guarantee the permanence of his achievements. I suspect that Taylor, like Bernard Williams,[16] would find even the latter arrangement no escape from infinite boredom, so that his final view, if he had finished his argument, would be that *almost* any conceivable form of life would be absurd, either because it fails to produce permanently lasting achievements or because it leads to boredom. The qualifier "almost" serves to give meaningful contrast to Taylor's absurdism since the remaining conception of nonabsurd existence rules out a relevant contrast (merciful death with the assurance of everlasting preservation of achievements).

Permanent preservation of personal achievement is not, however, a plausible requirement for nonabsurd meaningfulness. Indeed, there is something absurd in the idea that the gods would clutter up the universe to all eternity with modest monuments to everyone's best deeds. And if only Shakespearian and Beethovian triumphs are preserved, then by Taylor's standards, life becomes absurd for all the rest of us.

According to Camus, human beings necessarily crave a certain kind of cosmic order, significant culminations of their efforts, and a kind of transparent rational intelligibility in the world of experience. But the world has no such order; it works to destroy the point of whatever temporary achievements it permits; and it is in its central core alien, dense, and irrational. Hence the inevitable confrontation and the inevitable absurdity.

Camus seems to know exactly what he wants from the world. He believes also that the world, by its very nature, cannot provide him with what he wants, and that he, by his very nature, cannot modify or relinquish those wants, hopeless though they be. There is therefore a "divorce" in the nature of things, an ineradicable discrepancy between human nature and the rest of nature, and it is this irreconcilable clash that generates the absurdity of the human condition. He wants a universe that cares about him personally, a world that he can identify with instead of feeling alienated from, a world that can heal the deep sense of loneliness all sensitive beings experience when they encounter nature as an "other." Most of all, he cannot help wanting to live forever, although as a rational being he knows that death is inevitable. His unmodifiable yet unsatisfiable desires are more then mere wants; they are natural *needs*. "The absurd is born of this confrontation between human need and the unreasonable silence of the world."[17]

Camus eloquently describes the feeling of absurdity evoked in him by forests and oceans ("At the heart of all natural beauty lies something inhuman"), and by bustling human marketplaces. Always at its core is a vital yearning that he knows has no hope of satisfaction, yet no possibility of being extinguished. "At any street corner the feeling of absurdity can strike any person in the face."[18] One reliable evoker of that feeling is what Camus calls the "collapse of the stage setting." Individual lives proceed according to their fixed rhythms, and then suddenly "one day the 'why' arises and . . . [a] weariness tinged with amazement."[19] The feeling to which Camus here refers is one, I dare say, that almost all of us have experienced at one time or another, but for pessimistic philosophers it is more than a feeling, in that it contains the materials for an argument for human absurdity. I first remember experiencing the feeling and toying with the argument while observing crowds of shoppers in a supermarket. (Since then, I have come to call it the "supermarket regress.") Suddenly the stage setting collapsed, and the shoppers' life patterns seemed to make no more sense than the hole-digging in Taylor's example of the prisoners. Why are all those people standing in line before the cash registers? In order to purchase food. Why do they purchase food? In order to stay alive and healthy. Why do they wish to stay alive and healthy? So that they can work at their jobs. Why do they want to work? To earn money. Why do they want to earn money? So that they can purchase food. And so on, around the circle, over and over, with no "significant culmination" in sight. Vindicating purpose and meaning are constantly put off to another stage that never comes, and the whole round of activity looks more like a meaningless ritual-dance than something coherent and self-justifying.

As an argument for inevitable absurdity, the supermarket regress is only as strong as its premises. One presupposition of the argument in particular is weak, namely, the assumption that no human activity is ever valuable in *itself*, but that vindicating value is always postponed until some future consequence arrives, which in turn can never be valuable in itself but only valuable as a means to something else that cannot be valuable in itself, and so on, forever. This paradox is not an accurate picture of all human activity, striking as it may seem when it naturally suggests itself to an observer of crowds of human animals mechanically pursuing their ritualized goals. In fact, the impossibility of intrinsically valuable activity is itself an illusion produced by what Moritz Schlick in a remarkable essay[20] called "the tyranny of purpose."

There is another kind of insight, also natural and common, that can lead one too hastily to interpret human activity as absurd. Altogether unlike Camus, we can think of ourselves as part and parcel of nature, one biological species among many others. Then we can examine the life cycles of the lesser species and come to appreciate their absurd character, here responding not to apparent circularity as in the human case, but to a value regress proper, in which justifying purposes are put off forever. Various insects,[21] amphibians, and fish, for example, seem to have no ultimate purpose of their own but to stay alive long enough to reproduce, so that their progeny can also stay alive long enough to reproduce, and so on forever, as if simply keeping a species in existence were an end in itself with no further purpose needed. This has seemed to many human observers to be the very model of absurdity, an utterly pointless existence.

The absurdity is accentuated in the case of species like the salmon, whose members struggle and strive heroically, swimming against the currents, battered against rocks, plundered by predators, until the survivors reach the headwaters of their native streams, tattered, torn, and dying. Even then the ordeal is not over, for the males at least must fight off their own intraspecies competitors for an opportunity to entice females to lay eggs, to fertilize them, and only then to die. What is the point of all this effort? Simply to produce another generation of tiny salmon to start all over again, feeding and growing as they head down river toward the ocean, then after a time in salt water, heading back upstream amid the many dangers and against all odds, to reproduce and die. The whole process has no apparent point except its own further continuance. To some human observers that natural cycle is a kind of collective effort to discharge a task that makes no more sense than that assigned as punishment to the solitary Sisyphus. The human life style is perhaps less fixed and rigid, and surely more varied, but insofar as it resembles that of the insects, toads, and fish, it is equally self-contained and pointless.[22]

The best response to this argument is that it projects human needs and sensibilities into other species. The human observer simply does not have the salmon's point of view. A well-bred salmon will love the life of a salmon, which after all, is the only life it can know. The life cycle for it may seem to be its own point, with no further purpose, no further achievement external to it, needed to establish its rational credentials. To insist that without permanently preserved achievements and lasting monuments, the life of a salmon is absurd, is a piece of parochial prejudice on the part of human beings.

Both the supermarket circle and the biological regress purport to show that human life is pointless because justification for any of its parts or phases is indefinitely postponed, never coming to a final resting place. We choose to do $A$ only because it will lead to $B$, which we desire only because of its conducibility to $C$, which we value only as a means to $D$, and so on. In the biological regress argument the chain of justification proceeds in a straight line, so to speak, never coming to an end. It therefore fails to show how any component human activity can truly have a point beyond itself. In the supermarket version of the argument the chain does not proceed endlessly and infinitely only because it closes a circle at some point going round and round indefinitely, starting over again at regular intervals without ever having justified anything. Nagel thinks of these arguments as "standard" attempts to demonstrate absurdity, and although he is sympathetic to their motives and conclusions, he regards them as failures. Part of his ground for rejecting the arguments from circular and linear regression is factual. Some individual acts within life, he says, have a point even if the general statement of (say) the supermarket regression is correct. "Chains of justification come repeatedly to an end within life, and whether the process as a whole can be justified has no bearing on the finality of the end points. No further justification is needed to make it reasonable to take aspirin for a headache, attend an exhibit of the work of a painter one admires, or stop a child from putting his hand on a hot stove. No larger context or further purpose is needed to prevent these acts from being pointless."

Nagel's three examples of actions with a genuine point beyond themselves make a heterogeneous lot, but the aspirin and hot stove examples, at least, convincing as they are, do not substantially weaken the force of the supermarket circular regress. One can think of human life as an endlessly circular quest for a vindicating point that is never to be found, even though some individual acts in the generally pointless pursuit do have *their* points. It is possible after all to hold *both* that there is a point in taking aspirin and in keeping infantile hands off hot stoves *and* that in the main course of human life the activities that preoccupy us are inevitably absurd, forming an inescapable circle of activities each of which lacks a justifying point. It is not that aspirins are absurd, only that their use is not part of the central pattern that *is* absurd.

It is difficult to offer a sympathetic ear to Camus' other complaints, although one must acknowledge that he does know how to capture a mood that circumstances can induce in any of us, and that circumstances might understandably produce regularly in some of us. What Camus refers to as "needs," for example, that one live forever, or that we can have a full and perspicuous understanding of all the phenomena of nature that science struggles with piecemeal, are for others—indeed for most others—quite dispensable wants that can be relinquished or modified as the evidence suggests, without cost to one's integrity.

What sort of response does Camus recommend to what he takes to be the absurdity of human life? Suicide, he says, would be a pointless gesture. Self-deception is the common way out. But embracing consoling myths is inconsistent with one's integrity. There is in fact no way of reconciling the cravings inherent in our nature, as he sees it, with the uncompromising denials of the alien cosmos. The existentialist hero acknowledges his inherent absurdity without wincing; he cherishes his consciousness of it, keeping it forever alive as the evidence of his integrity. He has no hope that things could be different, but lives to the hilt and dies well, like a blind person who cannot relinquish his desire to see though he knows the desire is hopeless.[23] In his defiance of what is necessary, he claims to achieve his integrity, and in his revolt his happiness. If Camus were a Columbia River salmon, he would lead the way over the rocks and up the rapids and be the first to fertilize new eggs, but he would never for a moment abandon his conviction that the whole enterprise is absurd, and his stubborn scorn would enable him to feel quite good about himself. If only a fish could be like a man!

Before leaving Camus, it is interesting to note his suggestion of how absurdity might relate to self-fulfillment. If it is in my nature as a human being—ineluctably—to crave unity, intelligibility, and immortality, then according to Camus my absurdity consists in the "divorce" between my nature and the large world of which it is a part, which defeats rather than fulfills it. It is in my nature then, quite absurdly, to be out of harmony with the universe. Camus' prescription that I defiantly embrace this absurdity and live to the hilt, amounts to a recommendation that I attempt to fulfill that nature, absurd as it is, and be defiant of the uncooperative universe. One can interpret Camus as recommending *as a means to full self-fulfillment* that I be intensely and continuously conscious of my absurdity, that is, of the clash between larger nature and my nature. The beginnings of a paradox can be found in this conception: Can it be "fulfilling" to fulfill a nature in conflict with itself? Can one find one's fulfillment in frustration, one's triumph in defeat?

The absurdity of the human condition, according to the third theory, that of Nagel, derives from the clash of perspectives from which we can view ourselves: that of purposeful actors living out our lives and that of disinterested spectators of the very lives we earnestly live. Only human beings are capable of viewing themselves from a detached and impersonal perspective and making judgments from that viewpoint of their own insignificance. When we do view ourselves in that detached way, then the ordinary way of regarding our lives, which we cannot help but adopt if we are to pursue our lives at all, seems absurd to us. A mouse also regards his own life in the same serious everyday way that humans do, but since "he lacks the capacities for self-consciousness and self-transcendence that would enable him to see that he is only a mouse,"[24] he is not absurd. Human beings can diminish (but probably not eliminate) the absurdity of their own lives by allowing their individual animal natures to drift and respond to impulse, in short by becoming as much like mice as possible, but this would involve "considerable dissociative cost."[25]

Nagel is confusing when he talks as if he is making judgments about the absurdity of others' lives when he is only explaining the way in which those lives might come to *seem* absurd, either to those persons themselves or to a sensitive observer. Thus when he talks about possible "escapes" from absurdity and admits that a mindless life spent drifting with impulse is less absurd than more characteristically human lives despite its dissociative cost, he is using "absurd" to mean "seems absurd," much as psychoanalysts often equate "guilt" and "feelings of guilt." The life of a mouse is absurd when we look at it from an imaginatively extended perspective that the mouse itself cannot achieve. When Nagel denies the mouse's absurdity on the ground that *it* has no transcendental consciousness, he explains why the mouse's life cannot *seem* absurd to it. But the mouse's life can still seem absurd to *us*, and really be absurd nonetheless. Nagel, in short, at least in much of his discussion, takes the essential discrepancy in an absurd life to be a relation between two components of the being whose life it is—his natural and inevitable seriousness, and his awareness from a higher perspective of his own insignificance. But one could lack that kind of discrepancy, as mice do, and enjoy a more unified consciousness that in turn is discrepant with an external reality, the unaccommodating and alien universe. Nagel employs the latter conception of absurdity too when he speaks of the clash between subjective pretension and objective reality, and that is the notion that is used by Taylor and Camus when they make judgments of real, not merely apparent, absurdity.

The distinction between really being and only seeming absurd quickly suggests another, that between absurdity as a property of one's situation, and absurdity as a flaw in one's outlook or self-assessment—put tersely, between *absurd predicaments* and *absurd persons*. It does not follow, of course, from the fact that a person is in an absurd predicament that she is an absurd person, for she may have redeeming insights into, and attitudes toward her situation that put her beyond criticism or mockery. The human predicament that we all share is absurd according to Taylor because achievements do not last and there is thus a necessary and objective discrepancy between effort and outcome. It is absurd according to Camus because the universe is resistant to our inherent craving for order and intelligibility, and there is thus an ineradicable disharmony between our needs and the world's indifference. The human predicament is absurd according to Nagel because of the irresolvable clash between the importance we attach to our lives and the essential dubitability of all schemes of justification for that importance. All three writers agree that the absurdity of our human predicament is not a matter of "more or less" and not a matter that could be different from what it is. It is otherwise with the absurdity of persons. Some people are obviously more absurd than others in that there is a greater clash between their beliefs and their evidence, their mean and their ends, or their pretensions and their real characters and situations.

A person is also absurd—and this is the interesting point—when there is a radical discrepancy between her assessment of her situation and the actual nature of that situation. If one is really in an absurd predicament, if, for example, all of one's labors are bound to come to nothing in the end whatever one chooses to do about it, and one stubbornly denies that absurdity, adopting inappropriate attitudes and embracing vain hopes, then one becomes more than a little absurd oneself. Thus Sisyphus escapes personal absurdity by correctly appraising the absurdity of his predicament, realistically abandoning hope, and cooly proceeding with his labors in an existentialist spirit of "Let's get on with it,"[26] thus maintaining a kind of dignity and self-respect. But Sisyphus would surely be absurd if, like Don Quixote, he talked himself into believing that his labors had an intrinsic worth and importance and were essential to the maintenance of the world order. Indeed we could imagine a number of possible Sisyphuses varying in their degree of personal absurdity or unabsurdity as their beliefs, assessments, attitudes, and pretensions vary in their degrees of fittingness to their predicament. The situation of all these hypothetical Sisyphuses, however, is the same and as thoroughly absurd as a situation can be, for whatever any Sisyphus chooses to do about it, he must engage in endless repetitive cycles of pointless and unproductive labor.

How can a person be unabsurd if his life as a whole is unavoidably absurd? Some self-attitudes do not further anyone's escape from absurdity, and in the case of the person whose situation itself is absurd and whose projects and enterprises are pointless, they positively accentuate the personal absurdity of their possessor. Vanity, excessive pride or shame, pompous self-importance, even well-grounded self-esteem if taken too seriously, are absurd in a person whose situation guarantees the pointlessness or futility of his activities. Think of Shelley's Ozymandias, for example, who built a monument for posterity directing his descendants to "Look on my works, ye Mighty, and despair!" A tick of cosmic time later only "Two vast and trunkless legs of stone / stand in the desert. . . Near them, on the sand / Half sunk, a shattered visage lies."[27] How absurd was Old Ozymandias, self-declared "King of kings"! Almost equally absurd would be the towering self-regard of an eminent physicist for having won (and deserved) the Nobel Prize. Think of his proud medal found on some desert of the next millennium by beings whose school-children have a far more advanced understanding of physics than he did. A little bit of genuine humility, perhaps, is a virtue of anyone in any situation, but for a person in an absurd situation it is essential if the absurdity of his predicament is not to rub off on his character.

We can now venture some tentative conclusions. We can conclude first of all that there are elements properly characterized as absurd in every life. Moreover, some whole lives are predominately absurd, those, for example, spent largely in sheer drudgery to no further point, or those whose overriding pursuits were rendered futile by uncooperative circumstances or self-defeating strategies. Further arguments, however, to the conclusion that human life as such—and therefore each and every human life necessarily—is absurd are not convincing. Taylor and probably Camus (though he is less clear) are impressed by what they take to be the pointlessness (meaninglessness) of the human condition, a conclusion supported also by the arguments from the supermarket circle and the biological regress, but these arguments, because of confusions about the concept of pointlessness, are at best inconclusive. When we are speaking of activities *within* human life we characterize them as pointless when they are, first of all, apparently without worth for their own sakes, when, for example, they appear to be sheer drudgery, like pushing rocks and digging holes. If a given instance of sheer drudgery then appears to have no further point beyond itself that would confer instrumental value and intelligibility upon it, then and only then do we call it pointless. For an activity to be utterly without point or meaning then is first of all for it to have no value in its own right, and only then, for it to have no further purpose the achievement of which explains and justifies it. The supermarket circle and biological regress concentrate on showing that vindicating purposes never get wholly realized, but this would establish pointlessness only if all activities, human or animal, were sheer drudgery, without value in themselves. Some activities carry their own point within themselves, and for that reason, whatever their envisioned or actual consequences they are not "pointless." An adult salmon who has grown to maximum size and strength in the ocean, and is ready to begin his dangerous dash upstream to mating waters, is about to savor salmon existence in its purity, the salmon equivalent of "living to the hilt." "This is what being a salmon is all about," he might declare joyously. He will get battered about in the process, but if he could reason he might well conclude that the risk of injuries is justified by the inherent rewards, and like an adolescent football player preparing for his first game, he would be alive with anticipatory excitement.

Taylor asserts that human lives are absurd in the sense of having no point, but restricts the notion of a "point" to a state of affairs subsequent in time whose achievement confers instrumental value back on the life that created it, or at least is intended to do so whether successful or not. But there might be no such "point" outside of or after a person's life, yet nevertheless his life might have its own point—indeed it might *be* its own point. A fulfilled life may be absurd (pointless in Taylor's sense), yet not truly pointless because fulfillment is its point. This second kind of "point" looks backward in time, and exists because it fits some anticipatory condition, like an antecedent disposition. Actions producing the first kind of "point," in contrast, look forward to a time beyond their own termination, and to the production of lasting achievement. There is little point in that sense to the salmon's heroics, but they might yet escape absurdity if they discharge a fundamental native disposition of salmon nature—as they clearly do.

## THE CONCEPT OF SELF-FULFILLMENT

There are various technical concepts of self-fulfillment associated with the writings of such philosophers as Plato, Aristotle, Rousseau, and Hegel, whose histories go back to the earliest beginnings of Western philosophy and are equally venerable in Eastern thought. There also seem to be one or more notions of self-fulfillment, perhaps less clearly conceived and articulable, that are part of ordinary thought, as, for example, when people say that one kind of life, or one kind of marriage, hobby, or career, is preferred because it is more fulfilling.

In applying the ordinary concept of self-fulfillment, people seem, on different occasions, to use as many as four different models for their understanding. On the first model, fulfillment is simply the answering to *any* anticipatory condition, whether one's own or another's—promises, hopes, expectations, desires, requirements, or whatever. The second is "filling up, being made full." The third is the opposite of the second, namely, emptying, unwinding, discharging, untying—draining one's cup of life to the dregs. Each of these familiar models comes with its own metaphors to guide (or obscure) the understanding. It is the fourth model, however, that of "doing what comes naturally," that purports to be more "philosophical," and is the more important one for our present purposes. This model restricts itself to the basic dispositions of one's "nature," and where these differ or conflict, to the "higher" or "better" ones. Moreover, fulfillment on this model is not merely a discharging, but also a maturing and perfecting of our basic dispositions. Finally, fulfillment so interpreted is often said to be a "realizing of one's potential," where the word "potential" refers not only to one's basic natural proclivities to engage in activities of certain kinds, but also to one's natural capacities to acquire skills and talents, to exercise those abilities effectively, and thus to produce achievements. Insofar as one fails to "realize one's potential," one's life is thought, on this as well as the third model, to be "wasted."

This understanding of self-fulfillment is much too abstract to be useful, and the main challenge to the philosophers, from Aristotle on, who have tried to incorporate it, has been to give it specificity. Almost anything one does can be said to fulfill a prior disposition to act in precisely that way in circumstances of that kind, or to implant or strengthen the habit of acting that way in the future. Thus almost any action can be said to discharge a natural tendency, to be a doing of what it is in one's nature to do. Philosophers who have fashioned a technical concept of self-fulfillment from the vaguer everyday notion have for the most part assigned it a crucial role in the definition of "the good for man." For that reason, most of them have begun the task of specification by ruling out as self-fulfilling, actions that violate objective standards of morality or that are radically defective in other ways. If a man has the bad habit, acquired and reinforced over a lifetime, of stealing purses, then a given act of stealing a purse, even though it fulfills one of the basic dispositions of his (evil) character, cannot be allowed to count as self-fulfilling. The same kind of fiat has excluded evil actions that discharge native propensities, for example, the angry tirades or physical assaults of a person who is irascible, hotheaded, or aggressive "by nature." Such arbitrary exclusions do not shock common sense, but there does seem to be at least as much warrant in ordinary conceptions for saying that it may be a bad thing that certain kinds of self be fulfilled, but that the discharging of basic "evil" dispositions remains fulfillment, and properly so called, anyway.

Some philosophers in the grand tradition have also excluded from their conception of self-fulfillment, activities that fulfill dispositions peculiar to individual persons, so as to give special importance to activities that fulfill those dispositions that define our common human nature. The phrase "a person's nature" is of course ambiguous. It may refer to the nature he shares with all and only human beings, his "generic nature" as it were, the nature that makes him classifiable as the kind of being he is, or it may refer to the nature that belongs uniquely to him, his "individual nature," the character that distinguishes him from all other individuals of his kind. My generic nature includes my disposition to walk upright and to speak a language,[28] among other things. It is part of *my* individual nature, on the other hand, to be interested in philosophy, to be punctual at meetings, to be slow at mathematics, and to be irritable when very tired or hungry. Some of the traits that characterize me but not everybody else are not thought to be part of my individual nature because they are weak and tentative habits rather than governing propensities, or because they are trivial (like my habit of scratching my head when deliberating). My individual nature is partly acquired; my generic nature is derived entirely from heredity. I come into existence with it already "loaded and cocked."

Those philosophers of fulfillment who attach special significance to our generic natures tend to draw heavily on biological as well as mechanical metaphors. In a fulfilled life our preprogrammed potentialities "unfold" like the petals of a rose, each in its time, until the plant is fully flowered and "flourishing." Then there follows an equally natural, gradual withering and expiring, and the life of one plant, at least, has been fulfilled. Another plant, much like the first, is caught in a frost and nipped in the bud, never to achieve its "own good" as determined by its natural latencies—the very paradigm of a tragic waste. John Stuart Mill refers to qualities that are "the distinctive endowment" not of the individual in question but of a human being as such: "the human faculties of perception, judgment, discriminative feeling, mental activity, even moral preference,"[29] these understood as standing to human nature in the same relation as that in which unfolding and flourishing stand to the nature of a rose.

I believe it is a mistake, however (and not one committed in common thought), to exclude individual natures from one's conception of self-fulfillment. If we are told by philosophical sages to act always so as to unfold our generic human natures, we have not been given very clear directions at all. Any number of alternative lives might equally well fulfill one's generic nature, yet some might seem much more "fulfilling," in a perfectly ordinary and intelligible sense, than others. William James makes the point well:

> I am often confronted by the necessity of standing by one of my empirical selves and relinquishing the rest. Not that I would not, if I could, be both handsome and fat and well dressed, and a great athlete, and make a million a year, be a wit, a *bon vivant*, and a lady-killer, as well as philosopher, a philanthropist, statesman, warrior, and African explorer, as well as a "tone-poet" and saint. But the thing is simply impossible. The millionaire's work would run counter to the saint's; the *bon vivant* and the philanthropist would trip each other up; the philosopher and the lady-killer could not well keep house in the same tenement of clay. Such different characters may conceivably at the outset of life be alike possible to a man. But to make any one of them actual, the rest must more or less be suppressed.[30]

All James' possible careers might equally well fulfill his human nature, just as all the variously colored unfoldings of roses might equally well fulfill a rose's generic nature, but a rose cannot pick its own individual character, whereas a man has some choice. Since some of James' lives (presumably the philosophical one, to begin with) would be more fulfilling than others, it must be his individual nature qua William James that makes that so. The point would be even clearer if James had listed among the possibilities, "anchorite monk," "operatic *basso profundo*" "brain surgeon," and "drill sergeant." Some of these careers obviously accord more closely than others with *anyone's* native aptitudes, inherited temperament, and natural inclinations. How does one choose among them if one is seeking fulfillment? By "knowing oneself," of course, but not simply by knowing well the defining traits of *any* human being. To be sure, making the choice itself is a characteristically human act and calls into play all of the generic human traits of Mill's list— perception, discrimination, insight, and the like—but to exercise those traits effectively and well, and thus unfold one's generic human nature, one must first know one's individual character as so far formed, and make the decision that best fits it. Mill's final and favorite metaphor, indeed, is that of a life fitting an individual nature in the way a shoe fits a foot: "A man cannot get a coat or a pair of boots to fit him unless they are either made to his measure or he has a whole warehouseful to choose from; and is it easier to fit him with a life than with a coat.[?]"[31]

Some of a person's individual nature is native, for example, much of what we call aptitudes, temperamental dispositions, and physical strength. A fulfilling life therefore is one that "fits" these native endowments. But we make our own natures as we grow older, building on the native base. We begin, partly because of our inherited proclivities and talents, to develop tastes, habits, interests, and values. We cultivate the skills that grow naturally out of our aptitudes, and as we get better at them we enjoy them more and exercise them further so that they get better still, while we are inclined to neglect the tasks for which our skills are inadequate, and those abilities wither and decay on the vine.[32] The careers we then select as workers, players, and lovers, should be those that fit our well-formed individual natures, at least insofar as each stage in the emergence of the self grew naturally out of its predecessor in the direction of our native bent.

Emphasis should be given to the further point that fulfillment of one's generic and individual natures are interconnected and interdependent. The passages in *On Liberty* in which Mill urges fulfillment of the "distinctive endowment" of generic humanity occur, ironically, in a chapter entitled "Individuality as One of the Elements of Well-Being," and nowhere in that chapter can Mill discuss individuality for long without bringing in human nature and vice versa. His view clearly is that it is essential to the generic nature of human beings that each think and decide for himself rather than blindly follow all the rest, so that in cultivating the capacities that human beings share in common, each individual will at the same time be promoting his own distinctive individuality. If I pick a career that fits my individual nature instead of blindly drifting with custom or passively acceding to the choices of another, then I have exercised my generic nature as a thinker and chooser, at the same time that I have promoted the fulfillment of my individual nature as a person with a unique profile of interests and aptitudes.

Useful as it may be for some purposes the distinction between generic and individual natures is vague and ragged about the edges, a point we can appreciate by returning to the plight of Taylor's Sisyphus. Depending on the extent to which the gods had to tamper with him, he has either had a new individual nature grafted on to his basic human nature, or else a new (hence nonhuman) generic nature installed in him. If we say the former, then we must think of his infinite rock-pushing proclivities as merely personal eccentricities, only contingently unshared by other persons who share his human nature. If we say the latter, then the individual nature of Sisyphus and his generic nature coincide, since he is now one of a kind, the sole member of his new species. A rock-pushing instinct that is so specific would be such a departure from what we normally think of as human nature, so totally unshared by any other humans that perhaps there would be a point in saying that Sisyphus has a new generic nature, humanoid but not human, and that he is now the only member of the biological species *Homo sapiens geopetris*— sapient rock-pusher. Still more plausible, perhaps, we might think of the new

Sisyphus as a borderline case for our old classifications. Unless we hold to the discredited doctrine of fixed species, we can simply declare that there is no uniquely correct answer to the question of whether Sisyphus' generic nature has been changed, and that considerations of convenience and tidiness are as relevant to its resolution as are any questions of fact.

Moreover, when we consider thoughtfully the whole range of hypothetical Sisyphuses from which we might draw in order to flesh out Taylor's example, we are struck with how very vague the notion of a "nature" is, whether generic or individual. What is in Sisyphus's nature (or the nature of anyone else) is very much like what is in his (cluttered) closet or in his grab bag, including everything from aptitudes and interests to addictive compulsions. Think of all the variations on Taylor's theme: the gods might have implanted in Sisyphus an *appetite* for stone-pushing that makes regular and frequent demands on him, like hunger or the "sex urge" in others, and corresponding in its cycles to the time it takes to push a rock of standard size up Sisyphus' assigned mountain and then return again to the bottom of the hill. "Ye gods!" he might exclaim after each round of labors, "how I hunger for a nice big rock to push," and the accommodating deities always have one ready for him, like the next ball up in a pinball machine. Or the gods might have designed for him a peculiar talent for rock-pushing much like others' talents for piano-playing, tennis, or chess. The new Sisyphus starts all over as a perpetual youth, and from the start he is a veritable prodigy at rock-pushing. He comes to enjoy exercising his skills, and makes ever-new challenges for himself. He pushes the rock right-handed, then left-handed, then no-handed, then blindfolded, then does two at a time, then juggles three in the air all the way to the summit, eager to return for another rock so that he can break his record, or equal it next time while dancing a Grecian jig. Or the gods do their job by implanting an instinct for rock-pushing so that Sisyphus goes about his chores without giving them so much as a thought (except in rare reflective moments and then only to shrug his shoulders and get on with it). His work is as natural and unremarkable to him as having a language or standing upright is to us, or building a dam to a beaver, or peeling a banana to a chimpanzee. Or (perhaps more plausibly) the gods implant a drive or more general proclivity of which stone-pushing is only one of numerous possible fulfillments. If there were only opportunity to do so, Sisyphus would find it equally in his nature to push wooden logs, or plastic bags, or iron bars, or to pull, lift, carry, and throw objects, or to push them while swimming against a current, or to pile, hook, or nail them on to one another as in construction work, and the like. But pushing rocks up a mountain will do as well as any of the other activities as fulfillments of his drive to move and manipulate physical objects and he can be grateful to the gods for that. Or, the gods can use Taylor's own suggested method, and give Sisyphus (say) a shot in the arm after each trip so that he will feel a "compulsive impulse" to push the rock up once more in order to get relief in the form of another addicting shot. This technique would keep the gods busier than the others, but they could let some internal gland, timed to secrete the essential substance into Sisyphus's bloodstream at appropriate intervals, do the work for them. There is some-thing especially ingenious in this last scheme, for the "shot" given at the base of the hill creates the impulse to push the rock up the hill and also the addic-tive need, when its first effect wears off, to be renewed by another shot, and so on, ad infinitum.

If the gods' gift to Sisyphus is merely an appetite to push rocks he may yet fail to find self-fulfillment on balance in an indefinitely extended lifetime of rock-pushing, just as one of us might fail to be fulfilled in a life that gives us all the food we need, but nothing else. Sisyphus will have the periodic satisfac-tions of regular appetite satiation, and that is certainly some benefit to him, but the deepest yearnings of his nature will nevertheless be forever denied. Much the same can be said of his condition if the gods simply addict him chemi-cally to a substance that creates a rock-pushing itch, or if they implant in him an extrahuman instinct to push rocks that fails to dovetail or integrate with the human instincts he must continue to maintain if he is to preserve his identity with his earlier self. The model that makes talk of Sisyphean self-fulfillment most plausible is probably that in which the gods impart to him talents for rock-moving that he can forever after exercise and glory in. So endowed, he can find self-fulfillment through his developed virtuosity, in the same way others find fulfillment in lives of skilled cello-playing or cabinet-making.

No conception of self-fulfillment will make much sense unless it allows that fulfillment is a matter of degree. We begin life with a large number of potential careers some of which fit our native bent more closely than others but any of which, if pursued through a lifetime, would lead to substantial fulfill-ment, so that the pursuit of no *one* of them is indispensable to a fulfilled life. Imagine a warm and loving woman who is superbly equipped by her nature to be a parent, and has thought of herself throughout her girlhood as a potential mother. She marries and then discovers that she is barren. Had she not been infertile she would have achieved fulfillment in a long lifetime of nearly full-time motherhood. Is it now impossible for her to be fulfilled in a life without children? Clearly not, for the very traits that make her "superbly equipped" to be a mother will make her more than a little qualified for dozens of other roles, and a fulfilled life could stem from any one of these, from social work to school-teaching,[33] or even from a career based on independent specific aptitudes like poetry or basket-weaving. She may be disappointed that her chief ambition is squelched and her regrets may last a lifetime, but disappointment and fulfill-ment can coexist with little friction, as they do to some degree in most human lives. Thus, we each have within us a number of distinct individual possibili-ties, several (at least) of which would be sufficient for (a degree of) fulfillment, but no one of which is necessary. But the most fulfilling ones are those that best fit one's latent talents, interests, and initial bent and with one's evolving self-ideal (as opposed simply to one's conscious desires or formulated ambitions).

Some fulfilled human lives are relatively monochromatic, having a single dominant theme; others are diversely colored, having a harmonious orches-tration of themes with equal voices. All of them approach fulfillment insofar as they fill their natural allotment of years with vigorous activity. They need not be "successful," or "triumphant," or even contented on balance in order to be fulfilled, provided they are long lifetimes full of struggles and strivings, achievements and noble failures, contentments and frustrations, friendships and enmities, exertions and relaxations, seriousness and playfulness through all the programmed stages of growth and decay. Most important of all, a fulfilled human life will be a life of planning, designing, making order out of confusion and system out of randomness, a life of building, repairing, rebuilding, creating, pursuing goals, and solving problems. It is in the generic nature of the human animal to address the future, change its course, make the best of the situation. If one's house falls down, if one's cities are in rubble, if disaster comes and goes, the human inclination is to start all over again, rebuilding from scratch. There is no "fulfillment" in resignation and despair.

Sisyphus does seem very human after all, then, when he reshoulders his burden and starts back up his hill. But insofar as his situation is rigidly fixed by the gods, allowing him no discretion to select means, design strategies, and solve problems on his own, his life does not fulfill the governing human propensities. If he can fulfill his nature without these discretionary activities, then he has really assumed the nature of a different species.

In all the variations on the Sisyphus myth that we have spun thus far, the gods have assigned a very specific job to Sisyphus that requires no particular judgment or ingenuity on his part to be performed well. They have imposed a duty on him rather than assigning a responsibility.[34] He has a rote job to perform over and over, a mulish task for a mulish fellow, and his is not to reason why or how, but only to get on with it. Suppose, however, that the gods assign to Sisyphus an endless series of rather complex engineering problems and leave it up to him to solve them. Somehow rocks must be moved to mountain tops and there can be no excuses for, failure. "Get it up there somehow," they say. "The methods are up to you. Feel free to experiment and invent. Keep a record of your intermediate successes and failures and be prepared to give us an accounting of the costs. You may hire your own assistants and within certain well-defined limits you have authority to give them commands, so long as you are prepared to answer for the consequences of their work. Now good luck to you." If Sisyphus's subsequent labors are fulfilling, they will be so in a characteristically human way. His individual nature will be fulfilled by a life (endless and pointless though it may be) that fits his native bent and employs his inherited talents and dispositions to the fullest, as well as fitting his more specific individual tendencies, for example, a special fascination (perhaps also a gift of the gods) with rocks.

## WHY DOES SELF-FULFILLMENT MATTER?

Why should it "matter" that a person is unfulfilled if, despite his stunted and dwarfed self, the product perhaps of alienating work and other "unfitting" circumstances, he finds a steady diet of satisfactions in delusory occupations, escapist literature, drugs, drink, and television? Why should it "matter," to turn the question around, that a person finds fulfillment when his life looks as absurd from a longer perspective as the life of a shellfish appears to us?

Think first of what a substantially unfulfilled life involves. A person comes into existence with a set of governing dispositions that sets him off with others as a being of a certain kind. For twenty years he grows and matures, enlarging and perfecting his inherited propensities so that he becomes utterly unique, with a profile of talents and individual traits that, as a group, distinguish him from every other being who has ever existed, and constitute his individual nature. Perhaps he is capable of seeing, from time to time, that this "nature" of his is more than a little absurd. What he does best and most, let us imagine, is play chess and ping-pong and socialize with others who share those interests. He takes those pursuits more seriously than anything else in his life. But he knows that they are, after all, only games, of no cosmic significance whatever, and certainly of no interest to the indifferent universe, to posterity, to history, or to any of the other abstract tribunals by which humans in their more magniloquent moods are wont to measure significance. And yet, absurd as it is, it is *his* nature, and the only one he has, so somehow he must make the best of it and seek his own good in pursuit of its dominant talents. Whose nature could he try to fulfill, after all, but his own? Where else can his own good conceivably be found? It was not up to him to choose his own nature, for that would presuppose that the choosing self already had a nature of its own determining its choice. But given the nature with which he finds himself indissolubly identified for better or worse, he must follow the path discovered in it and identify his good with the goals toward which his nature is already inclined.

Now suppose that he makes a mess of it through imprudence, frivolity, or recklessness; or imagine that the world withdraws its opportunities; or that lightning strikes and leaves him critically incapacitated for the realization of his potential. That leaves him still the pleasure of his diminished consciousness, his soma pills and television programs, his comic books and crossword puzzles, but his deepest nature will forever remain unfulfilled. Now we think of that nature, with all of its elaborate neurochemical equipment underlying its distinctive drives and talents and forming its uniquely complex character, as largely unused, wasted, all for naught. All wound up, it can never discharge or wind down again. In contrast, the life of fulfillment strikes us as one that comes into being prone and equipped to do its thing, and then uses itself up doing that thing, without waste, blockage, or friction.

When any nature is left unfulfilled it is likely to strike us as a bad thing, an objectively regrettable fact. Perhaps we would withdraw or modify that judgment when we come to appreciate how absurd that nature's preoccupations really were. But from the point of view of the self whose nature it is, nonfulfillment is more than a bad or regrettable thing to be graded down in some negative but modifiable "value judgment." It may or may not be all those things in some final balancing-up, all things considered. But from the point of view of the individual involved, nonfulfillment marks the collapse of his whole universe, the denial once and for all of his own good. There is a world of difference in the use of the word "good" as a predicate of evaluation, and its use in the venerable phrase of the philosophers—"one's own good." My good is something peculiarly mine, as determined by my nature alone, and particularly by its most powerful trends and currents. Anything else that is good for me (or in my interest) is good because it contributes to my good, the fulfillment of my strongest stable tendencies. One can judge or evaluate that good from some other standpoint, employing some other standard, and the resultant judgment may use the words "good," "bad," or "indifferent." It may not be a good thing that my good be achieved or that it be achieved in a given way, or at a given cost. But it is logically irrelevant to the question of *what my good is* whether my good is itself "good" when judged from an external position. My nonfulfillment may not be a "bad thing on balance" in another's judgment or even in my own. My nonfulfillment may not be "objectively regrettable" or tragic. But my nonfulfillment cannot be *my good* even if it is from all other measuring points, a good thing.

It is perhaps not quite self-evident that my good consists in fulfillment. A hedonist might hold out for the position that my good consists in a balance of pleasant over unpleasant experiences while denying that the basic disposition of my nature is to seek pleasure, thus denying that pleasant experiences as such are fulfilling. I cannot refute such a heroic (and lonely) philosopher. But I would like to urge against the philosopher who is overly impressed with the fact of human absurdity, that if my good is fulfillment, it must be fulfillment of *my* nature and not of something else. That my nature is eccentric, absurd, laughable, trivial, cosmically insignificant, is neither here nor there. Such as it is, it is my nature for better or worse. The self whose good is at issue is the self I am and not some other self that I might have been. If I had had any choice in the matter I might have preferred to come into existence with the nature (that is the potential) of William James, John F. Kennedy, or Michael Jordan, but I cannot spend all my days lamenting that the only nature whose fulfillment constitutes my good is my own!

The prerequisite to self-fulfillment is a certain amount of clear-eyed, nondeluded self-love. A moment ago I spoke of one's own nature "such as it is," "for better or worse." These phrases recall the wedding ceremony and its conception of marital love as loyalty and devotion without condition or reservation. Totally unconditional devotion may be too much to ask from any lover, but within wide limits, various kinds of human love of others have a largely unconditional character. Gregory Vlastos describes parental love, for example, in a way that makes it quite familiar: "Constancy of affection in the face of variations of merit is one of the surest tests of whether a parent does love a child."[35] Judgments of merit have nothing to do with love so construed. A child's failures, even moral failures, may disappoint his parents' hopes without weakening their loyalty or affection in the slightest. A parent may admire one child more than another, or like (in the sense of "enjoy") one more than another, as well as judge one higher than the other, but it is a necessary condition of parental love that, short of limiting extremes, it not fluctuate with these responses to merit.

The love that any stable person has toward himself will be similarly constant and independent of perceived merits and demerits. I may (realistically) assign myself very low grades for physique, intellect, talent, even character—indeed I may ascribe deficiencies even to my individual nature itself—while still remaining steadfastly loyal and affectionate to myself. Aristotle was right on target when he said that a wise man ought to have exactly that degree of self-esteem that is dictated by the facts, neither more nor less. But self-esteem is not self-love. I have self-love for myself when I accept my nature as given, without apology or regret, even as I work, within the limits it imposes, for self-improvement. We have been through a lot together, my self and I, sharing everything alike, and as long as I have supported him, he has never let me down. I have scolded him, but never cursed his nature. He is flawed all right, and deeply so, but when the warts show, I smile, fondly and indulgently. His blunders are just what one would expect from anyone with his nature. One cannot come to hate a being with whom one has been so very intimate. Indeed, I would not know how to begin to cope with another self after all my years of dependency, "for better or worse," on this one. In this way self-identity can be conceived as a kind of arranged marriage (I did not select the self that was to be me) that in a stable person ripens into true love, but in an unstable one sours into rancor and self-destruction. And the truest expression of one's self-love is devotion toward one's own good, which is the fulfillment of one's own (who else's?) nature—absurd as that may be.


## THE CRITIQUE OF COSMIC ATTITUDES


Some lives are manifestly and incontrovertibly absurd. Lives spent moving metaphoric rocks back and forth to no further end and lives spent tangling with metaphoric windmills are cases in point. Other lives are full of achievement and design. In these lives, intermediate goals lend meaning to the pursuits that are instrumental to their achievement, and they in turn are given a point by the more ultimate goals they subserve. No goal is *the* ultimate one, however, for the most general ends are themselves means to a great variety of other ends, all tied together in an intricate and harmonious web of purpose. There may be no purpose to the whole web except its service to its own component parts, but each constituent has a place and a vindicating significance to the person whose life it is. Such a life is, relatively speaking, not absurd. There is no doubt an important practical point in distinguishing human lives in terms of their degree of absurdity, even in highlighting and emphasizing the distinctions. (Marx's doctrine of alienation is an example of the social utility of making such distinctions.) As we have seen, however, philosophers have found reason to claim that there is a kind of cosmic absurdity inherent in the human condition as such. As we stand back and look at ourselves from an extended temporal position, the distinction between absurd and nonabsurd lives begins to fade into insignificance, and finally vanishes altogether.

We also make useful distinctions between relatively fulfilled and unfulfilled selves, or fulfilling and unfulfilling lives. However we interpret "fulfillment—as the development of one's chief aptitudes into genuine talents in a life that gives them scope, or an unfolding of all basic tendencies and inclinations, or an active realization of the universally human propensities to plan, design, make order—there are wide differences among persons in the degree of fulfillment they achieve. Some lives are wasted; some are partially wasted and partially fulfilled; others are nearly totally fulfilled. Unlike the contrast between absurd and nonabsurd lives, these distinctions seem to be time-resistant. If Hubert Humphrey's life was fulfilling to him, that is a fact like any other, and it never ceases to be true that it was a fact. From any temporal distance from which it can be observed at all it will continue to appear to be a fact (though a diminishingly interesting or important one).

Consider a human life that is near-totally fulfilled, yet from a quite accessible imaginary vantage point is apparently absurd. Insofar as the person in question is fulfilled, he ought to "feel good" about his life, and rejoice that he has achieved his good. Suppose that he realizes then how futile it all was, "coming to nothing in the end." What would be the appropriate attitude in that event to hold toward his life? Unchanged pride and satisfaction? Bitterness and despair? Haughty existential scorn? We can call such responsive attitudes taken toward one's whole life and by implication toward the whole human condition, "cosmic attitudes." One of the traditional tasks of philosophy (and what philosophy is entirely about in the minds of innocent persons unacquainted with the academic discipline of that name) is to perform a kind of literary criticism of cosmic attitudes. It used to be the custom for philosophers not only to describe the universe in its more general aspects but to recommend cosmic attitudes toward the world as so described.

I welcome the suggestion of Nagel that the appropriate responsive attitude toward human lives that are both absurd and fulfilled is *irony*,[36] and I shall conclude by elaborating that suggestion somewhat beyond the bare recommendation that Nagel offers.

None of the familiar senses of irony in language or in objective occurrences seem to make any sense out of the advice that we respond to absurdity with irony. What Nagel has in mind clearly is another sense in which irony is a kind of outlook on events, namely, "an attitude of detached awareness of incongruity."[37] This is a state of mind halfway between seriousness and playfulness. It may even seem to the person involved that he is both very serious and playful at the same time. The tension between these opposed elements pulling in their opposite ways creates at least temporarily a kind of mental equilibrium not unlike that of the boy in Lincoln's story who was "too scared to laugh and too big to cry," except that the boy squirms with discomfort whereas irony is on balance an *appreciative* attitude.[38] One appreciates the perceived incongruity much as one does in humor, where the sudden unexpected perception of incongruity produces laughter. Here the appreciation is more deliberate and intellectual. The situation is too unpleasant in some way—sad, threatening, disappointing—to permit the relaxed playfulness of spirit prerequisite to the comic response. There *is* a kind of bittersweet pleasure in it, but not the pleasure of amusement. The situation is surely not seen as funny, although perhaps it would be if only one could achieve a still more detached outlook on it. One contemplates a situation with irony when one looks the facts in the eye and responds in an appreciative way to their incongruous aspects as such. Irony is quite different from despair-cum-tears, scornful defiance-cum-anger, and amusement-cum-laughter. It is pleasant enough to be expressed characteristically in a smile, but a somewhat tired smile, with a touch both of gentleness and mischievousness in it, as befitting the expression of a tempered pleasure.

In one of the most moving scenes of the twenty-seven-part BBC documentary film on the First World War, a group of British reinforcements is shown marching toward the front. We know that they are cannon fodder marching to their own slaughter, and they know it too. They are foot-sore and bone-weary, and splattered with mud, and a steady rain is falling. The song they sing as they march is not a rousing anthem like "La Marseillaise" or "Rule, Britannia!," not a cocky fight song like "Over There," not a jolly drinking song like "Waltzing Matilda," not a sentimental ballad, hymn of lamentation, or mournful dirge. Instead they sing to the stirring tune of "Auld Lang Syne" the famous nonsense verse they created for the occasion:

> We're here because we're here
> Because we're here because we're here;
> We're here because we're here
> Because we're here because we're here . . .

The observer of the film feels a sudden pang and finds himself near tears, but quickly he perceives the absurdity in the lyrics and responds appreciatively to it, just as the troops, by selecting those words, are responding to the perceived absurdity in their situation. The sensitive observer sees how fitting the ironic response of the soldiers is (and how dreadfully false any of its standard alternatives would have been) and himself takes a quiet sad pleasure in it. The soldiers were in an inescapably absurd predicament, without hope, and only by their unflinching acceptance of the absurdity of their situation are they saved from absurdity themselves. For us, the unseen audience, there is an inspiration in their example that makes the scene noble.

I do not mean to suggest for a moment that the march of the doomed soldiers is an apt metaphor for the whole of human life. The soldiers' brief lives were tragically wasted. If they had been specially bred military animals they might have found both a personal and biological fulfillment in their peculiar demises, but they were ordinary humans whose bizarre and untimely deaths climaxed their undeveloped and unfinished lives. In contrast, many individuals do achieve fulfillment in long, active, creative lives. These lives are more than just "worthwhile"; they represent to those who lead them the achievement of the only condition that can plausibly be deemed "their good." So philosophical "pessimism," the view of Schopenhauer and others that *no* life can *possibly* be worth living given the absurdity of the human condition, must be rejected. Its logical contrary, that cosmic optimism that holds that all human lives necessarily are, or always can be, good and worthwhile, must also be rejected, in favor of the commonsense view that fulfillment requires luck, and luck is not always good in a world that contains violent passions, accidents, disease, and war.

In this chapter, however, I have tried not only to sketch a conception of the good life and the bad but also to recommend an appropriate attitude toward the human condition generally. Imagine a person who both through his own virtues and good luck has led a maximally fulfilling life into his final declining years. He has realized his highest individual potential in a career that perfectly fit his inherited temperamental proclivities. His talents and virtues have unfolded steadily in a life that gave them limitless opportunity for exercise, and he has similarly perfected his generic human powers of discrimination, sympathy, and judgment in a life full of intermeshing purposes and goals. All of this is a source of rich satisfaction to him, until in the philosophical autumn of his days, he chances upon the legend of Sisyphus, the commentary of Camus, and the essays of Taylor and Nagel. In a flash he sees the vanity of all his pursuits, the total permeability of his achievements by time, the lack of any long-term rationale for his purposes, in a word the absurdity of his (otherwise good) life. At first he will feel a keen twinge. But unless he be misled by the sophistries of the philosophical pessimists who confuse the empty ideal of long-term coherence with the Good for Man, he will soon recover. And then will come a dawning bittersweet appreciation of the cosmic incongruities first called to his attention by the philosophers. The thought that there should be a modest kind of joke at the heart of human existence begins to please (if not quite tickle) him. Now he can die not with a whine or a snarl, but with an ironic smile.

## NOTES

1. Richard Taylor, *Good and Evil* (London: Macmillan, 1970), p. 259.

2. Ibid.

3. The various essays in which Camus gives his most thorough account of absurdity have been translated into English by Justin O'Brien and published in one volume under the title *The Myth of Sisyphus and Other Essays* (New York: Random House, 1955).

4. Taylor, *Good and Evil*, p. 258.

5. Thomas Nagel, "The Absurd," *Journal of Philosophy* 68 (1971): 718.

6. Camus, *Myth of Sisyphus*, p. 22.

7. Nagel, "Absurd," pp. 716–27. See also his *The View from Nowhere* (New York: Oxford University Press, 1986), pp. 208–32.

8. Cartoon by Handelsman, *New Yorker*, July 6, 1981, p. 34.

9. Or first taking away and then giving, as in the unfunny example of absurdity from the Civil War: "Lincoln and Brooks lingered at the cot of a wounded soldier who held with a weak white hand a tract given him by a well-dressed lady performing good works that morning. The soldier read the title of the tract and then began laughing. Lincoln noticed that the lady of good works was still nearby, and told the soldier that undoubtedly the lady meant well. 'It is hardly fair of you to laugh at her gift.' The soldier gave Lincoln something to remember. 'Mr. President, how can I help laughing a little? She has given me a tract on the "Sin of Dancing," and both my legs are shot off'" (Carl Sandburg, *Abraham Lincoln: The War Years* [New York: Harcourt, Brace, 1926], 2:293).

10. W. D. Joske, "Philosophy and the Meaning of Life," *Australasian Journal of Philosophy* 52 (August 1974): 93–104. Joske gives an example of a whole individual life that could seem absurd because trivial in this sense. "We find ourselves bewildered by the school master in Guthrie Wilson's novel, *The Incorruptibles*, who devotes his life to parsing and analyzing every sentence of *Paradise Lost*." A contrasting example of a life that is absurd because futile would be one devoted full-time to an attempt to square the circle.

11. Taylor, *Good and Evil*, p. 262.

12. Ibid., p. 263.

13. Ibid., p. 260.

14. Ibid., p. 263.

15. Ibid., p. 264.

16. Bernard Williams, "The Makropoulos Case: Reflections on the Tedium of Immortality," in *Problems of the Self* (Cambridge: Cambridge University Press, 1973), pp. 82–100. Jonathan Glover replies to Williams: "But I am not convinced that someone with a fairly constant character *need* eventually become intolerably bored, so long as [he] can watch the world continue to unfold and go on asking new questions and thinking, and so long as there are other people to share their feelings and thoughts with. Given the company of the right people, I would be glad of the chance to sample a few million years and see how it went" (*Causing Death and Saving Lives* [Harmondsworth: Penguin, 1977], p. 57).

17. Camus, *Myth of Sisyphus*, p. 21.

18. Ibid., p. 9.

19. Ibid., p. 10.

20. Moritz Schlick, "On the Meaning of Life," in *Philosophical Papers* (Dordrecht: Reidel, 1979), 2:112–28.

21. See Taylor's illustration of the New Zealand Cave Gloworm (*Good and Evil*, pp. 261–62).

22. Nagel, "Absurd," p. 724.

23. Camus, *Myth of Sisyphus*, p. 91.

24. Nagel, "Absurd," p. 718.

25. Ibid., p. 726.

26. This is the final line of Jean-Paul Sartre's play, *No Exit (Huis Clos)*, translated by Stewart Gilbert (New York: Alfred A. Knopf, 1946).

27. Percy Bysshe Shelley, *Ozymandias*, lines 2–4, 11, 12.

28. There have been feral children who have permanently lost their ability to learn a language and children born without legs who never acquire the ability to walk. But insofar as these persons are human beings, they are born with the innate *capacity* to acquire the dispositions and skills involved in walking and talking even though circumstances

prevent that capacity from being realized. The capacities in question are often conditional ones: all human children have the capacity to learn a language, which is activated
between the ages of two and twelve only, and only if they are made part of a language-
speaking community during those years. That conditional capacity to acquire the
dispositions and skills involved in language use is common to all human beings.

29. John Stuart Mill, *On Liberty* (Oxford: Blackwell, 1946), p. 51.

30. William James, *Psychology* (New York: Henry Holt, 1893), 1:309; as quoted in Lucius
Garvin, *A Modern Introduction to Ethics* (Boston: Houghton-Mifflin, 1953), p. 333.

31. Mill, *On Liberty*, p. 60.

32. John Rawls calls the statement of this psychological tendency "the Aristotelian
Principle" and states it as follows: "Other things being equal, human beings enjoy the
exercise of their realized capacities (their innate or trained abilities), and this enjoyment increases the more the capacity is realized, or the greater its complexity. The
intuitive idea here is that human beings take more pleasure in doing something as
they become more proficient at it, and of two activities they do equally well, they
prefer the one calling for a larger repertoire of more intricate and subtle discrimina-
tions." Rawls cites the preference among good players for chess over checkers and
among good mathematicians for algebra over arithmetic (*A Theory of Justice* [Cam-
bridge, Mass.: Harvard University Press, 1971], p. 426).

33. Aptitudes and basic dispositions differ in an important way from ordinary
desires, plans, and ambitions. The latter characteristically tend to be more precise and
determinate than the former, and therefore less flexible and easy to "fulfill." Many
ambitions are for some relatively specific object and when that object does not come
into existence the ambition is denied: General interests, talents, and drives, however,
can typically find substitute objects that do equally well. If one has a highly developed mechanical aptitude, for example, one can employ it equally well as an airplane
or an automobile mechanic, as well as a carpenter or a plumber, or in a hundred other
callings. One's ambition to be an automobile mechanic, on the other hand, is
squelched once and for all, by the denial of opportunity to enter that particular field.
For this reason, fulfillment is, on the whole, less difficult to achieve than successful
ambition or "satisfaction."

34. The distinction between duty and responsibility is well made by J. Roland
Pennock in "The Problem of Responsibility," *Nomos III: Responsibility*, ed.
C. J. Friedrich (New York: "Atherton, 1960), p. 13: "We normally reserve [the word
'responsibility'] for cases where the performance of duty requires discernment and
choice. We might well say, to a child, 'It is your responsibility to take care of your
room,' but we would not be likely to say, 'It is your responsibility to do as you are
told.'"

35. Gregory Vlastos, "Justice and Equality," in *Social Justice*, ed. Richard B. Brandt
(Englewood Cliffs, N.J.: Prentice-Hall, 1962), p. 44.

36. Nagel, "Absurd," p. 707: "If *sub specie aeternitatis* there is no reason to believe that
anything matters, then that doesn't matter either, and we can approach our absurd
lives with irony instead of heroism or despair."

37. *Webster's New Collegiate Dictionary* (1976), based on *Webster's Third New International
Dictionary of the English Language*. Of the five English dictionaries I consulted, only this
newest one contained any definition of irony as an attitude. Is that because this sense is
relatively new or because dictionary-makers have heretofore overlooked it?

38. "The President takes the result of the New York election [a defeat for his party]
philosophically, and will doubtless profit by the lesson. When Colonel Forney inquired
of him how he felt he replied: 'Somewhat like the boy in Kentucky who stubbed his toe
while running to see his sweetheart. The boy said he was too big to cry, and far too
badly hurt to laugh'" (*Frank Leslie's Illustrated Weekly*, November 22, 1862).

CHAPTER 15        E .  D .  K L E M K E

## Living Without Appeal:
## An Affirmative
## Philosophy of Life

From time to time, philosophers get together at congresses and symposia in which some philosophers read papers and others criticize and raise questions. To the layman, I am sure, the topics which are discussed seem highly technical and inaccessible, and the vocabulary used is, doubtless, unintelligible. Indeed, if the ordinary man were to drop in on such meetings, he would, I suspect, find the proceedings to be either totally incomprehensible or the occasion for howling laughter. To give some indication of what I am referring to, I shall list the titles of some recent philosophical papers, many of which are acknowledged to be very important works:

The meaning of a word
Performative–constative
Negative existentials
Excluders
Reference and referents
Proper names
On referring
Parenthetical verbs
Bare particulars
Elementarism, independence, and ontology
The problem of counterfactual conditionals

This paper was first read in the Last Lecture Series, at DePauw University, and was repeated, by request, three times. In a revised form, it was read as the Top Prof lecture at Roosevelt University. It was again revised for this volume.

Is existence a predicate?

Etc.

Upon hearing (or reading) papers such as these, the ordinary man would probably exclaim "What's this all got to do with philosophy?" And he would, no doubt, be in agreement with Kierkegaard, who once wrote:

> What the philosophers say about Reality is often as disappointing as a sign you see in a shop window which reads: Pressing Done Here. If you brought your clothes to be pressed, you would be fooled; for the sign is only for sale. (*Either/Or*, v. 1, p. 31)

Now I have no quarrel with what goes on at these professional gatherings. I engage in such activities myself. I believe that most philosophical problems are highly technical and that the making of minute distinctions and the employment of a specialized vocabulary are essential for the solution of such problems. Philosophy here is in the same boat as any other discipline. For this reason, there is (and perhaps always will be) something aristocratic about the pursuit of philosophy, just as there is about the pursuit of theoretical physics or Peruvian excavation. The decriers of philosophy often overlook the fact that any discipline which amounts to more than a type of verbal diarrhea must proceed by making subtle distinctions, introducing technical terminology, and striving for as much rigor and precision as is possible. And the critics fail to see that, in philosophy as in other fields, by the very nature of the discipline, some problems will be somewhat rarified, and of interest mainly to the specialist.

On the other hand, I am inclined to think that the philosopher ought occasionally to leave the study, or the philosophical association lecture hall, or even the classroom, and, having shed his aristocratic garments, speak as a man among other men. For the philosopher is, after all, human too. Like other men, he eats, sleeps, makes love, drinks martinis (or perhaps cognac), gets the flu, files income tax, and even reads the newspapers. On such more democratic occasions, he ought to employ his analytical tools as diligently as ever. But he should select as his topic some issue which is of concern to all men, or at least most men, at some time in their lives. It is my hope that I have chosen such a topic for this essay.

The problem which I wish to discuss has been formulated in a single sentence by Camus (in *The Myth of Sisyphus*), which I take as a kind of "text." The sentence to which I am referring is: "Knowing whether or not one can live *without appeal* is all that interests me."[1] I say that I take this as a *kind* of text because, as so often, Camus overstates the point. Thus I would not—and perhaps most of us would not—say that, knowing whether or not one can live without appeal is *all* that interests me. But I believe that most of us would say that it certainly is one of those crucial problems which each man must confront as he tries to make sense of his life in this wondrously strange existence.

I

Prophets of doom and redemption seem to exist in almost every age, and ours is no exception. It is commonly held by many present-day thinkers, scholars, and poets, that the current state of the world and of many of the individuals within it is one of disintegration and vacuity. As they see it: Men of our age grope for disrupting principles and loyalties, and often reveal a destructive tension, a lack of wholeness, or an acute anxiety. Whether or not this is a unique situation in history, as an account of the present state of things, such disintegration is commonly mentioned. And theorists in almost every discipline and pursuit have given analyses of the current predicament and offered solutions. For example, philosophers and theologians (Jaspers, Marcel, Swenson, Tillich, Schweitzer, Niebuhr), scientists and scientific writers (Einstein, DeNuoy), sociologists (Sorokin), historians (Butterfield), among others, have waved warning signs, sometimes in a last effort to "save civilization from utter destruction." I would like to consider some points which are held in common by many of these writers (and others whom I have not indicated) and then to comment about those views. In this section, I shall state the common core of this position. In the next section, I shall make my comments and show that there is another genuine alternative.

According to many of the above writers (and others whom I have not mentioned), our age is one in which a major catastrophe has taken place. This has been designated as an increasing lack of a determining principle, the severing of a determining bond, the loss of a determining passion, or the rejection of a determining ultimate. What is the nature of this ultimate? It has been described as a principle by which finite forces are held in equilibrium, a bond which relates all horizontally functioning powers vertically to a realm beyond the finite. It is said to be a unifying and controlling power by which the varied inclinations, desires, and aims of an individual may be kept in balance. It is characterized as an agency which removes those oppositions and dichotomies which tend to destroy human selfhood. It has been held, by writers such as the above, to be a *transcendent* and *unconditional ultimate,* the one indispensable factor for the attainment of a *meaningful* and *worthwhile* existence. In their view, in order to prevent the destruction of individuals and cultures, and to provide a sense of direction and wholeness, the awareness of and relationship to such an ultimate are absolutely necessary.

Many of the writers have noted that, not only in intellectual circles, but at a much wider level, many individuals are increasingly refusing to accept the reality of this controlling ultimate. As they see it, such individuals have either remained content with a kind of vacuum in "the dimension of the spiritual," or they have "transvaluated and exalted immanent, finite forces" into a substitute for the transcendent. Men have tried—say these writers—to find equilibrium and unity through "natural," non-authoritative, self-regulating, temporal aims and principles, which they hold to be capable of an innate self-integration which requires no outside aid. According to these writers, this hope is futile, for as soon as reliance upon the transcendent ultimate ceases, disintegration results. Only when finite relationships, processes, and forces are referred back to a transhistorical order can integration, wholeness, meaning, and purpose be achieved. As long as men lack confidence in, or sever the bond to, the transcendent, their accomplishments and goals, no matter how noble or worthy, can have no final consistency or solidity. Rather, their efforts are mere remnants of an "atrophied world," shut up within the realm of immanence, intoxicated with itself, lured by "phantasms and idolatrous forces."

According to this view, the integrity of the individual is today threatened by the loss of belief in the transcendent ultimate and its replacement by a "devitalized" and "perverse" confidence in the all-sufficiency of the finite. The only remedy, we are told, is the recognition of the determining regulation of a dimension beyond the fleeting pace of the temporal world, by which alone existence can have worth and value.

At this point, one might be tempted to ask several questions of these writers:

(1) "Even if the above characterization of the world has some truth, must one look to transcendentalism as the remedy? Cannot a 'natural' philosophy or principle help us?"

The usual answer is: No. All naturalistic views reduce existence to mere finite centers and relationships. But all of these finite agencies are conditioned by others. All are therefore transitory and unstable. None can become a determining ultimate. Only a transcendent ultimate is capable of sustaining the kind of faith which gives human existence meaning and value.

(2) "But isn't this supernaturalism all over again? And doesn't it (as usual) imply either an unbridgeable gulf between the finite and the infinite or an external control or suppression of the finite by the so-called infinite?"

The customary reply is that this view may indeed be called supernaturalism. But (we are told) this does not imply the impossibility of any association of the finite and the infinite. For the ultimate, according to these writers, is not transcendent in the sense of being totally isolated from the finite, but, rather, is operative within the natural world. Furthermore (so the reply goes), the existence of a transcendent order does not entail either external control or suppression of the finite. It merely implies a human receptivity to a non-natural realm. That is, human achievement and value result from the impingement of the infinite upon the finite in moments of *kairos*, providing fullness and meaning but not at the price of denying the human activity which is involved. There always remains the awareness that the human subject is in a personal relation to another subject, a relation of supreme importance.

(3) "And how does one come to this relation?"

Perhaps mainly (say many of these writers) through suffering and sorrow, through a sense of sin and despair. When an individual sees that all finite centers and loyalties are fleeting and incapable of being lasting objects of faith, then he will renounce all previous efforts in despair, repent in humility, and gratefully make *the movement of faith* by which alone his life can become meaningful and worthwhile.

This, then, is the view which I propose to comment on. It is an all-or-nothing position. Its central thesis is that of a transcendent ultimate of absolute supremacy, which reigns over all finite things and powers, and *which alone is capable of providing meaning and worth to human existence.* Finite, historical centers can at best bring temporary assistance. They all wither with time and circumstances. Only when men turn from the finite to the infinite can they find (in the words of Kierkegaard) a hope and anticipation of the eternal which holds together all the "cleavages of existence."

## II

I shall refer to the above view (which I have tried to portray justly) as transcendentalism. It contains three component theses. These are:

(1) There *exists* a transcendent being or ultimate with which man can enter into some sort of relation.

(2) Without such a transcendent ultimate, and the relation of faith to it, human life lacks *meaning, purpose,* and *integration.*

(3) Without such meaning or integration, human life is not *worthwhile.*

It is necessary to comment upon all three of these points.

(1) First, the thesis that there *exists* such a transcendent ultimate or power. I assume that those who assert the existence of a transcendent being intend their assertion to be a *cognitive* one. That is, they claim to be saying something which states a fact and which is capable of being either true or false. Thus they would not admit that their claim is merely an expression of feelings or attitudes. I also assume that those who make this assertion intend their statement to be interpreted *literally.* That is, they mean to say that the transcendent *really exists.* The transcendent presumably does not exist in the same sense in which Santa Claus may be said to "exist." These persons would, I assume, hold that the transcendent exists in actuality, although it may not exist in any empirical sense.

I ask: What *reasons* are there for holding that such an entity as the transcendent exists? I take it that I do not have to linger on such an answer as the testimony of a sacred book. The fact that the Bible or any other sacred writing asserts the existence of a transcendent is no more evidential to the existence of such a being than it is to the non-existence. All that a scriptural writing proves is that someone *believed* that a transcendent ultimate exists. And that is not at all the same as showing that such a being actually exists. The same may be said for the testimony of some unusual person—Moses, Jesus, Mohammed, etc. Furthermore, the fact that the testimony is made by a large number of persons does not substantiate the view. An impartial reading of history often shows that, on major issues, the majority is almost always wrong.

I also shall not linger on the traditional arguments for the existence of a god: The ontological, cosmological, teleological arguments, etc. Many theologians themselves now acknowledge that these are not so much arguments for the existence of such a being as they are explications of the affirmation of faith. Therefore, the fact that a certain segment of the universe is orderly, that it exhibits beauty, that it shows an adaptation of means to ends does not in any way provide evidence that there is one who orders, beautifies, and adapts.

Arguments from religious experience are also unconvincing. Due to their lack of intersubjective testability, the most that such arguments can demonstrate is that someone has had an unusual experience. They do not provide any evidence that the *object* of such an experience exists. That object may, of course, exist. But the occurrence of such an experience does not verify the existence of an actual, rather than imaginary, object. Suppose that, while a dentist is drilling my tooth, I have an experience of a blinding light or an unusual voice. I do not take this to be an adequate reason for saying that I *know* that I have now communed with the Absolute. I trust that you do not do so either.

What evidence, then, is there for the existence of a transcendent? I submit that there is *none*. And my reading of religious writings and my conversations with many of those who maintain the existence of the transcendent lead me to affirm that they also would agree that there is none. For they hold that the existence of the transcendent (although a cognitive claim) is apprehended, *not* in a cognitive relationship but in the relationship of *faith*.

Thus in the usual sense of the term "evidence," there seems to be no evidence for the existence of a transcendent ultimate. Why, then, should I accept such a claim? After all, throughout the rest of my philosophical activity *and* throughout my normal, everyday activities, I constantly rely upon criteria of evidence before accepting a cognitive claim. I emphasize that this holds for my *everyday* life and not merely for any philosophical or scientific beliefs which I may entertain. Not only do I accept or reject (say) the Principle of Rectilinear Propagation of Light because of evidence. I also ask for evidence in order to substantiate such simple claims as "The stylus in my stereo tone arm is defective," or "Jones eloped with his secretary."

It is clear that both believers and non-believers share this desire for evidence with me. At least, believers agree up to the point of the transcendent-claim. If I reject this claim because of lack of evidence, I do not think that I can be justly accused of being an extremist. Rather, I should be commended for my consistency!

The transcendentalist will reply: "But the usual criteria do not apply in this case. They work only for natural entities. The transcendent is not a natural being." I answer: Then the only reasonable procedure seems to be that of suspending my judgment, for I do not know of any non-natural criteria. The transcendentalist replies: "No, merely suspending your judgment implies that you think that some evidence might eventually be found. We are in a different dimension here. An act of *faith* is required."

I reply with two points: (a) In its normal usage, the term "faith" still implies evidence and reasons. Why do I have faith in Smith, but not in Jones? Obviously because of *reasons*. I do not have faith in people haphazardly and without evidence. (b) If I am told that faith in the transcendent is not faith in the normal sense, but a special act of commitment, then I can only honestly reply: *I have no need for such faith.* The transcendentalist retorts: "Ah, but you do, for only through faith in the transcendent can life have meaning; and surely you seek a life that is significant and worthwhile." And this leads us to the second thesis.

(2) The transcendentalist claims that without the transcendent and faith in the transcendent, human existence is without *meaning, purpose, integration.* Is this true? And if true in some sense, what follows?

(A) Let us take *meaning* first. Is there any reason to believe that without the existence of the transcendent, life has no meaning? That is, does the existence of meaning presuppose the existence of the transcendent?

It is necessary to distinguish between *objective* meaning and *subjective* meaning. An objective meaning, if there were such, would be one which is either structurally *part of* the universe, apart from human subjective evaluation; or dependent upon some *external agency* other than human evaluation. Two comments are in order: (i) *If* the notion of objective meaning is a plausible one, then I see no reason why it must be tied up with the existence of a transcendent being, for it certainly is not self-contradictory to hold that an objective meaning could conceivably exist even though a transcendent being did not. That is, the two concepts of "transcendent being" and "objective meaning" are not logically related in the way in which the two concepts "three" and "odd" (for example) are related. (ii) But, more fundamental, I find the notion of an objective meaning as difficult to accept as I do the notion of a transcendent being. Therefore I cannot rely upon the acceptance of objective meaning in order to substantiate the existence of the transcendent.

Further comment is needed on this point. It seems to me that there is no shred of evidence for the existence of an objective meaning in the universe. If I were to characterize the universe, attempting to give a complete description, I would do so in terms of matter in motion, or energy, or forces such as gravitation, or events, etc. Such a description is *neutral.* It can have no nondescriptive components. The same holds for a description of any segment of the universe. Kepler, for example, was entitled to say that the paths of the planets are elliptical, etc. But he was not entitled to say that this motion exhibits some fundamental, objective purpose more so than some other type of motion would. From the standpoint of present evidence, evaluational components such as meaning or purpose are not to be found in the universe as objective aspects of it. Such values are the result of human evaluation. With respect to them, we must say that the universe is valueless; it is *we* who evaluate, upon the basis of our subjective preferences. Hence, we do not discover values such as meaning to be inherent within the universe. Rather, we "impose" such values upon the universe.

When the transcendentalist holds that, without the transcendent, no objective meaning for human existence is possible, he assumes that the notion of an objective meaning is an intelligible one. But if one can show, as I believe one can, that the idea of objective meaning is an implausible one, then his argument has no point. In no way does it give even the slightest evidence for the existence of a transcendent ultimate.

However, it is possible that some transcendentalist would want to take a different position here. There are at least two alternatives which he might hold.

(i) The transcendentalist might *agree* that there is no *objective* meaning in the universe, that meaning *is* a function of human subjectivity. His point now is that *subjective* meaning is found if and only if there exists a transcendent. I reply with two points (1) This is a grandiose generalization, which might wow an imbecile but not anyone of normal intelligence, and, like most such generalizations, it is false. (I shall return to this point in connection with the transcendentalist's third thesis.) (2) The meaning which the transcendentalist here affirms cannot be subjective meaning, for it is dependent upon some external, non-human factor, namely, the existence of the transcendent. This sort of meaning is *not* a function of human subjectivity. Thus we are back where we were. The transcendentalist's views about meaning do not provide any evidence at all for the existence of a transcendent ultimate.

(ii) I mentioned that the transcendentalist may take a second alternative. He might want to hold: "Of course, the fact of meaning in human existence does not in any way prove, demonstratively or with probability, that there *is* a transcendent being. Therefore, I won't say that meaning in life is impossible unless the transcendent exists. I will merely say that one cannot find meaning unless *one has faith in* the transcendent. The fact of meaning testifies to the necessity of *faith.*"

I reply again with two points. (1) This generalization is also false. I know of many humans who have found a meaningful existence without faith in the transcendent. (2) However, even if this statement were true—even if heretofore not a single human being had found meaning in his life without faith in the transcendent—*I should reject such meaning and search for some other kind.* To me, the price which the transcendentalist pays for his meaning is too dear. If I am to find any meaning in life, I must attempt to find it without the aid of crutches, illusory hopes, and incredulous beliefs and aspirations. I am perfectly willing to admit that *I may not find any meaning at all* (although I think I can, even if it is not of the noble variety of which the transcendentalist speaks). But at least *I must try* to find it on my own. And this much I know: I can strive for a meaning only if it is one which is within the range of my comprehension as an inquiring, rational *man*. A meaning which is tied to some transcendent entity—or to faith in such—is not intelligible to me. Again, I here maintain what I hold throughout the rest of my existence, both philosophically and simply as a living person. I can accept only what is comprehensible to me, i.e., that which is within the province of actual or possible experience, or that for which I find some sound reasons or evidence. Upon these grounds, I must reject any notion of meaning which is bound with the necessity of faith in some mysterious, utterly unknowable entity. If my life should turn out to be less happy thereby, then I shall have to endure it as such. As Shaw once said: "The fact that a believer is happier than a skeptic is no more to the point than the fact that a drunken man is happier than a sober one. The happiness of credulity is a cheap and dangerous quality."

(B) I shall not say much about the transcendentalist's claim that, without the transcendent, or without faith in it, human existence is *purposeless*. For if I were to reply in detail, I should do so in about the same manner as I did with respect to the matter of meaning. An objective purpose is as difficult to detect in the universe as an objective meaning. Hence, again, one cannot argue that there must be a transcendent or that faith in such is necessary.

(C) What about the transcendentalist's claim that, without the transcendent, or, without *faith* in the transcendent, no integration is possible?

(i) In one sense of the term, this assertion, too, is obviously false. There are many persons who have attained what might be called psychological integration, i.e., self-integration, integration of personality, etc., without faith in the transcendent. I know of dozens of people whose lives are integrated in this sense, yet have no transcendental commitments.

(ii) But perhaps the transcendentalist means something much more fundamental than this psychological thesis by his claim. Perhaps he is making some sort of metaphysical assertion—a statement about man and his place in the universe. Thus his assertion must be taken to mean that *metaphysical* integration is not achievable without the transcendent or without faith in it. Like Kierkegaard, he holds that the cleavages of existence cannot be held together without the transcendent. What shall we say to this interpretation?

I am not sure that I understand what such integration is supposed to be. But insofar as I do, it seems to me that it is not possible. I am willing to admit that, if such integration were achievable, it might perhaps be attained only by virtue of something transcendent. But I find no conclusive or even reasonable evidence that such integration has been achieved either by believers in the transcendent or by non-believers. Hence one cannot infer that there is a transcendent ultimate or that faith in such an entity is necessary.

What about the mystics? you ask. It would be silly for me to say that the mystics have not experienced something very unusual which they have *interpreted* as some sort of unity with the universe, or whatever it may be. They may, indeed, have *felt* that, at rare moments, they were "swallowed up in the infinite ocean of being," to quote James. But again, peculiar and non-intersubjectively testable experiences are not reliable evidence for any truth-claim.

Besides, suppose that the mystics *had* occasionally achieved such unity with the universe. Still, this is somewhat irrelevant. For the point is, that I, and many beings like myself (perhaps most of you), have not been favored with such experiences. In fact, it appears that most people who have faith in the transcendent have not had such experiences. This is precisely *why* they have faith. If they had complete certainty, no faith would be needed. Thus faith itself does not seem to be enough for the achievement of integration; and if integration were obtained, faith would be unnecessary. Hence the transcendentalist's view that integration is achieved *via* faith in the transcendent is questionable.

But even if this last thesis were true, it does me no good. Once again, I cannot place my faith in an unknown X, in that which is incomprehensible to me. Hence I must accept the fact that, for me, life will remain without objective meaning, without purpose, and without metaphysical integration. *And I must go on from there.* Rather than crying for the moon, my task must be, as Camus said, to know whether or not one can live *without appeal.*

(3) This leads us to the transcendentalist's third (and most crucial) thesis: That without meaning, purpose, and integration, life is not *worthwhile.* From which he draws the conclusion that without a *transcendent* or *faith* in it, life is not worthwhile. I shall deal only with the claim that without *meaning,* life is not worthwhile. Similar comments could be made regarding purpose and integration.

If the transcendentalist's claim sounds plausible at all, it is only because he continues to confuse objective meaning with subjective meaning. It is true that life has no objective meaning. Let us face it once and for all. But from this it does not follow that life is not *worthwhile,* for it can still be subjectively meaningful. And, really, the latter is the only kind of meaning worth shouting about. An objective meaning—that is, one which is inherent within the universe or dependent upon external agencies—would, frankly, leave me cold. It would not be *mine.* It would be an outer, neutral thing, rather than an inner, dynamic achievement. I, for one, am *glad* that the universe has no meaning, for thereby is *man all the more glorious.* I willingly accept the fact that external meaning is non-existent (or if existent, certainly not apparent), for this leaves me free to *forge my own meaning.* The extent of my creativity and thereby my success in this undertaking depends partly on the richness of my own psyche. There are some persons whose subjectivity is poor and wretched. Once they give up the search for objective meaning, they may perhaps have a difficult time in finding life to be worthwhile. Such is the fate of the impoverished. But those whose subjectivity is enlarged—rationally, esthetically, sensually, passionally—may find life to be worthwhile by means of their creative activity of subjective evaluation, in which a neutral universe takes on color and light, darkness and shadow, becomes now a source of profound joy, now a cause for deep sorrow.

What are some ways by which such worthwhileness can be found? I can speak only for myself. I have found subjective meaning through such things as *knowledge, art, love, and work.* Even though I realize that complete and perfect knowledge of matters of fact is not attainable, this does not lessen my enthusiasm to know and to understand. Such pursuits may have no practical utility; they are not thereby any less significant. To know about the nature of necessary truth or the probable structure of the atom is intrinsically fascinating, to me. And what a wealth of material lies in the arts. A Bach fugue, a Vlaminck painting, a Dostoevsky novel; life is intensely enriched by things such as these. And one must not neglect mention of one's relationships of friendship and love. Fragmentary and imperfect as these often are, they nevertheless provide us with some of our most heightened moments of joy and value. Finally, of all of the ways which I listed, none is more significant and constantly sustaining to me than work. There have been times when I, like many others, no doubt, have suffered some tragedy which seemed unendurable. Every time, it has been my work that has pulled me through.

In short, even if life has no meaning, in an external, objective sense, this does not lead to the conclusion that it is not worth living, as the transcendentalist naively but dogmatically assumes. On the contrary, this fact opens up a greater field of almost infinite possibilities. For as long as I am *conscious*, I shall have the capacity with which to *endow* events, objects, persons, and achievements with value. Ultimately, it is through my *consciousness* and it alone that worth or value are obtained. Through consciousness, the scraping of horses' tails on cats' bowels (to use James' phrase) become the beautiful and melodic lines of a Beethoven string quartet. Through consciousness, a pile of rock can become the memorable Mount Alten which one has climbed and upon which one almost perished. Through consciousness, the arrangements of *P*s and *Q*s on paper can become the symbols of the formal beauty and certain truth of the realm of mathematical logic. Through consciousness, the gift of a carved little piece of wood, left at one's door by a friend, can become a priceless treasure. Yes, it is a *vital* and *sensitive consciousness* that counts. Thus there is a sense in which it is true, as many thinkers and artists have reminded us, that everything begins with my consciousness, and nothing has any worth except through my consciousness.

## III

I shall conclude with an ancient story. "Once a man from Syria led a camel through the desert; but when he came to a dark abyss, the camel suddenly, with teeth showing and eyes protruding, pushed the unsuspecting paragon of the camel-driving profession into the pit. The clothes of the Syrian were caught by a rosebush, and he was held suspended over the pit, at the bottom of which an enormous dragon was waiting to swallow him. Moreover, two mice were busily engaged in chewing away the roots of the already sagging plant. Yet, in this desperate condition, the Syrian was thralled to the point of utmost contentment by a rose which adorned the bush and wafted its fragrance into his face."[2]

I find this parable most illuminating. We are all men hanging on the thread of a few rapidly vanishing years over the bottomless pit of death, destruction, and nothingness. Those objective facts are starkly real. Let us not try to disguise them. Yet I find it marvelously interesting that man's *consciousness*, his reason and his passion, can elevate these routine, objective, external events, in a moment of lucidity and feeling, to the status of a personally appropriated ideal—an ideal which does not annul those objective facts, but which *reinterprets* them and clothes them with the apparel of *man's subjectivity*.

It is time, once again, to speak personally. What your situation is, I cannot say. But I know that I am that Syrian, and that I am hanging over the pit. My doom is inevitable and swiftly approaching. If, in these few moments that are yet mine, I can find no rose to respond to, or rather, if I have lost the ability to respond, then I shall moan and curse my fate with a howl of bitter agony. But *if* I can, in these last moments, respond to a rose—or to a philosophical argument or theory of physics, or to a Scarlatti sonata, or to the touch of a human hand—I say, if I can so respond and can thereby transform an external and fatal event into a moment of conscious insight and significance, then I shall go down *without hope or appeal yet passionately triumphant and with joy*.

## NOTES

1. A. Camus, *The Myth of Sisyphus*, tr. by J. O'Brien (New York: Vintage Books, 1959), p. 45.
2. R. Hertz, *Chance and Symbol* (Chicago: University of Chicago, 1948), pp. 142–143. Another version of this parable appears in Tolstoy's *My Confession*.

PART THREE    Questioning the
Question

the answer is always a matter of describing at a higher level not why things are as they are, but simply how they are. And so, to whatever level our explanations may be carried, the final statement is never an answer to the question "Why?" but necessarily only an answer to the question "How?"

It follows, if my argument is correct, that there is no sense in asking what is the ultimate purpose of our existence, or what is the real meaning of life. For to ask this is to assume that there can be a reason for our living as we do which is somehow more profound than any mere explanation of the facts; and we have seen that this assumption is untenable. Moreover it is untenable in logic and not merely in fact. The position is not that our existence unfortunately lacks a purpose which, if the fates had been kinder, it might conceivably have had. It is rather that those who inquire, in this way, after the meaning of life are raising a question to which it is not logically possible that there should be an answer. Consequently, the fact that they are disappointed is not, as some romanticists would make it, an occasion for cynicism or despair. It is not an occasion for any emotional attitude at all. And the reason why it is not is just that it could not conceivably have been otherwise. If it were logically possible for our existence to have a purpose, in the sense required, then it might be sensible to lament the fact that it had none. But it is not sensible to cry for what is logically impossible. If a question is so framed as to be unanswerable, then it is not a matter for regret that it remains unanswered. It is, therefore, misleading to say that life has no meaning; for that suggests that the statement that life has a meaning is factually significant, but false; whereas the truth is that, in the sense in which it is taken in this context, it is not factually significant.

There is, however, a sense in which it can be said that life does have a meaning. It has for each of us whatever meaning we severally choose to give it. The purpose of a man's existence is constituted by the ends to which he, consciously or unconsciously, devotes himself. Some men have a single overriding purpose to which all their activities are subordinated. If they are at all successful in achieving it, they are probably the happiest, but they are the exceptions. Most men pass from one object to another; and at any one time they may pursue a number of different ends, which may or may not be capable of being harmonized. Philosophers, with a preference for tidiness, have sometimes tried to show that all these apparently diverse objects can really be reduced to one: but the fact is that there is no end that is common to all men, not even happiness. For setting aside the question whether men ought always to pursue happiness, it is not true even that they always do pursue it, unless the word "happiness" is used merely as a description of any end that is in fact pursued. Thus the question what is the meaning of life proves, when it is taken empirically, to be incomplete. For there is no single thing of which it can truly be said that this is the meaning of life. All that can be said is that life has at various times a different meaning for different people, according as they pursue their several ends.

That different people have different purposes is an empirical matter of fact. But what is required by those who seek to know the purpose of their existence is not a factual description of the way that people actually do conduct themselves, but rather a decision as to how they should conduct themselves. Having been taught to believe that not all purposes are of equal value, they require to be guided in their choice. And thus the inquiry into the purpose of our existence dissolves into the question "How ought men to live?" . . .

The question . . . is one that would seem to fall within the province of moral philosophy; but . . . the end of moral philosophy is "not knowledge but action."[1] . . . [O]nce the philosopher who wishes to be practical has said this, there is very little more that he can say. Like anyone else, he can make moral recommendations, but he cannot legitimately claim for them the sanction of philosophy. He cannot prove that his judgments of value are correct, for the sufficient reason that no judgment of value is capable of proof. Or rather, if it is capable of proof, it is only by reference to some other judgment of value, which must itself be left unproved. The moral philosopher can sometimes affect men's conduct by drawing their attention to certain matters of fact; he may show, for example, that certain sorts of action have unsuspected consequences, or that the motives for which they are done are different from what they appear to be; and he may then hope that when his audience is fully aware of the circumstances it will assess the situation in the same way as he does himself. Nevertheless there may be some who differ from him, not on any question of fact, but on a question of value, and in that case he has no way of demonstrating that his judgment is superior. He lays down one rule, and they lay down another; and the decision between them is a subject for persuasion and finally a matter of individual choice.

Since judgments of value are not reducible to statements of fact, they are strictly speaking neither true nor false; and it is tempting to infer from this that no course of conduct is better or worse than any other. But this would be a mistake. For the judgment that no course of conduct is better or worse than any other is itself a judgment of value and consequently neither true nor false. And while an attitude of moral indifference is legitimate in itself, it is not easily maintained. For since we are constantly faced with the practical necessity of action, it is natural for most of us to act in accordance with certain principles; and the choice of principles implies the adoption of a positive set of values. That these values should be consistent is a necessary condition of their being fully realized; for it is logically impossible to achieve the complete fulfilment of an inconsistent set of ends. But, once their consistency is established, they can be criticized only on practical grounds, and from the standpoint of the critic's own moral system, which his adversary may or may not accept. No doubt, in practice, many people are content to follow the model rules that are prescribed to them by others; but the decision to submit oneself to authority on such a point is itself a judgment of value. In the last resort, therefore, each individual has the responsibility of choice; and it is a responsibility that is not to be escaped.

# NOTE

1. See [Aristotle's] *Nicomachean Ethics*, Book I, Section 3.

# CHAPTER 17

K A I   N I E L S E N

# Linguistic Philosophy and "The Meaning of Life"

## II

How ... is it possible for our life to have a meaning or a purpose? For a while ... Ayer in his "The Claims of Philosophy" is a perfectly sound guide.[1] We do know what it is for a man to have a purpose. "It is a matter," Ayer remarks, "of his intending, on the basis of a given situation, to bring about some further situation which for some reason or other he conceives to be desirable."

But, Ayer asks, how is it possible for life *in general* to have a meaning or a purpose?

Well, there is one very simple answer. Life in general has a purpose if all living beings are tending toward a certain specifiable end. To understand the meaning of life or the purpose of existence it is only necessary to discover this end.

As Ayer makes perfectly clear, there are overwhelming difficulties with such an answer. In the first place there is no good reason to believe living beings are tending toward some specifiable end. But even if it were true that they are all tending toward this end such a discovery would not at all answer the question "What is the meaning or purpose of life?" This is so because when we human beings ask this exceedingly vague question we are not just asking for *an explanation* of the facts of existence; we are asking for a *justification* of these facts. In asking this question we are seeking a way of life, trying as suffering, perplexed, and searching creatures to find what the existentialists like to call an "authentic existence." And as Ayer goes on to explain,

a theory which informs them merely that the course of events is so arranged as to lead inevitably to a certain end does nothing to meet their need. For the end

From *Cross Currents*, Summer 1964. Used by permission of the author.

in question will not be one that they themselves have chosen. As far as they are concerned it will be entirely arbitrary; and it will be a no less arbitrary fact that their existence is such as necessarily to lead to its fulfillment. In short, from the point of view of justifying one's existence, there is no essential difference between a teleological explanation of events and a mechanical explanation. In either case, it is a matter of brute fact that events succeed one another in the ways that they do and are explicable in the ways that they are.

In the last analysis, an attempt to answer a question of why events are as they are must always resolve itself into saying only *how* they are. Every explanation of why people do such and such and why the world is so and so finally depends on a very general description. And even if it is the case, as Charles Taylor powerfully argues, that teleological explanations of human behavior are irreducible, Ayer's point here is not all weakened, for in explaining, teleologically or otherwise, we are still showing how things are; we are not justifying anything.[2]

When we ask: "What is the meaning of life?" we want an answer that is more than *just* an explanation or description of *how* people behave or *how* events are arranged or *how* the world is constituted. We are asking for a *justification* for our existence. We are asking for a justification for why life is as it is, and not even the most complete explanation and/or description of *how* things are ordered can answer this quite different question. The person who demands that some general description of man and his place in nature should entail a statement that man ought to live and die in a certain way is asking for something that can no more be the case than it can be the case that ice can gossip. To ask about the meaning of our lives involves asking how we should live, or whether any decision to live in one way is more *worthy* of acceptance than any other. Both of these questions are clearly questions of value; yet no statement of *fact* about how we in fact do live can by itself be sufficient to answer such questions. No statement of what ought to be the case can be deduced from a statement of what is the case. If we are demanding such an answer, then Ayer is perfectly right in claiming the question is unanswerable.

Let me illustrate. Suppose, perhaps as a result of some personal crisis, I want to take stock of myself. As Kierkegaard would say, I want to appropriate, take to heart, the knowledge I have or can get about myself and my condition in order to arrive at some decision as to what sort of life would be most meaningful for me, would be the sort of life I would truly want to live if I could act rationally and were fully apprised of my true condition. I might say to myself, though certainly not to others, unless I was a bit of an exhibitionist, "Look Nielsen, you're a little bit on the vain side and you're arrogant to boot. And why do you gossip so and spend so much of your time reading science fiction? And why do you always say what you expect other people want you to say? You don't approve of that in others, do you? And why don't you listen more? And weren't you too quick with Jones and too indulgent with Smith?"

In such a context I would put these questions and a host of questions like them to myself. And I might come up with some general explanations, good or bad, like "I act this way because I have some fairly pervasive insecurities." And to my further question, "Well, why do you have these insecurities?" I might dig up something out of my past such as "My parents died when I was two and I never had any real home." To explain why this made me insecure I might finally evoke a whole psychological theory and eventually perhaps even a biological and physiological theory, and these explanations about the nature of the human animal would themselves finally rest, in part at least, on various descriptions of how man does behave. In addition, I might, if I could afford it and were sufficiently bedevilled by these questions, find my way to a psychiatrist's couch and there, after the transference had taken place, I would eventually get more quite personalized explanations of my behavior and attitudes. But none of these things, in themselves, could tell me the meaning of life or even the meaning of my life, though they indeed might help me in this search. I might discover that I was insecure because I could never get over the wound of the loss of my father. I might discover that unconsciously I blamed myself. As a child I wished him dead and then he died so somehow I did it, really. And I would, of course, discover how unreasonable this is. I would come to understand that people generally react this way in those situations. In Tolstoy's phrase, we are all part of the "same old river." And, after rehearsing it, turning it over, taking it to heart, I might well gain control over it and eventually gain control over some of my insecurities. I could see and even live through again what *caused* me to be vain, arrogant and lazy. But suppose, that even after all these discoveries I really didn't want to change. After stocktaking, I found that I was willing to settle for the *status quo*. Now I gratefully acknowledge that this is very unlikely, but here we are concerned with the *logical* possibilities. "Yes, there are other ways of doing things," I say to myself, "but after all is said and done I have lived this way a long time and I would rather go on this way than change. This sort of life, is after all, the most meaningful one. This is how I really want to act and this is how I, and others like me, ought to act." What possible facts could anyone appeal to which would prove, in the sense of logically entail, that I was wrong and that the purpose of life or the meaning of life was very different than I thought it was? It is Ayer's contention, and I think he is right, that there are none.

"But you have left out God," someone might say. "You have neglected the possibility that there is a God and that God made man to His image and likeness and that God has a plan for man. Even Sartre, Heidegger and Camus agree that to ask 'What is the Meaning of Life?' or 'What is the purpose of human existence?' is, in effect, to raise the question of God. If there is a God your conclusion would not follow, and, as Father Copleston has said, if there is *no* God human existence can have no end or purpose other than that given by man himself."[3]

I would want to say, that the whole question of God or no God, Jesus or no Jesus, is entirely beside the point. Even if there were a God human existence can, in the relevant sense of "end," "purpose" or "meaning," have no other end, purpose or meaning than what we as human beings give it by our own deliberate choices and decisions.

Let us see how this is so. Let us suppose that everything happens as it does because God intends that it should. Let us even assume, as we in reality cannot, that we can know the purpose or intentions of God. Now, as Ayer points out, either God's "purpose is sovereign or it is not. If it is sovereign, that is, if everything that happens is necessarily in accordance with it, then this is true also of our behavior. Consequently, there is no point in our deciding to conform to it, for the simple reason that we cannot do otherwise." No matter what, we do God's purpose. There is no sense in saying it is *our* purpose, that it is something we have made our own by our own deliberate choice. I have not *discovered* a meaning for my life and other people have not *discovered* a meaning for their lives. If it were possible for us *not* to fulfill it, the purpose would not be God's *sovereign* purpose and if it is His sovereign purpose, it cannot, in the requisite sense, be *our* purpose, for it will not be something of which it would make sense to say that we chose it. It is just something that necessarily happens to us because of God's intentions. If we are compelled to do it, it is not *our* purpose. It is only our purpose if we want to do it and if we could have done otherwise.

On the other hand, if God's purpose is not sovereign and we are not inexorably compelled to do what God wills, we have no reason to conform to God's purpose unless we independently judge it to be *good* or by our own independent decision make it our purpose. We cannot derive the statement "x is good" from "that Being whom people call 'God' says 'x is good'" or from "that Being whom people call 'God' wills x" unless we *independently* judge that whatever this Being *says* is good *is good* or whatever that Being wills *ought* to be done. Again, as Ayer remarks, this "means that the significance of our behavior depends finally upon our own judgments of value; and the concurrence of a deity then becomes superfluous."[4]

The basic difficulty, as Ayer makes clear, is that in trying to answer the questions as we have above, we have really misunderstood the question. "What-is-the-meaning-of-that?" and "What-is-the-purpose-of-that?" questions can be very different. . . . "What is the meaning of Life?" in many contexts at least can well be treated as a "What-is-the-purpose-of-that?" question. But "What is the purpose of life?" is only very superficially like "What is the purpose of a blotter?" "What is the purpose of brain surgery?" or "What is the purpose of the liver?" The first is a question about a human artifact and in terms of certain assumed ends we can say quite explicitly, independently of whether or not we want blotters, what the purpose of blotters is. Similarly brain surgery is a well-known human activity and has a well-known rationale. Even if we are Christian Scientists and disapprove of surgery altogether, we can understand and agree on what the purpose of brain surgery is, just as we all can say Fearless Fosdick is a good safecracker, even though we disapprove of safecrackers. And again, in terms of the total functioning of the human animal we can say what livers are for, even though the liver is not an artifact like a blotter. If there is a God and God made man, we *might* say the question "What is the purpose of human life?" is very like "What is the purpose of umbrellas?" The human animal then becomes a Divine artifact. But, even if all this were so, we would not—as we have already seen—have an answer to the *justificatory* question we started with when we asked, "What is the meaning of life?" If we knew God's purpose for man, we would know what man was made for. But we would not have an answer to our question about the meaning of life, for we would not know if there was purpose *in* our lives or if we could find a point in acting one way rather than another. We would only know that there was some-thing—which may or may not be of value—that we were constructed, "cut out," to be.

Similarly, if an Aristotelian philosophy is correct, "What is the purpose of life?" would become very like "What is the purpose of the liver?" But here again a discovery of what end man is as a matter of fact tending toward would not answer the perplexity we started from, that is to say, it would not answer the question, "What is the meaning of life, how should men live and die?" We would only learn that "What is the purpose of life?" could admit of two very different uses. As far as I can see, there are no good reasons to believe either that there is a God or that the human animal has been ordered for some general end: but even if this were so it would not give us an answer to the question: "What is the meaning of life?"

This is so because the question has been radically misconstrued. When we ask: "What is the meaning of life?" or "What is the purpose of human existence?" we are normally asking, as I have already said, questions of the following types: "What should we seek?" "What ends—if any—are worthy of attainment?" Questions of this sort require a very different answer than any answer to: "What is the meaning of 'obscurantism'?" "What is the pur-pose of the ink-blotter?" and "What is the purpose of the liver?" Ayer is right when he says: "what is required by those who seek to know the purpose of their existence is not a factual description of the way that people actually do conduct themselves, but rather a decision as to how they *should* conduct themselves." Again he is correct in remarking: "There is . . . a sense in which it can be said that life does have a meaning. It has for each of us whatever meaning we severally *choose* to give it. The purpose of a man's existence is constituted by the ends to which he, consciously or unconsciously, devotes himself."

Ayer links this with another crucial logical point, a point which the exis-tentialists have dramatized as some kind of worrisome "moral discovery." Ayer points out that "[i]n the last resort . . . each individual has the responsi-bility of choice" and that it is logically impossible that someone else, in some authoritative position, can make that choice for him. If someone gives me moral advice in the nature of the case I must decide whether or not to follow his advice, so again the choice is finally my own. This is true because moral questions are primarily questions about what to do. In asking how I ought to live, I am trying to make up my mind how to act. And to say I deliberately acted in a certain way implies that I decided to do it. There is no avoiding personal choice in considering such questions.

But Ayer, still writing in the tradition of logical empiricism, often writes as if it followed from the truth of what we have said so far, that there could be no reasoning about "How ought man to live?" or "What is the meaning of life?" Thus Ayer says at one point in "The Claims of Philosophy": "He [the moral agent] cannot prove that his judgments of value are correct, for the sufficient reason that no judgment of value is capable of proof." He goes on to argue that people have no way of demonstrating that one judgment of value is superior to another. A decision between people in moral disagreement is a "subject for persuasion and finally a matter of individual choice."

As we have just seen there is a sound point to Ayer's stress on choice vis-a-vis morality, but taken as a whole his remarks are at best misleading. There is reasoning about moral questions and there are arguments and proofs in morality. There are principles in accordance with which we appraise our actions, and there are more general principles, like the principle of utility or the principles of distributive justice in accordance with which we test our lower-level moral rules. And there is a sense of "being reasonable" which . . . has distinctive application to moral judgments. Thus, if I say, "I ought to be relieved of my duties, I'm just too ill to go on" I not only must believe I am in fact ill, I must also be prepared to say, of any of my colleagues or anyone else similarly placed, that in like circumstances they too ought to be relieved of their duties if they fall ill. There is a certain *generality* about moral discourse and a man is not reasoning morally or "being reasonable" if he will not allow those inferences. Similarly, if I say "I want x" or "I prefer x" I need not, though I may, be prepared to give reason why I want it or prefer it, but if I say "x is the right thing to do" or "x is good" or "I ought to do x" or "x is worthy of attainment," I must—perhaps with the exception of judgments of intrinsic goodness—be prepared to give *reasons* for saying "x is the right thing to do," "x is good," "I ought to do x" and the like . . .

It is indeed true in morals and in reasoning about human conduct generally that justification must come to an end; but this is also true in logic, science and in common sense empirical reasoning about matters of fact; but it is also true that the end point in reasoning over good and evil is different than in science and the like, for in reasoning about how to act, our judgment finally terminates in a choice—a decision of principle. And here is the truth in Ayer's remark that moral judgments are "finally a matter of individual choice." But, unless we are to mislead, we must put the emphasis on "finally," for a dispassioned, neutral analysis of the uses of the language of human conduct will show, as I have indicated, that there is reasoning, and in a relevant sense, "objective reasoning," about moral questions. It is not at all a matter of pure persuasion or goading someone into sharing your attitudes.

I cannot, of course, even begin to display the full range of the reasoning which has sought to establish this point. But I hope I have said enough to block the misleading implications of Ayer's otherwise very fine analysis. . . .

## III

There are, however, other considerations that may be in our minds when we ask "What is the meaning of life?" or "Does life have a meaning?" In asking such questions, we may *not* be asking "What should we seek?" or "What goals are worth seeking really?" Instead we may be asking "Is *anything* worth seeking?" "Does it matter finally what we do?" Here, some may feel, we finally meet the real tormenting "riddle of human existence."

Such a question is not simply a moral question: it is a question concerning human conduct, a question about how to live one's life or about whether to continue to live one's life. Yet when we consider what an answer would look like here we draw a blank. If someone says "Is anything worthwhile?" we gape. We want to reply: "Why, sitting in the sunshine in the mornings, seeing the full moon rise, meeting a close friend one hasn't seen in a long time, sleeping comfortably after a tiring day, all these things and a million more are most assuredly worthwhile. Any life devoid of experiences of this sort would most certainly be impoverished."

Yet this reply is so obvious we feel that something different must be intended by the questioner. The questioner knows that we, and most probably he, ordinarily regard such things as worthwhile, but he is asking if these things or *anything* is worthwhile *really*? These things *seem* worthwhile but are they in reality? And here we indeed do not know what to say. If someone queries whether it is really worthwhile leaving New York and going to the beach in August we have some idea of what to say; there are some criteria which will enable us to make at least a controversial answer to this question. But when it is asked, in a philosophical manner, *if anything, ever* is really worthwhile, it is not clear that we have a genuine question before us. The question borrows its form from more garden-variety questions but when we ask it in this general way do we actually know what we mean? If someone draws a line on the blackboard, a question over the line's straightness can arise only if some criterion for a line's being straight is accepted. Similarly only if some criterion of worthiness is accepted can we intelligibly ask if a specific thing or anything is worthy of attainment.

But if a sensitive and reflective person asks, "Is anything worthwhile, really?" could he not be asking this because, (1) he has a certain vision of human excellence, and (2) his austere criteria for what is worthwhile have developed in terms of that vision? Armed with such criteria, he might find nothing that man can in fact attain under his present and foreseeable circumstances *worthy* of attainment. Considerations of this sort seem to be the sort of considerations that led Tolstoy and Schopenhauer to come to such pessimistic views about life. Such a person would be one of those few people, who as one of Hesse's characters remarks, "demand the utmost of life and yet cannot come to terms with its stupidity and crudeness." In terms of his ideal of human excellence nothing is worthy of attainment.

To this, it is natural to respond, "If this is our major problem about the meaning of life, then this is indeed no intellectual or philosophical riddle about human destiny. We need not like Steppenwolf return to our lodging lonely and disconsolate because life's 'glassy essence' remains forever hidden, for we can well envisage, in making such a judgment, what would be worthwhile. We can say what a meaningful life would look like even though we can't attain it. If such is the question, there is no 'riddle of human existence,' though there is a pathos to human life and there is the social-political pattern problem of how to bring the requisite human order into existence. Yet only if we have a conception of what human life should be can we feel such pathos."

If it is said in response to this that what would really be worthwhile could not possibly be attained, an absurdity has been uttered. To say something is worthy of attainment implies that, everything else being equal, it ought to be attained. But to say that something ought to be attained implies that it *can* be attained. Thus we *cannot* intelligibly say that something is worthy of attainment but that it cannot possibly be attained. So in asking "Is anything worthy of attainment?" we must acknowledge that there are evaluative criteria operative which guarantee that what is sincerely said to be worthy of attainment is at least in principle attainable. And as we have seen in speaking of morality, "x is worthy of attainment" does not mean "x is preferred," though again, in asserting that something is worthy of attainment, or worthwhile, we imply that we would choose it, everything else being equal, in preference to something else. But we cannot intelligibly speak of a choice if there is no possibility of doing one thing rather than another.

Life is often hard and, practically speaking, the ideals we set our hearts on, those to which we most deeply commit ourselves, may in actual fact be impossible to achieve. A sensitive person may have an ideal of conduct, an ideal of life, that he assents to without reservation. But the facts of human living being what they are, he knows full well that this ideal cannot be realized. His ideals are intelligible enough, logically their achievement is quite possible, but as a matter of *brute fact* his ideals are beyond his attainment. If this is so, is it worthwhile for him and others like him to go on living or to strive for anything at all? Can life, under such circumstances, be anything more than an ugly habit? For such a man, "What is the meaning of life?" has the force of "What *point* can a life such as mine have under these circumstances?" And in asking whether such a life has a point he is asking the very question we put above, viz. can life be worth living under such conditions.

Again such a question is perfectly intelligible and is in no way unanswerable any more than any other question about how to act, though here too we must realize that the facts of human living *cannot* be sufficient for a man simply to read off an answer without it in any way affecting his life. Here, too, *any* answer will require a decision or some kind of effective involvement on the part of the person involved. A philosopher can be of help here in showing what kind of answers we cannot give, but it is far less obvious that he can provide us with a set of principles that together with empirical facts about his condition and prospects, will enable the perplexed man to know what he ought to do. The philosopher or any thoughtful person who sees just what is involved in the question can give some helpful advice. Still the person involved must work out an answer in anguish and soreness of heart.

However, I should remind him that no matter how bad his own life was, there would always remain something he could do to help alleviate the sum total of human suffering. This certainly has value and if he so oriented his life, he could not say that his life was without point. I would also argue that in normal circumstances he could not be sure that his ideals of life would permanently be frustrated, and if he held ideals that would be badly frustrated under almost any circumstances, I would get him to look again at his ideals. Could such ideals really be adequate? Surely man's reach must exceed his grasp, but how far should we go? Should not any ideal worth its salt come into some closer involvement with the realities of human living? And if one deliberately and with self-understanding plays the role of a Don Quixote can one justifiably complain that one's ideals are not realized? Finally, it does not seem to me reasonable to expect that *all* circumstances can have sufficient meaning to make them worthwhile. Under certain circumstances life is not worth living. As a philosopher, I would point out this possibility and block those philosophical-religious claims that would try to show that this could not possibly be.

Many men who feel the barbs of constant frustration, come to feel that their ideals have turned out to be impossible, and ask in anguish—as a consequence—"Does life really have any meaning?" To a man in such anguish I would say all I have said above and much more, though I am painfully aware that such an approach may seem cold and unfeeling. I know that these matters deeply affect us; indeed they can even come to obsess us, and when we are so involved it is hard to be patient with talk about what can and cannot be said. But we need to understand these matters as well; and, after all, what more can be done along this line than to make quite plain what is involved in his question and try to exhibit a range of rational attitudes that could be taken toward it, perhaps stressing the point that though Dr. Rieux lost his wife and his best friend, his life, as he fought the plague, was certainly not without point either for him or for others. But I would also try to make clear that finally an answer to such a question must involve a decision or the having or adopting of a certain attitude on the part of the person involved. This certainly should be stressed and it should be stressed that the question "Is such a life meaningful?" is a sensible question, which admits of a non-obscurantist, non-metaphysical treatment.

## IV

There are many choices we must make in our lives and some choices are more worthwhile than others, though the criteria for what is worthwhile are in large measure at least context-dependent. "It's worthwhile going to

Leningrad to see the Hermitage" is perfectly intelligible to someone who knows and cares about art. Whether such a trip to Leningrad is worthwhile for such people can be determined by these people by a visit to the Museum. "It's worthwhile fishing the upper Mainistee" is in exactly the same category, though the criteria for worthwhileness are not the same. Such statements are most assuredly perfectly intelligible; and no adequate grounds have been given to give us reason to think that we should philosophically tinker with the ordinary criteria of "good art museum" or "good trout fishing." And why should we deny that these and other things are really worthwhile? To say "Nothing is worthwhile since all pales and worse still, all is vain because man must die" is to mistakenly assume that because an eternity of even the best trout fishing would be not just a bore but a real chore, that trout fishing is therefore not worthwhile. Death and the fact (if it is a fact) that there is nothing new under the sun need not make all vanity. That something must come to an end can make it all the more precious: to know that love is an old tale does not take the bloom from your beloved's cheek.

Yet some crave a more general answer to "Is anything worthwhile?" This some would say, is what they are after when they ask about the meaning of life.

As I indicated, the criteria for what is worthwhile are surely in large measure context-dependent, but let us see what more we can say about this need for a more general answer.

In asking "Why is anything worthwhile?" if the "why" is a request for *causes*, a more general answer can be given. The answer is that people have preferences, enjoy, admire and approve of certain things and they can and sometimes do reflect. Because of this they find some things worthwhile. This, of course, is not what "being worthwhile" *means*, but if people did not have these capacities they would not find anything worthwhile. But *reasons* why certain things are worthwhile are dependent on the thing in question.

If people find x worthwhile they generally prefer x, approve of x, enjoy x, or admire x on reflection. If people did not prefer, approve of, enjoy or admire things then nothing would be found to be worthwhile. If they did not have these feelings the notion of "being worthwhile" would have no role to play in human life; but it does have a role to play and, as in morality, justification of what is worthwhile must finally come to an end with the reflective choices we make.

Moral principles, indeed, have a special onerousness about them. If something is a moral obligation, it is something we ought to do through and through. It for most people at least and from a moral point of view for everyone overrides (but does not exhaust) all non-moral considerations about what is worthwhile. If we are moral agents and we are faced with the necessity of choosing either A or B, where A, though very worthwhile, is a nonmoral end and where B is a moral one, we must choose B. The force of the "must" here is logical. From a moral point of view there is no alternative but to choose B. Yet we do not escape the necessity of decision for we still must *agree* to *adopt* a moral point of view, to *try* to act as moral agents. Here, too, we must finally make a decision of principle.[5] There are good Hobbesian reasons for adopting the moral point of view but if one finally would really prefer "a state of nature" in which all were turned against all, rather than a life in which there was a freedom from this and at least a minimum of cooperation between human beings, then these reasons for adopting the moral point of view would not be compelling to such a person. There is, in the last analysis, no escape from making a choice.

In asking "What is the meaning of Life?" we have seen how this question is in reality a question concerning human conduct. It asks either "What should we seek?" or "What ends (if any) are really worthwhile?" I have tried to show in what general ways such questions are answerable. We can give reasons for our moral judgments and moral principles and the whole activity of morality can be seen to have a point, but not all questions concerning what is worthwhile are moral questions. Where moral questions do not enter we must make a decision about what, on reflection, we are going to seek. We must ascertain what—all things considered—really answers to our interests or, where there is no question of anything answering to our interests or failing to answer to our interests, we should decide what on reflection we prefer. What do we really want, wish to approve of, or admire? To ask "Is anything worthwhile?" involves our asking "Is there nothing that we, on reflection, upon knowledge of ourselves and others, want, approve of, or admire?" When we say "So-and-so is worthwhile" we are making a normative judgment that cannot be derived from determining what we desire, admire or approve of. That is to say, these statements do not entail statements to the effect that so and so is worthwhile. But in determining what is worthwhile this is finally all we have to go on. In saying something is worthwhile, we (1) *express* our preference, admiration or approval; (2) in some sense imply that we are prepared to defend our choice with *reasons;* and (3) in effect, indicate our belief that others like us in the relevant respects and similarly placed, will find it worthwhile too. And the answer to our question is that, of course, there are things we humans desire, prefer, approve of, or admire. This being so, our question is not unanswerable. Again we need not fly to a metaphysical enchanter.

As I said, "Is anything really worthwhile, really worth seeking?" makes us gape. And "atomistic analyses," like the one I have just given, often leave us with a vague but persistent feeling of dissatisfaction, even when we cannot clearly articulate the grounds of our dissatisfaction. "The real question," we want to say, "has slipped away from us amidst the host of distinctions and analogies. We've not touched the deep heart of the matter at all."

Surely, I have not exhausted the question for, literally speaking, it is not one question but a cluster of loosely related questions all concerning "the human condition"—how man is to act and how he is to live his life even in the face of the bitterest trials and disappointments. Questions here are diverse, and a philosopher, or anyone else, becomes merely pretentious and silly when he tries to come up with some formula that will solve, resolve or dissolve the perplexities of human living. But I have indicated in skeletal fashion how we can approach general questions about "What (if anything) is worth seeking?" And I have tried to show how such questions are neither meaningless nor questions calling for esoteric answers.

## V

We are not out of the woods yet. Suppose someone were to say: "Okay, you've convinced me. Some things are worthwhile and there is a more or less distinct mode of reasoning called moral reasoning and there are canons of validity distinctive of this sui generis type reasoning. People do reason in the ways that you have described, but it still remains the case that here one's attitudes and final choices are relevant in a way that isn't necessarily the case in science or an argument over plain matters of fact. But when I ask: 'How ought men act?' 'What is the meaning of life?' and 'What is the meaning of *my* life?, how should I live and die?' I want an answer that is logically independent of any human choice or any pro-attitude toward any course of action or any state of affairs. Only if I can have that kind of warrant for my moral judgments and ways-of-life will I be satisfied."

If a man demands this and continues to demand this after dialectical examination we must finally leave him unsatisfied. As linguistic philosophers there is nothing further we can say to him. In dialectical examination we can again point out to him that he is asking for the logically impossible, but if he recognizes this and persists in asking for that which is impossible there are no further rational arguments that we can use to establish our point. But, prior to this last-ditch stand, there are still some things that we can say. We can, in detail and with care, point out to him, describe fully for him, the rationale of the moral distinctions we do make and the functions of moral discourse. A full description here will usually break this kind of obsessive perplexity. Furthermore, we can make the move Stephen Toulmin makes in the last part of his *The Place of Reason in Ethics.* We can describe for him another use of "Why" that Toulmin has well described as a "limiting question."[6]

Let me briefly explain what this is and how it could be relevant. When we ask a "limiting question" we are not really asking a question at all. We are in a kind of "land of shadows" where there are no clear-cut uses of discourse. If we just look at their grammatical form, "limiting questions" do not appear to be extra-rational in form, but in their depth grammar—their actual function—they clearly are. "What holds the universe up?" looks very much like "What holds the Christmas tree up?" but the former, in common sense contexts at least, is a limiting question while the latter usually admits of a perfectly obvious answer. As Toulmin himself puts it, limiting questions are "questions expressed in a form borrowed from a familiar mode of reasoning, but not doing the job which they normally do within that mode of reasoning."[7] A direct answer to a limiting question never satisfies the questioners. Attempted "answers" only regenerate the question, though often a small change in the questions themselves or their context will make them straight-forward questions. Furthermore, there is no standard interpretation for limit-ing questions sanctioned in our language. And limiting questions do not present us with any genuine alternatives from which to choose.

Now "limiting questions" get used in two main contexts. Sometimes, they merely express what Ryle, rather misleadingly, called a "category mis-take." Thus someone who was learning English might ask: "How hot is blue?" or "Where is anywhere?" And, even a native speaker of English might ask as a *moral* agent, "Why ought I to do what is right?" We "answer" such questions by pointing out that blue cannot be hot, anywhere is not a particu-lar place, and that if something is indeed right, this entails that it ought to be done. Our remarks here are grammatical remarks, though our speaking in the material mode may hide this. And if the questioner's "limiting question" merely signifies that a category mistake has been made, when this is pointed out to the questioner, there is an end to the matter. But more typically and more interestingly, limiting questions do not *just* or at all indicate category mistakes but express, as well or independently, a *personal predicament*. Limit-ing questions may express anxiety, fear, hysterical apprehensiveness about the future, hope, despair, and any number of attitudes. Toulmin beautifully illustrates from the writings of Dostoevsky an actual, on-the-spot use, of lim-iting questions:

> He was driving somewhere in the steppes. . . . Not far off was a village, he could see the black huts, and half the huts were burnt down, there were only the charred beams sticking out. As they drove in, there were peasant women drawn up along the road . . .
>
> "Why are they crying? Why are they crying?" Mitya [Dmitri] asked, as they dashed gaily by.
>
> "It's the babe," answered the driver, "the babe is weeping."
>
> And Mitya was struck by his saying, in his peasant way, "the babe," and he liked the peasant's calling it a "babe." There seemed more pity in it.
>
> "But why is it weeping?" Mitya persisted stupidly. "Why are its little arms bare? Why don't they wrap it up?"
>
> "The babe's cold, its little clothes are frozen and don't warm it."
>
> "But why is it? Why?" foolish Mitya still persisted.
>
> "Why, they're poor people, burnt out. They've no bread. They're begging because they've been burnt out."
>
> "No, no," Mitya, as it were still did not understand. "Tell me why it is those poor mothers stand there? Why are people poor? Why is the babe poor? Why is the steppe barren? Why don't they hug each other and kiss? Why don't they sing songs of joy? Why are they so dark from black misery? Why don't they feed the babe?"
>
> And he felt that, though his questions were unreasonable, and senseless, yet he wanted to ask just that, and he had to ask it just in that way. And he felt that a passion of pity, such as he had never known before, was rising in his heart, that he wanted to cry, that he wanted to do something for them all, so that the babe should weep no more, so that the dark-faced, dried-up mother should not weep, that no one should shed tears again from that moment . . .

"I've had a good dream, gentlemen," he said in a strange voice, with a new light, as of joy, in his face.[8]

It is clear that we need not, may not, from the point of view of analysis, condemn these uses of language as illicit. We can point out that it is a muddle to confuse such questions with literal questions, and that such questions have no fixed *literal* meaning, and that as a result there are and can be no fixed literal ways of answering them, but they are indeed, genuine uses of language, and not the harum-scarum dreams of undisciplined metaphysics. When existentialist philosophers and theologians state them as profound questions about an alleged ontological realm there is room for complaint, but as we see them operating in the passage I quoted from *The Brothers Karamazov,* they seem to be not only linguistically proper but also an extremely important form of discourse. It is a shame and a fraud when philosophers "sing songs" as a substitute for the hard work of philosophizing, but only a damn fool would exclude song-singing, literal or metaphorical, from the life of reason, or look down on it as a somehow inferior activity. Non-literal "answers" to these non-literal, figurative questions, when they actually express personal predicaments or indeed more general human predicaments may, in a motivational sense, *goad* people to do one thing or another that they *know* they ought to do or they may comfort them or give them hope in time of turmoil and anxiety. I am not saying this is their only use or that they have no other respectable rationale. I do not at all think that; but I am saying that here is a rationale that even the most hard nosed positivist should acknowledge.

The man who demands "a more objective answer" to his question, "How ought men to live?" or "What is the meaning of Life?" may not be just muddled. If he is *just* making a "category mistake" and this is pointed out to him, he will desist, but if he persists, his limiting question probably expresses some anxiety. In demanding an answer to an evaluative question that can be answered independently of any attitudes he might have or choices he might make, he may be unconsciously expressing his fear of making decisions, his insecurity and confusion about what he really wants, and his desperate desire to have a Father who would make all these decisions for him. And it is well in such a context to bring Weston LaBarre's astute psychological observation to mind. "Values," LaBarre said, "must from emotional necessity be viewed as absolute by those who use values as compulsive defenses against reality, rather than properly as tools for the exploration of reality."[9] This remark, coming from a Freudian anthropologist, has unfortunately a rather metaphysical ring, but it can be easily enough de-mythologized. The point is, that someone who persists in these questions, persists in a demand for a totally different and "deeper" justification or answer to the question "What is the meaning of Life?" than the answer that such a question admits of, may be just expressing his own insecurity. The heart of rationalism is often irrational. At such a point the only reasoning that will be effective with him, if indeed any reasoning will be effective with him, may be psychoanalytic reasoning. And by then, of course you have left the philosopher and indeed all questions of justification far behind. But again the philosopher can describe the kinds of questions we can ask and the point of these questions. Without advocating anything at all he can make clearer to us the structure of "the life of reason" and the goals we human beings do prize.

## VI

There is another move that might be made in asking about this haunting question: "What is the meaning of Life?" Suppose someone were to say: "Yes I see about these 'limiting questions' and I see that moral reasoning and reasoning about human conduct generally are limited modes of reasoning with distinctive criteria of their own. If I am willing to be guided by reason and I can be reasonable there are some answers I can find to the question: 'What is the meaning of Life?' I'm aware that they are not cut and dried and that they are not simple and that they are not even by any means altogether the same for all men, but there are some reasonable answers and touchstones all the same. You and I are in perfect accord on that. But there is one thing I don't see at all, 'Why ought I to be guided by reason anyway?' and if you cannot answer this for me I don't see why I should think that your answer—or rather your schema for an answer—about the meaning of Life is, after all, really any good. It all depends on how you *feel*, finally. There are really no answers here."

But again we have a muddle; let me very briefly indicate why. If someone asks: "Why ought I to be guided by reason anyway?" or "Is it really good to be reasonable?" one is tempted to take such a question as a paradigm case of a "limiting question," and a very silly one at that. But as some people like to remind us—without any very clear sense of what they are reminding us of—reason has been challenged. It is something we should return to, be wary of, realize the limits of, or avoid, as the case may be. It will hardly do to take such a short way with the question and rack it up as a category mistake.

In some particular contexts, with some particular people, it is (to be paradoxical, for a moment) reasonable to question whether we ought to follow reason. Thus, if I am a stubborn, penny-pinching old compulsive and I finally take my wife to the "big-city" for a holiday, it might be well to say to me: "Go on, forget how much the damn tickets cost, buy them anyway. Go on, take a cab even if you can't afford it." But to give or heed such advice clearly is not, in any fundamental sense, to fly in the face of reason, for on a deeper level— the facts of human living being what they are—we are being guided by reason.

It also makes sense to ask, as people like D. H. Lawrence press us to ask, if it really pays to be reasonable. Is the reasonable, clear-thinking, clear-visioned, intellectual animal really the happiest, in the long run? And can his life be as rich, as intense, as creative as the life of Lawrence's sort of man? From Socrates to Freud it has been assumed, for the most part, that self-knowledge, knowledge of our world, and rationality will bring happiness, if anything will. But is this really so? The whole Socratic tradition may be wrong at this point. Nor is it obviously true that the reasonable man, the man who sees life clearly and without evasion, will be able to live the richest, the most intense or the most creative life. I hope these things are compatible but they may not be. A too clear understanding may dull emotional involvement. Clear-sightedness may work against the kind of creative intensity that we find in a Lawrence, a Wolfe or a Dylan Thomas.

But to ask such questions is not in a large sense to refuse to be guided by reason. Theoretically, further knowledge could give us at least some vague answers to such unsettling questions; and, depending on what we learned and what decisions we would be willing to make, we would then know what to do. But clearly, we are not yet flying in the face of reason, refusing to be guided by reason at all. We are still playing the game according to the ground rules of reason.

What is this question, "Why should I be guided by reason?" or "Why be reasonable?" if it isn't any of these questions we have just discussed? If we ask this question and take it in a very general way, the question is a limiting one and it does involve a category mistake. What could be *meant* by asking: "Why ought we *ever* use reason at all?" That to ask this question is to commit a logical blunder, is well brought out by Paul Taylor when he says:

> . . . it is a question which would never be asked by anyone who thought about what he was saying, since the question, to speak loosely, answers itself. It is admitted that no amount of arguing in the world can make a person who does not want to be reasonable want to be. For to argue would be to give reasons, and to give reasons already assumes that the person to whom you give them is *seeking* reasons. That is it assumes he is reasonable. A person who did not want to be reasonable in any sense would never ask the question, "Why be reasonable?" For in asking the question, Why? he is seeking reasons, that is, he is being reasonable in asking the question. The question calls for the use of reason to justify *any* use of reason, including the use of reason to answer the question.[10]

In other words, to ask the question, as well as answer it, commits one to the use of reason. To ask: "Why be guided by reason at all?" is to ask "Why be reasonable, ever?" As Taylor puts it, "The questioner is thus seeking good reasons for seeking good reasons," and this surely is an absurdity. Anything that would be a satisfactory answer would be a "tautology to the effect that it is reasonable to be reasonable. A negative answer to the question, Is it reasonable to be reasonable? would express a self-contradiction."

If all this is pointed out to someone and he still persists in asking the question in this logically senseless way there is nothing a philosopher qua philosopher can do for him, though a recognition of the use of limiting questions in discourse may make this behavior less surprising to the philosopher himself. He might give him all five volumes of *The Life of Reason* or *Vanity Fair* and say, "Here, read this, maybe you will come to see things differently." The philosopher himself might even sing a little song in praise of reason, but there would be nothing further that he could say to him, philosophically: but by now we have come a very long way.

## NOTES

1. The rest of the references to Ayer in the text are from this essay. His brief remarks in his "What I Believe" in *What I Believe* (London: 1966), pp. 15–16 and in his introduction to *The Humanist Outlook*, A. J. Ayer (ed.) (London: 1968), pp. 6–7 are also relevant as further brief statements of his central claims about the meaning of life.

2. Charles Taylor, *The Explanation of Behavior* (Routledge and Kegan Paul, 1964).

3. See his discussion of existentialism in his *Contemporary Philosophy*.

4. While I completely agree with the central thrust of Ayer's argument here, he has, I believe, overstated his case. Even if our behaviour finally depends on our own standards of value, it does not follow that the concurrence of the deity, if there is one, is superfluous, for we could still find crucial moral guidance from our grasp of something of God's wisdom.

5. I have discussed the central issues involved here at length in my "Why Should I Be Moral?" *Methods*, 15 (1963).

6. Stephen Toulmin, *An Examination of the Place of Reason in Ethics* (Cambridge University Press, 1950).

7. Ibid., p. 205.

8. Ibid., p. 210.

9. Weston LaBarre, *The Human Animal* (University of Chicago, 1954).

10. Paul Taylor, "Four Types of Relativism," *Philosophical Review* (1956).

# CHAPTER 18

J O H N   W I S D O M

## *The Meanings of the Questions of Life*

When one asks "What is the meaning of life?" one begins to wonder whether this large, hazy and bewildering question itself has any meaning. Some people indeed have said boldly that the question has no meaning. I believe this is a mistake. But it is a mistake which is not without excuse. And I hope that by examining the excuse we may begin to remedy the mistake, and so come to see that whether or not life has a meaning it is not senseless to enquire whether it has or not. First, then, what has led some people to think that the whole enquiry is senseless?

There is an old story which runs something like this: A child asked an old man "What holds up the world? What holds up all things?" The old man answered "A giant." The child asked "And what holds up the giant? You must tell me what holds up the giant." The old man answered "An elephant." The child said, "And what holds up the elephant?" The old man answered "A tortoise." The child said "You still have not told me what holds up all things. For what holds up the tortoise?" The old man answered "Run away and don't ask me so many questions."

From this story we can see how it may happen that a question which looks very like sensible meaningful questions may turn out to be a senseless, meaningless one. Again and again when we ask "What supports this?" it is possible to give a sensible answer. For instance what supports the top-most card in a house of cards? The cards beneath it which are in their turn supported by the cards beneath them. What supports all the cards? The table. What supports the table? The floor and the earth. But the question "What supports all things, absolutely all things?" is different. It is absurd, it is senseless, like the question "What is bigger than the largest thing in the world?" And it is easy to see why the question "What supports all things?" is absurd. Whenever we ask, "What supports thing A or these things A, B, C," then we can answer this question only by mentioning some thing other than the thing A or things A, B, C about which we asked "What supports it or them." We must if we are to answer the question mention something D other than those things which form the subject of our question, and we must say that this thing is what supports them. If we mean by the phrase "all things" absolutely all things which exist then obviously there is nothing outside that about which we are now asked "What supports all this?" Consequently any answer to the question will be self-contradictory just as any answer to the question "What is bigger than the biggest of all things" must be self-contradictory. Such questions are absurd, or, if you like, silly and senseless.

In a like way again and again when we ask "What is the meaning of this?" we answer in terms of something other than this. For instance imagine that there has been a quarrel in the street. One man is hitting another man on the jaw. A policeman hurries up. "Now then" he says, "what is the meaning of all this?" He wants to know what led up to the quarrel, what caused it. It is no good saying to the policeman "It's a quarrel." He knows there is a quarrel. What he wants to know is what went before the quarrel, what led up to it. To answer him we must mention something other than the quarrel itself. Again suppose a man is driving a motor car and sees in front of him a road sign, perhaps a red flag, perhaps a skull and crossbones. "What does this mean?" he asks and when he asks this he wants to know what the sign points to. To answer we must mention something other than the sign itself, such as a dangerous corner in the road. Imagine a doctor sees an extraordinary rash on the face of his patient. He is astonished and murmurs to himself "What is the meaning of this?" He wants to know what caused the strange symptoms, or what they will lead to, or both. In any case in order to answer his question he must find something which went before or comes after and lies outside that about which he asks "What does this mean?" This need to look before or after in order to answer a question of the sort "What is the meaning of this?" is so common, so characteristic, a feature of such questions that it is natural to think that when it is impossible to answer such a question in this way then the question has no sense. Now what happens when we ask "What is the meaning of life?"

Perhaps someone here replies, the meaning, the significance of this present life, this life on earth, lies in a life hereafter, a life in heaven. All right. But imagine that some persistent enquirer asks, "But what I am asking is what is the meaning of all life, life here and life beyond, life now and life hereafter? What is the meaning of all things in earth and heaven?" Are we to say that this question is absurd because there cannot be anything beyond all things while at the same time any answer to "What is the meaning of all things?" must point to some thing beyond all things?

Imagine that we come into a theatre after a play has started and are obliged to leave before it ends. We may then be puzzled by the part of the play that we are able to see. We may ask "What does it mean?" In this case we want to know what went before and what came after in order to understand the part we saw. But sometimes even when we have seen and heard a play from the beginning to the end we are still puzzled and still ask what does the whole thing mean. In this case we are not asking what came before or what came after, we are not asking about anything outside the play itself. We are, if you like, asking a very different sort of question from that we usually put with the words "What does this mean?" But we are still asking a real question, we are still asking a question which has sense and is not absurd. For our words express a wish to grasp the character, the significance of the whole play. They are a confession that we have not yet done this and they are a request for help in doing it. Is the play a tragedy, a comedy or a tale told by an idiot? The pattern of it is so complex, so bewildering, our grasp of it still so inadequate, that we don't know what to say, still less whether to call it good or bad. But this question is not senseless.

In the same way when we ask "What is the meaning of all things?" we are not asking a senseless question. In this case, of course, we have not witnessed the whole play, we have only an idea in outline of what went before and what will come after that small part of history which we witness. But with the words "What is the meaning of it all?" we are trying to find the order in the drama of Time. The question may be beyond us. A child may be able to understand, to grasp a simple play and be unable to understand and grasp a play more complex and more subtle. We do not say on this account that when he asks of the larger more complex play "What does it mean?" then his question is senseless, nor even that it is senseless for him. He has asked and even answered such a question in simpler cases, he knows the sort of effort, the sort of movement of the mind which such a question calls for, and we do not say that a question is meaningless to him merely because he is not yet able to carry out quite successfully the movement of that sort which is needed in order to answer a complex question of that sort. We do not say that a question in mathematics which is at present rather beyond us is meaningless to us. We know the type of procedure it calls for and may make efforts which bring us nearer and nearer to an answer. We are able to find the meaning which lies not outside but within very complex but still limited wholes whether these are dramas of art or of real life. When we ask "What is the meaning of all things?" we are bewildered and have not that grasp of the order of things the desire for which we express when we ask that question. But this does not render the question senseless nor make it impossible for us to move towards an answer.

We must however remember that what one calls answering such a question is not giving an answer. I mean we cannot answer such a question in the form: "The meaning is this."

Such an idea about what form answering a question must take may lead to a new despair in which we feel we cannot do anything in the way of answering such a question as "What is the meaning in it all?" merely because we are not able to sum up our results in a phrase or formula.

When we ask what is the meaning of this play or this picture we cannot express the understanding which this question may lead to in the form of a list of just those things in the play or the picture which give it its meaning. No.

The meaning eludes such a list. This does not mean that words quite fail us. They may yet help us provided that we do not expect of them more than they can do.

A person who is asked what he finds so hateful or so lovable in another may with words help himself and us in grasping what it is that so moves him. But he will only mislead us and himself if he pretends that his words are a complete account of all that there is in the matter.

It is the same when we ask what is it in all things that makes it all so good, so bad, so grand, so contemptible. We must not anticipate that the answer can be given in a word or in a neat list. But this does not mean that we can do nothing towards answering these questions nor even that words will not help us. Indeed surely the historians, the scientists, the prophets, the dramatists and the poets have said much which will help any man who asks himself: Is the drama of time meaningless as a tale told by an idiot? Or is it not meaningless? And if it is not meaningless is it a comedy or a tragedy, a triumph or a disaster, or is it a mixture in which sweet and bitter are for ever mixed?

# CHAPTER 19

R O B E R T   N O Z I C K

## Philosophy and the Meaning of Life

The question of what meaning our life has, or can have, is of utmost importance to us. So heavily is it laden with our emotion and aspiration that we camouflage our vulnerability with jokes about seeking for the meaning or purpose of life: A person travels for many days to the Himalayas to seek the word of an Indian holy man meditating in an isolated cave. Tired from his journey, but eager and expectant that his quest is about to reach fulfillment, he asks the sage, "What is the meaning of life?" After a long pause, the sage opens his eyes and says, "Life is a fountain." "What do you mean, life is a fountain?" barks the questioner. "I have just traveled thousands of miles to hear your words, and all you have to tell me is that? That's ridiculous." The sage then looks up from the floor of the cave and says, "You mean it's not a fountain?" In a variant of the story, he replies, "So it's not a fountain."

The story is reassuring. The supposed sages are frauds who speak nonsense, nonsense they either never thought to question ("You mean it's not a fountain?") or do not care very much about ("So it 's not a fountain"). Surely, then, we have nothing to learn from these ridiculous people; we need not seek their ludicrous "wisdom."

But why was it necessary for the joke to continue on after the sage said "life is a fountain," why was it necessary for the story to include the seeker's objection and the sage's reply? Well, perhaps the sage *did* mean something by "life is a fountain," something profound which we did not understand. The challenge and his reply show his words were empty, that he can give no deep and illuminating interpretation to his remark. Only then are we in a secure position to laugh, in relief.

However, if we couldn't know immediately that his answer "life is a fountain" was ridiculous, if we needed further words from him to exclude the lingering possibility of a deeper meaning to his apparently preposterous first reply, then how can we be sure that his second answer also does not have a deeper meaning which we don't understand? He says "You mean it's not a fountain?"; but who are *you* to mean? If you know so much about it, then why have you gone seeking him; do you even know enough to recognize an appropriate answer when you hear it?

The questioner apparently came in humility, seeking the truth, yet he assumed he knew enough to challenge the answer he heard. When he objects and the sage replies, "so it's not a fountain," was it to gain this victory in discussion that the questioner traveled so far? (The story is told that Gershom Scholem, the great scholar of kabbalism, as a young man sought out practitioners of kabbalah in Jerusalem, and was told he could study with them on the condition that he not ask any questions for two years. Scholem, who has a powerful, critical, and luminous intelligence, refused.)

When he set out on his trip, did the questioner hope for an intellectual formula presenting the meaning of life? He wanted to know how he should live in order to achieve a life with meaning. What did he expect to hear from this meditating man in a cave high in the mountains? "Go back to the posh suburb and continue your present life, but shift to a less pressured job and be more accessible to your children?" Presumably, the man in the cave is following what he takes to be the path to a meaningful life; what else can he answer except "follow my path, be like me?" "Are you crazy; do you think I am going to throw everything over to become a scruffy person sitting in a cave?" But does the seeker know enough to exclude that life as the most (or only) meaningful one, the seeker who traveled to see *him*?

Could *any* formula answer the question satisfactorily? "The meaning of life is to seek union with God"—oh yeah, that one. "A meaningful life is a full and productive life"—sure. "The purpose of life is to pursue the task of giving meaning to life"—thanks a lot. "The meaning of life is love"—yawn. "The meaning of life is spiritual perfection"—the upward and onward trip. "The meaning of life is getting off the wheel of life and becoming annihilated"—no thanks. No one undertakes the trip to the sage who hasn't already encountered all the known formulas and found them wanting. Does the seeker think the sage has some *other* words to tell him, words which somehow have not reached print? Or is there a secret formula, an esoteric doctrine that, once heard, will clarify his life and point to meaning? If there were such a secret, does he think the wise man will tell it to *him*, fresh from Los Angeles with two days of travel by llama and foot? Faced with such a questioner, one might as well tell him that life is a fountain, perhaps hoping to shock him into reconsidering what he is doing right then. (Since he will not understand anything, he might as well be told the truth as best he can understand it—the joke would be that life *is* a fountain. Better yet would be for that to get embodied in a joke.)

If it is not words the questioner needs—certainly no short formula will help—perhaps what he needs is to encounter the person of the sage, to be in his presence. If so, questions will just get in the way; the visitor will want to observe the sage over time, opening himself to what he may receive. Perhaps he will come eventually to find profundity and point in the stale formulas he earlier had found wanting.

Now, let us hear another story. A man goes to India, consults a sage in a cave and asks him the meaning of life. In three sentences the sage tells him, the man thanks him and leaves. There are several variants of this story also: In the first, the man lives meaningfully ever after; in the second he makes the sentences public so that everyone then knows the meaning of life; in the third, he sets the sentences to rock music, making his fortune and enabling everyone to whistle the meaning of life; and in the fourth variant, his plane crashes as he is flying off from his meeting with the sage. In the fifth version, the person listening to me tell this story eagerly asks what sentences the sage spoke.

And in the sixth version, I tell him.

. . .

# GOD'S PLAN

One prevalent view, less so today than previously, is that the meaning of life or people's existence is connected with God's will, with his design or plan for them. Put roughly, people's meaning is to be found and realized in fulfilling the role allotted to them by God. If a superior being designed and created people for a purpose, in accordance with a plan for them, the particular purpose he had for them would be what people are *for*. This is distinct from the view that finds meaning in the goal of merging with God, and also from the view which holds that if you do God's will you will be rewarded—sit at his right hand, and receive eternal bliss—and that the meaning and purpose of life is to achieve this reward which is intrinsically valuable (and also meaningful?).

Our concern now is not with the question of whether there is a God; or whether, if there is, he has a purpose for us; or whether if there is and he has a purpose for us, there is any way to discover this purpose, whether God reveals his purpose to people. Rather, our question is how all this, even if true, would succeed in providing meaning for people's lives.

First, we should ask whether any and every role would provide meaning and purpose to human lives. If our role is to supply $CO_2$ to the plants, or to be the equivalent within God's plan of fixing a mildly annoying leaky faucet, would this suffice? Is it enough to be an absolutely trivial component within God's grand design? Clearly, what is desired is that we be important; having merely some role or other in God's plan does not suffice. The purpose God has for us must place us at or near the center of things, of his intentions and goals. Moreover, merely playing some role in a central purpose of God's is not sufficient—the role itself must be a central or important one. If we describe God's central purpose in analogy with making a painting, we do not want to play the role of the rag used to wipe off brushes, or the tin in which these rags are kept. If we are not the central focus of the painting, at least we want to be like the canvas or the brush or the paint.

Indeed, we want more than an important role in an important purpose; the role itself should be positive, perhaps even exalted. If the cosmic role of human beings was to provide a negative lesson to some others ("don't act like them") or to provide needed food for passing intergalactic travelers who *were* important, this would not suit our aspirations—not even if afterwards the intergalactic travelers smacked their lips and said that we tasted good. The role should focus on aspects of ourselves that we prize or are proud of, and it should use these in ways connected with the reasons why we prize them. (It would not suffice if the exercise of our morality or intelligence, which we prize, affects our brain so that the intergalactic travelers find it more *tasty*.)

Do all these conditions guarantee meaning? Suppose our ingenuity was to be used to aid these travelers on their way, but that their way was no more important than ours. There was no more reason why we were aiding them (and perishing afterwards) than the other way around—the plan just happened to go that way. Would this cruel hoax leave us any more content than if there were no plan or externally given role at all?

There are two ways we individually or collectively could be included in God's plan. First, our fulfilling our role might depend upon our acting in a certain way, upon our choices or cooperation; second, our role might not depend at all upon our actions or choices—willy-nilly we shall serve. (In parallel to the notion of originative value, we can say that under the first our life can have originative meaning.) About the first way we can ask why we should act to fulfill God's plan, and about both ways we can ask why fitting God's plan gives meaning to our existence.[1] That God is good (but also sometimes angry?) shows that it would be good to carry out his plan. (Even then, perhaps, it need not be good *for us*—mightn't the good overall plan involve sacrificing us for some greater good?) Yet how does doing what is good provide meaning? Those who doubt whether life has meaning, even if transparently clearheaded, need not have doubted that it is good to do certain things.

How can playing a role in God's plan give one's life meaning? What makes this a meaning-giving process? It is not merely that some being created us with a purpose in mind. If some extragalactic civilization created us with a purpose in mind, would that by itself provide meaning to our lives? Nor would things be changed if they created us so that we also had a feeling of indebtedness and a feeling that something was asked of us. It seems it is not enough that God have some purpose for us—his purpose itself must be meaningful. If it were sufficient merely to play some role in some external purpose, then you could give meaning to your life by fitting it to my plans or to your parents' purpose in having you. In these instances, however, one immediately questions the meaningfulness of the other people's purposes. How do God's purposes differ from ours so as to be guaranteed meaningfulness and importance? Let me sharpen this question by presenting a philosophical fable.[2]

# TELEOLOGY

Once you come to feel your existence lacks purpose, there is little you can do. You can keep the feeling, and either continue a meaningless existence or end it. Or you can discover the purpose your existence already serves, the meaning it has, thereby eliminating the feeling. Or you can try to dispose of the feeling by giving a meaning and purpose to your existence.

The first dual option carries minimal appeal; the second, despite my most diligent efforts, proved impossible. That left the third alternative, where, too, there are limited possibilities. You can make your existence meaningful by fitting it into some larger purpose, making yourself part of something else that is independently and incontestably important and meaningful. However, a sign of really having been stricken is that no preexisting purpose will serve in this fashion—each purpose that in other moods appears sufficiently fructifying then seems merely arbitrary. Alternatively, one can seek meaning in activity that itself is important, in something self-sufficiently intrinsically valuable. Preeminent among such activities, if there are any such, is creative activity. So, as a possible route out of my despair, I decided to create something that itself would be marvelous. (No, I did not decide to write a story beginning "Once you come to feel your existence lacks purpose." Why am I always suspected of gimmicks?)

The task required all of my knowledge, skill, intuitive powers, and craftsmanship. It seemed to me that my whole existence until then had been merely a preparation for this creative activity, so completely did it draw upon and focus all of my experience, abilities, and knowledge. I was excited by the task and fulfilled, and when it was completed I rested, untroubled by purposelessness.

But this contentment was, unfortunately, only temporary. For when I came to think about it, although it *had* taxed my ingenuity and energy to make the heavens, the earth, and the creatures upon it, what did it all amount to? I mean, the whole of it, when looked at starkly and coldly, was itself just an object, of no intrinsic importance, containing creatures in a condition as purposeless as the one I was trying to escape. Given the possibility that my talents and powers were those of a being whose existence might well be meaningless, how could their exercise endow my existence with purpose and meaning if it issued only in a worthless object?

At this point in my thoughts I came upon the solution to my problem. If I were to create a plan, a grand design into which my creation fit, in which my creatures, by serving the pattern and purpose I had ordained for them, would find their purpose and goal, then this very activity of endowing their existence with meaning and purpose would be my purpose and would give my existence meaning and point. Also, giving their existence meaning would, retroactively, make meaningful my previous activity of creation, it having issued in something that turned out to be of value and worth.

The arrangement has served. Only occasionally, out of the corner of my mind, do I wonder whether my arbitrarily having picked a plan for them can really have succeeded in giving meaning to the lives of the role-fulfillers among them. (It was necessary, of course, that I pick some plan or other for them, but no special purpose was served by my picking the particular plan I did. How could it have been? For my sole purpose then was to give meaning to my existence, and this one purpose was insufficient to determine any particular plan into which to fit my creatures.) However, lacking any conception of a less defective route to meaningfulness, I refuse to examine whether such a symbiotic arrangement truly is possible, whether different beings can provide meaning and point to each other's existence in a fashion so seemingly circular. Such questions press me toward the alternative I tremble to contemplate, yet to which I find my thoughts recurring. The option of ending it all, by now familiar, is less alien and terrifying than before. I walk through the valley of the shadow of death.

To imagine God himself facing problems about the meaningfulness of his existence forces us to consider how meaning attaches to his purposes. Let us leave aside my fancy that since it is important that our lives be provided with meaning, God's existence is made meaningful by his carrying out that task, so that—since his plans for us thereby become meaningful—our meaning is found in fitting those plans. For if it were possible for man and God to shore up each other's meaningfulness in this fashion, why could not two people do this for each other as well? Moreover, a plan whose *only* purpose is to provide meaning for another's life (or the planner's) cannot succeed in doing the trick; the plan must have some independent purpose and meaning itself.

Nor will it help to escalate up a level, and say that if there is a God who has a plan for us, the meaning of our existence consists in finding out what this plan asks of us and has in store for us. To know the meaning of life, on this view, would consist in our knowing where we came from, why we are here, where we are going. But apart from the fact that many religions hold such knowledge of God's purposes to be impossible (see, for example, *Ecclesiastes* and *Job*), and condemn various attempts to gain such knowledge (such as occult techniques and necromancy), and apart even from the fact that this seems too much a metapurpose, no more satisfying than saying "the purpose of life is the quest for the purpose of life," this view merely postpones the question of wherein God's plan itself is meaningful.

What is it about God's purposes that makes them meaningful? If our universe were created by a child from some other vast civilization in a parallel universe, if our universe were a toy it had constructed, perhaps out of prefabricated parts, it would not follow that the child's purposes were meaningful. Being the creator of all we see is not sufficient to endow his purposes with meaningfulness. Granted, the purposes of God are the purposes of a powerful and important being (as compared to us). However, it is difficult to see why that suffices for those purposes to ground our existence in meaning. Could the purposes of scientists so give meaning to artificially created short-lived animal life they maintained in a controlled laboratory environment? The scientists, creators of the animals' universe and life, would be as gods to them. Yet it would be unbearably poignant if the most intelligent animal, in a leap of intuition, did its equivalent of worshiping the absent scientist. . . .

These diverse possibilities about the intentional and purposeful creation of our universe . . . press home the question of how, or in virtue of what, a religious view can ground the meaning of our lives. Just as the direct experience of God might unavoidably provide one with a motive to carry out his wishes, so it might be that such an experience (of which type of creator?) always would resolve all doubts about meaning. To experience God might leave one with the absolute conviction that his existence was the fountain of meaning, watering your own existence. I do not want to discount testimony reporting this. But even if we accepted it fully, it leaves unanswered the question of how meaning is possible. What is it about God, as usually conceived, in virtue of which he can ground meaning? How *can* there be a ball of meaning? Even if we are willing to treat the testimony in the way we treat accurate perceptual reports, there still remains the problem of understanding how meaning can be encountered in experience, of how there can be a stopping place for questions about meaning. How in the world (or out of it) can there be something whose nature contains meaning, something which just glows meaning?

# NOTES

1. The question of why we should act to fulfill God's plan, in case it is up to us, may appear foolish. After all, this is God, the creator of the universe, omniscient and omnipotent. But what is it about God, in virtue of which we should carry out our part in his plan? Put aside the consideration that if we do not, he will punish us severely; this provides a prudential reason of the sort a slave has for obeying his more powerful master. Another reason holds that we should cooperate in fulfilling God's plan because we owe that to him. God created us, and we are indebted to him for existence. Fulfilling his purpose helps to pay off our debt of gratitude to him. (See Abraham Heschel, *Who is Man?*, Stanford University Press, 1965, p. 108.) Even if we don't want to play that role, it not being the sort of activity we prize, nevertheless must we do it to repay the debt? We might think so on the following grounds. You were created for the role, and if not for God's desire that you fulfill the role, you wouldn't exist at all; furthermore, existing while performing that role is better than not existing at all, so you should be thankful you were created at all, even if only for that role. Therefore, you are obligated to carry it out.

However, we do not think this form of reasoning is cogent when it concerns parents and children. The purposes parents have when they plan to have children (provided only these stop short of making the child's life no better than nonexistence) do not fix the obligations of the child. Even if the parents' only purpose was to produce a slave, and a slave's life is better than nonexistence, the offspring does not owe to his parents acquiescence in being enslaved. He is under no obligation to cooperate, he is not owned by his parents even though they made him. Once the child exists, it has certain rights that must be respected (and other rights it can assert when able) even if the parents' very purpose was to produce something without these rights. Nor do children owe to their parents whatever they would have conceded in bargaining before conception (supposing this had been possible) in order to come into existence.

Since children don't owe their parents everything that leaves their lives still a net plus, why do people owe their ultimate creator and sustainer any more? Even if they owe God no more, still, don't children owe their parents something for having produced and sustained them, brought them to maturity and kept them alive? To the extent that this debt to parents arises from their trouble and labor, since we don't cost an omnipotent God anything, there's nothing to pay back to him and so no need to. However, it is implausible that a child's whole debt to his parents depends merely on the fact that he was trouble. (When a parent takes great delight in his child's growth, so that any inconveniences caused are counterbalanced by the pleasures of parenthood, doesn't this child still owe something to the parent?) Still, at best, these considerations can lead to a limited obligation to our creator and sustainer—there is no arriving at Abraham by this route. To speak of a limited obligation may sound ludicrous here; "we owe everything to him." Everything may come from him, but do we owe it all back?

Our discussion thus far might leave a believer uncomprehending: he might speak as follows. "Why should one do what is wanted by an omnipotent, omniscient creator of you who is wholly good, perfect, and so on? What better reason could there be than that such a being wants you to do it? Catching the merest glimpse of the majesty and greatness and love of such a being, you would want to serve him, you would be filled with an overwhelming desire to answer any call. There would be a surrender rather than a calculation. The question 'why do it?' would not arise to someone who knew and felt what God was. That experience transforms people. You would do it out of awe and love." I do not want to deny that the direct experience of God would or might well provide an overwhelming motive to serve him. However, there remains the second question: why and how does fitting God's plan and carrying out his will provide meaning to our lives?

2. This first appeared in *Mosaic*, Vol. Ill, no. 1, Spring 1971 (published by the Harvard-Radcliffe Hillel Society), pp. 27–28, as one of "Two Philosophical Fables," and is reprinted here with only minor changes.

CHAPTER 20 SUSAN WOLF

# Meaning in Life

A meaningful life is, first of all, one that has within it the basis for an affirmative answer to the needs or longings that are characteristically described as needs for meaning. I have in mind, for example, the sort of questions people ask on their deathbeds, or simply in contemplation of their eventual deaths, about whether their lives have been (or are) worth living, whether they have had any point, and the sort of questions one asks when considering suicide and wondering whether one has any reason to go on. These questions are familiar from Russian novels and existentialist philosophy, if not from personal experience. Though they arise most poignantly in times of crisis and intense emotion, they also have their place in moments of calm reflection, when considering important life choices. Moreover, paradigms of what are taken to be meaningful and meaningless lives in our culture are readily available. Lives of great moral or intellectual accomplishment—Gandhi, Mother Teresa, Albert Einstein—come to mind as unquestionably meaningful lives (if any are); lives of waste and isolation—Thoreau's "lives of quiet desperation," typically anonymous to the rest of us, and the mythical figure of Sisyphus—represent meaninglessness.

To what general characteristics of meaningfulness do these images lead us and how do they provide an answer to the longings mentioned above? Roughly, I would say that meaningful lives are lives of active engagement in projects of worth. Of course, a good deal needs to be said in elaboration of this statement. Let me begin by discussing the two key phrases, "active engagement" and "projects of worth."

A person is actively engaged by something if she is gripped, excited, involved by it. Most obviously, we are actively engaged by the things and people about which and whom we are passionate. Opposites of active engagement are boredom and alienation. To be actively engaged in something is not

From "Happiness and Meaning: Two Aspects of the Good Life," *Social Philosophy & Policy*, Vol. 24, 1997. Reprinted with the permission of Cambridge University Press.

always pleasant in the ordinary sense of the word. Activities in which people are actively engaged frequently involve stress, danger, exertion, or sorrow (consider, for example: writing a book, climbing a mountain, training for a marathon, caring for an ailing friend). However, there is something good about the feeling of engagement: one feels (typically without thinking about it) especially alive.

That a meaningful life must involve "projects of worth" will, I expect, be more controversial, for the phrase hints of a commitment to some sort of objective value. This is not accidental, for I believe that the idea of meaningfulness, and the concern that our lives possess it, are conceptually linked to such a commitment.[1] Indeed, it is this linkage that I want to defend, for I have neither a philosophical theory of what objective value is nor a substantive theory about what has this sort of value. What is clear to me is that there can be no sense to the idea of meaningfulness without a distinction between more and less worthwhile ways to spend one's time, where the test of worth is at least partly independent of a subject's ungrounded preferences or enjoyment.

Consider first the longings or concerns about meaning that people have, their wondering whether their lives are meaningful, their vows to add more meaning to their lives. The sense of these concerns and resolves cannot fully be captured by an account in which what one does with one's life doesn't matter, as long as one enjoys or prefers it. Sometimes people have concerns about meaning despite their knowledge that their lives to date have been satisfying. Indeed, their enjoyment and "active engagement" with activities and values they now see as shallow seems only to heighten the sense of meaninglessness that comes to afflict them. Their sense that their lives so far have been meaningless cannot be a sense that their activities have not been chosen or fun. When they look for sources of meaning or ways to add meaning to their lives, they are searching for projects whose justifications lie elsewhere.

Second, we need an explanation for why certain sorts of activities and involvements come to mind as contributors to meaningfulness while others seem intuitively inappropriate. Think about what gives meaning to your own life and the lives of your friends and acquaintances. Among the things that tend to come up on such lists, I have already mentioned moral and intellectual accomplishments and the ongoing activities that lead to them. Relationships with friends and relatives are perhaps even more important for most of us. Aesthetic enterprises (both creative and appreciative), the cultivation of personal virtues, and religious practices frequently loom large. By contrast, it would be odd, if not bizarre, to think of crossword puzzles, sitcoms, or the kind of computer games to which I am fighting off addiction as providing meaning in our lives, though there is no question that they afford a sort of satisfaction and that they are the objects of choice. Some things, such as chocolate and aerobics class, I choose even at considerable cost to myself (it is irrelevant that these particular choices may be related); so I must find them worthwhile in a sense. But they are not the sorts of things that make life worth living.[2]

"Active engagement in projects of worth," I suggest, answers to the needs an account of meaningfulness in life must meet. If a person is or has been thus actively engaged, then she does have an answer to the question of whether her life is or has been worthwhile, whether it has or has had a point. When someone looks for ways to add meaning to her life, she is looking (though perhaps not under this description) for worthwhile projects about which she can get enthused. The account also explains why some activities and projects but not others come to mind as contributors to meaning in life. Some projects, or at any rate, particular acts, are worthwhile but too boring or mechanical to be sources of meaning. People do not get meaning from recycling or from writing checks to Oxfam and the ACLU. Other acts and activities, though highly pleasurable and deeply involving, like riding a roller coaster or meeting a movie star, do not seem to have the right kind of value to contribute to meaning.

Bernard Williams once distinguished categorical desires from the rest. Categorical desires give us reasons for living—they are not premised on the assumption that we will live. The sorts of things that give meaning to life tend to be objects of categorical desire. We desire them, at least so I would suggest, because we think them worthwhile. They are not worthwhile simply because we desire them or simply because they make our lives more pleasant.

Roughly, then, according to my proposal, a meaningful life must satisfy two criteria, suitably linked. First, there must be active engagement, and second, it must be engagement in (or with) projects of worth. A life is meaningless if it lacks active engagement with anything. A person who is bored or alienated from most of what she spends her life doing is one whose life can be said to lack meaning. Note that she may in fact be performing functions of worth. A housewife and mother, a doctor, or a busdriver may be competently doing a socially valuable job, but because she is not engaged by her work (or, as we are assuming, by anything else in her life), she has no categorical desires that give her a reason to live. At the same time, someone who is actively engaged may also live a meaningless life, if the objects of her involvement are utterly worthless. It is difficult to come up with examples of such lives that will be uncontroversial without being bizarre. But both bizarre and controversial examples have their place. In the bizarre category, we might consider pathological cases: someone whose sole passion in life is collecting rubber bands, or memorizing the dictionary, or making handwritten copies of War and Peace. Controversial cases will include the corporate lawyer who sacrifices her private life and health for success along the professional ladder, the devotee of a religious cult, or—an example offered by Wiggins[3]—the pig farmer who buys more land to grow more corn to feed more pigs to buy more land to grow more corn to feed more pigs.

We may summarize my proposal in terms of a slogan: "Meaning arises when subjective attraction meets objective attractiveness." The idea is that in a world in which some things are more worthwhile than others, meaning arises when a subject discovers or develops an affinity for one or typically several of the more worthwhile things and has and makes use of the opportunity to engage with it or them in a positive way.

## NOTES

1. This point is made by David Wiggins in his brilliant but difficult essay "Truth, Invention, and the Meaning of Life," *Proceedings of the British Academy*, vol. 62 (1976).

2. Woody Allen appears to have a different view. His list of the things that make life worth living at the end of *Manhattan* includes, for example "the crabs at Sam Woo's," which would seem to be on the level of chocolates. On the other hand, the crabs' appearance on the list may be taken to show that he regards the dish as an accomplishment meriting aesthetic appreciation, where such appreciation is a worthy activity in itself; in this respect, the crabs might be akin to other items on his list such as the second movement of the *Jupiter Symphony*, Louis Armstrong's recording of "Potatohead Blues," and "those apples and pears of Cèzanne." Strictly speaking, the appreciation of great chocolate might also qualify as such an activity.

3. See Wiggins, "Truth, Invention, and the Meaning of Life," p. 342.

# CHAPTER 21

# STEVEN M. CAHN

## *Meaningless Lives?*

A person's life can be judged as long or short, as moral or immoral, or as successful or unsuccessful in terms of worldly fame, creative achievements, material acquisitions, and loving relationships. But does judging a person's life as meaningful or meaningless make sense? Susan Wolf thinks so. I do not.

She claims that "meaningful lives are lives of active engagement in projects of worth," and that to be actively engaged is to be "gripped, excited, involved." According to Wolf, "projects of worth" are those that are "worthwhile," a term she recognizes as suggesting "a commitment to some sort of objective value," while also admitting she has "neither a philosophical theory of what objective value is nor a substantive theory about what has this sort of value."[1]

She does, however, offer numerous examples of activities that are sources of meaning and ones that are not. Among those that yield meaning are moral or intellectual accomplishments, relationships with friends and relatives, aesthetic enterprises, religious practices, climbing a mountain, training for a marathon, and caring for an ailing friend. Among those that do not yield meaning are collecting rubber bands, memorizing the dictionary, making handwritten copies of *War and Peace*, riding a roller coaster, meeting a movie star, watching sitcoms, playing computer games, solving crossword puzzles, recycling, or writing checks to Oxfam and the ACLU. Controversial cases include a life single-mindedly given to corporate law, one devoted to a religious cult, and, an example she takes from David Wiggins, a pig farmer who buys more land to grow more corn to feed more pigs to buy more land to grow more corn to feed more pigs.

Numerous questions jump to mind regarding the items in these categories. Why are involvements with religious practices clearly meaningful but not devotion to a religious cult? Why is caring for an ailing friend meaningful but not providing financial support for a sick stranger? Why is solving challenging crossword puzzles not an intellectual accomplishment? Why is meeting a movie star meaningless? Does Wolf suppose that meeting a famous philosopher would be more meaningful? Why is having met David Lewis more meaningful than having met W. C. Fields? Why is single-minded concentration on corporate law a controversial case? Would single-minded concentration on labor law, patent law, or constitutional law also be controversial? Does single-minded concentration on epistemology escape controversy?

Collecting rubber bands is no doubt an unusual hobby, but people have devoted their lives to collecting stamps, coins, baseball memorabilia, bottle tops, theatrical programs, medieval works on astrology, comic books, and numerous other objects. Are some of these collections meaningful and others not?

One of my best friends, a philosopher, has devoted innumerable hours to practicing and playing golf. Another friend, also a philosopher, finds golf an utter waste of time. Is one of them right and the other wrong?

Wolf suggests that "mindless, futile, never-ending tasks" are not likely to be meaningful. These criteria, however, are questionable. For instance, physical conditioning is mindless, trying to persuade all others of your solutions to philosophical problems is futile, and seeking to eliminate all diseases is never-ending. Are these activities, therefore, without meaning? Lifting heavier and heavier weights may be mindless, futile, and never-ending, but I see no reason to derogate weightlifting.

Why not allow others to pursue their own ways of life without disparaging their choices and declaring their lives meaningless? After all, others might declare meaningless a life devoted to philosophical speculation that leads to writing articles that leads to others reading those articles that leads to more philosophical speculation that leads to writing more articles that leads to others reading more articles. Why is such activity more meaningful than that engaged in by Wiggins's pig farmer?

In trying to explain why Woody Allen in *Manhattan* includes in his list of the things that make life worth living the crabs at Sam Woo's, Wolf hypothesizes that "he regards the dish as an accomplishment meriting aesthetic appreciation." A simpler and more obvious explanation, however, is that he finds the crabs especially tasty.

Wolf herself admits that she enjoys eating chocolate, exercising in aerobics class, and playing computer games. Why then does she insist on devaluing these activities?

If a person can find delights that bring no harm, such a discovery should not be denigrated but appreciated. For as was said wisely more than two thousand years ago in the Book of Ecclesiastes: "Even if a man lives many years, let him enjoy himself in all of them, remembering how many the days of darkness are going to be."[2]

# NOTES

1. All quotations are from Susan Wolf, "Happiness and Meaning: Two Aspects of the Good Life," *Social Philosophy & Policy* Vol. 24 (1997), 207–225.

2. Ecclesiastes 11:8. The translation is from *Tanakh: The Holy Scriptures* (Philadelphia: Jewish Publication Society, 1988).

CHAPTER 22  JOHN KEKES

# The Meaning of Life

## I

Most of our lives are spent in routine activities. We sleep, wash, dress, eat; go to work, work, shop, relax; balance the checkbook, clean house, do the laundry, have the car serviced; chat, pay bills, worry about this or that, take small pleasure in small things. We do all this in the intervals between familiar milestones: we are born, mature, age, and die; we have children and lose our parents; we graduate, find a job, get married, divorce, fall in and out of love, set up house; succeed at some things, fail at others; make friends and have fights; move house, change jobs, get fired or promoted, fall ill and recover, save for retirement and retire. So life goes for me, you, and just about everyone, allowing for small individual and cultural variations that affect the form but not the fact of routine. These activities constitute everyday life. Everyday life is what life mostly is. Keeping it going, however, involves constant struggle. From a birth we did not choose to a death we rarely desire, we have to cope with endless problems. If we fail, we suffer. And what do we gain from success? No more than some pleasure, a brief sense of triumph, perhaps a little peace of mind. But these are only interludes of well-being, because our difficulties do not cease. It is natural to ask then why we should continue on this treadmill. After all, we could stop.

The tough-minded answer is that the question falsely suggests that we need reasons for continuing to live. The truth is that our nature impels us to carry on. We have wants and the capacity to satisfy them, and instinct and training dictate that we do so. We live as long as we can, as well as we can, and we do so because we are the kind of organisms we are. It is our nature to struggle. To look for reasons beyond this is to misuse the respite we occasionally enjoy from the difficult business of living.

From *Midwest Studies in Philosophy*, Vol. 24, 2000. Reprinted with the permission of Blackwell Publishing, Ltd.

This bleak view correctly depicts the past and present condition of the majority of humanity. People struggle because they are hungry, cold, and threatened, and they want comfort. One should have compassion for the multitudes living in this way. The fact is, however, that many of us, living in civilized societies, no longer face such unrelenting adversity. For us, fortunate ones, the primitive struggle is over. We enjoy the comforts for which the less favored billions yearn. The point of the struggle in primitive conditions is to overcome obstacles to living. But what should we live for once the obstacles are overcome? What should we do with our comfortable lives? Having a comfortable life does not mean that the struggle is over, only that it takes less deadly forms. The threat is to income, prestige, status, self-esteem; the dangers are social and psychological. Nonetheless, these we also want to avoid. Why should we not say then that in primitive conditions our aim is to attain comfort, whereas in civilized conditions it is to protect and enhance the comfort we already have? We struggle to win such prizes as our society affords and to avoid being adversely judged by the prevailing standards.

This is a superficial view. No doubt, in civilized societies many are motivated in this way, but we also have some freedom and opportunity to stand back and reflect. Much of this reflection needs to be concentrated on the strategy and tactics of the daily struggle. Yet we often have some time and energy left to ponder life and our own lives, to ask why we should live in whatever happen to be the socially accredited ways. We know the standards by which success is judged and the rewards and costs of failure. If we are honest, we admit that we care about success and want to avoid failure, at least in the projects that matter to us. Reflection, however, may prompt us to ask whether they should matter. It may seem to us that the whole business we are caught up in is bogus. We see that children are indoctrinated, adolescents are goaded and guided, and adults are rewarded by the vast, impersonal, ubiquitous molds into which civilized societies press their members. And we may ask why we should put up with it. Why should we care about the emblems of success and the stigma of failure? What does it really matter to us in the dark hours of a sleepless night what our neighbors, acquaintances, or colleagues think about us? They employ standards and judge according to them, but we have come to question the standards. Life will seem hollow if we reflect in this way and we shall rightly ask what meaning it has.

Maybe it has none. Maybe evolution has brought it about that we have a capacity to ask questions about our condition, and in civilized societies some even have the opportunity to employ their capacity. But it is folly to suppose that just because we can ask a question there is going to be an answer to it that we like. There are plenty of useless things in nature, and perhaps this capacity is one of them. Maybe life just is, as black holes, electrons, and hurricanes are. Each has an explanation in terms of the laws of nature and antecedent conditions, but there is no meaning beyond that.

One may meet this answer with despair or cynicism. Both are injurious. They poison the enjoyment there is in life by corrupting the innocent connection between a want and its satisfaction. There intrudes the gnawing question about the point of it all. Despair and cynicism cleave us into a natural self and a preying, harping, jeering, or self-pitying reflective self. We are thus turned against ourselves. Reflection sabotages our own projects. If this is the truth, then the human prospect is dim. Maybe a capacity has evolved in us, and it will undo us.

It is not surprising, therefore, that many people of sturdy common sense simply ignore the question. They go on with the business of living, do as well as they can, enjoy the comforts they may, and prudently keep out of deep waters. This evasion, however, is likely to be possible only for those who are succeeding in navigating life's treacherous waters. The young who are about to start tend to ask why they should follow their elders' mode of life. The old who look back may wonder about whether it was worth it. And the sick, poor, unlucky, and untalented may well ask, with various degrees of resentment, about the point of the enterprise in which they have not done well. It is not possible to ignore the question because it is persistently asked.

Nor is it reasonable to avoid putting the question to ourselves, quite independently of external challenges. It is demeaning to participate in all manner of activities, expending great effort, giving and getting hard knocks, obeying rules we have not made, chasing goals said by others to be rewarding, without asking why we should do all this. Is it not the very opposite of prudence and common sense to invest our lives in projects whose value we have not ascertained? Furthermore, there are exceptionally few lives uninterrupted by serious crises. Grief, ill health, social cataclysms, injustice, setbacks, lack of merited appreciation, being in the power of those who abuse it, and many similar adversities are likely to interfere with even the most prudently lived lives. The questions such adversities raise in us can be answered, if at all, only by reminding ourselves of the point of facing them. Doing that, however, requires having thought about the meaning of our lives.


## II


In chapter 5 of his *Autobiography*,[1] John Stuart Mill makes wonderfully concrete what it is like for one's life to have meaning and then to lack it. He writes:

> I had what might truly be called an object in life: to be a reformer of the world. My conception of my own happiness was entirely identified with this object. The personal sympathies I wished for were those of my fellow labourers in this enterprise. . . . [A]s a serious and permanent personal satisfaction . . . my whole reliance was placed on this; and I was accustomed to felicitate myself on the certainty of a happy life which I enjoyed, through placing my happiness in something durable and distant, in which some progress might always be making, while it could never be exhausted by complete attainment. This did very well for several years, during which the general improvement

going on in the world and the idea of myself as engaged with others in struggling to promote it, seemed enough to fill up an interesting and animated existence.

Mill lived in this manner until "the time came when I was awakened from this as from a dream. . . . [I]t occurred to me to put the question directly to myself: 'Suppose that all your objects in life were realized; that all the changes in institutions and opinions which you are looking forward to, could be completely effected at this very instant: would this be a great joy and happiness to you?' And an irrepressible self-consciousness answered: 'No!' At this my heart sank within me: the whole foundation on which my life was constructed fell down. . . . The end has ceased to charm, and how could there ever again be any interest in the means? I seemed to have nothing left to live for."

Reflecting on what has gone wrong, Mill offers the following diagnosis:

> All those to whom I looked up, were of the opinion that the pleasure of sympathy with human beings, and the feelings which made the good of others . . . the objects of existence, were the greatest and surest sources of happiness. Of the truth of this I was convinced, but to know that a feeling would make me happy if I had it, did not give me the feeling. My education, I thought, had failed to create these feelings in sufficient strength to resist the dissolving influence of analysis, while the whole course of my intellectual cultivation had made . . . analysis the inveterate habit of my mind. I was thus left stranded . . . without any desire for the ends which I had been so carefully fitted out to work for: no delight in virtue, or the general good, but also as little in anything else.

Mill's explanation of what has deprived his life of meaning is convincing, but we can go beyond it. He became indifferent to his projects and ceased to care about the goals he used to pursue because he became disengaged from them. The circumstances of his disengagement and the nature of his projects are peculiar to Mill, and so is the extraordinary education that was partly responsible for both his achievements and his life's lost meaning. But we can abstract from these peculiarities and recognize Mill's case as typical of many lives whose meaning has been lost. The precipitating experience is that we awaken, as if from a dream, and realize that what mattered before no longer does. Loss of religious faith, the death of a deeply loved person, the recognition that our decisive choices were based on self-deception, the realization that we have devoted our lives to pursuing a hollow goal, the discovery that our passionate commitment is to an irremediably tainted cause are such experiences. The result is disillusion, and life becomes a tedious burden.

These experiences may bring us to regard our activities as worthless. We see ourselves as engaged in the endless drudgery of some soul-destroying job. We do what we do, not to attain some positive good, but to avoid poverty or starvation. Yet some intrinsically worthless activities may have a point if they lead to goals we value. If, however, chores lacking in either intrinsic or instrumental value dominate in our lives, such as tightening screws day in, day out, as in Chaplin's *Modern Times*, then we can rightly judge them meaningless because they are pointless. In other cases, the activities that dominate our lives may have a point, and yet our lives may still be meaningless, because our goals are destructive, like having enough drugs to support an addiction. Lives of this sort are misdirected. Other lives are meaningless because their goals are trivial, like keeping our childhood toys in working order. There are also lives directed at goals impossible even of approximation, like communicating with the dead. These lives are futile.

It will deepen our understanding of what it would be like for our lives to have meaning if we see that it is not enough to avoid these defects. Mill reasonably judged his life meaningless, yet it had worth, for it was dedicated to a good cause; it aimed at the important goal of bettering the condition of humanity, thus it was not pointless, misdirected, destructive, or trivial; and it was not futile either, for the amelioration of misery and the increase of general happiness are feasible goals. Mill recognized that his project in life had these meaning-conferring attributes, yet they were insufficient to give it meaning.

One element that Mill's life lacked was his wanting to continue to be engaged in his project. Before his crisis, he identified himself with it, he actively wanted to pursue it; after it, he did not. There appeared a break between Mill and the worthwhile, purposeful, well-directed, important, and possible project of improving the condition of humanity. The connecting link is Mill's identification with his project, and that is what has come to an end. Mill's case shows that it is a mistake to suppose that there are some types of lives in which meaning is inherent, so that if we live them, we cannot fail to find them meaningful. Meaningful lives must have the features just described, but we must also identify with them, we must want to engage in them. Our motivation is as essential as the intrinsic features of the lives.

The fact is, however, that the combination of the intrinsic features and our motivation is still not sufficient for meaning. We may come to think that reflection excludes the possibility of meaning because it brings home to us the absurdity of even the most reasonable projects. Thomas Nagel gives an account of the philosophical sense of absurdity that "must arise from the perception of something universal—some respect in which pretension and reality inevitably clash for all of us."[2] What is this clash? "Two inevitable standpoints collide in us, and that is what makes life absurd." One is that we "cannot live lives without energy and attention, nor without making choices which show that we take some things more seriously than others. . . . Think of how an ordinary individual sweats over his appearance, his health, his sex life, his emotional honesty, his social utility, his self-knowledge, the quality of his ties with family, colleagues, and friends, how well he does his job, whether he understands the world and what is going on in it." The other viewpoint is that "humans have the capacity to stand back and survey themselves, and the lives to which they are committed, with that detached amazement which comes from watching an ant struggle up a heap of sand. Without developing the illusion that they are able to escape from their specific and idiosyncratic position, they can view it *sub specie aeternitatis*. . . . Yet when we take this view . . . it does not disengage us from life, and there lies our absurdity: not in the fact that such an external view can be taken of us, but in the fact that we ourselves take it, without ceasing to be the persons whose ultimate concerns are so coolly regarded."[3]

This is a perceptive analysis of the philosophical sense of absurdity, but it does not help to understand the kind of meaninglessness that overtook Mill. It is true that we have a capacity to view ourselves from an impersonal cosmic perspective, but the fact is that few of us do so and those who do are by no means uniformly assailed by a sense of meaninglessness. Plato, Spinoza, and Kant among philosophers, Sophocles and Wordsworth among poets, Einstein among scientists come to mind as combining a cosmic view with an intense concern with human welfare. The truths that in the long run we shall all be dead and that from Alpha Centauri we seem like ants lead many reflective people to a heightened appreciation of the importance of human concerns. Nor do people find their lives meaningless, as Mill did, because of a philosophical sense of absurdity. Mill's trouble was not that from a cosmic perspective it appeared absurd to care about his project. What bothered him was that he lost the capacity to "sweat over his appearance, his health, his sex life . . . whether he understands the world and what is going on in it." His life became desultory because he stopped caring, not because his caring appeared to be absurd from a nonhuman point of view.

The experience we need to understand is the break that sometimes occurs in everyday life between us and our projects. The projects used to matter, but they no longer do. This may happen because our projects are worthless, pointless, misdirected, trivial, destructive, or futile. Or it may happen because although our projects have none of these defects, they may still lack meaning because of our attitude toward them. Our attitudes may sometimes be sapped by a sense of absurdity, but they are more often sapped by a disengagement of our will and emotions that has nothing to do with absurdity. It must also be allowed that people may find their lives meaningless because they are meaningless. But not all lives are. The question is: what is it that engages our will and emotions, gives meaning to our lives, given that our projects are not defective and we do not suffer from a sense of absurdity? There are two types of answers: the religious and the moral, and we shall examine them in turn.

### III

The religious approach to the question is pithily expressed by Wittgenstein: "The sense of the world must lie outside the world. In the world everything is as it is, and everything happens as it does happen: *in* it no value exists. . . .

If there is any value . . . it must lie outside the whole sphere of what happens and is the case."[4] The world is the natural world, and it is a world of facts, not of values. If anything in the natural world has meaning or value, it must come from the outside of it. And it is on the outside that the religious answer concentrates. As Wittgenstein puts it, "Ethics is transcendental,"[5] and he means that "Ethics is the enquiry into what is valuable, or, into what is really important, or . . . into the meaning of life, or into what makes life worth living, or into the right way of living."[6]

We know then the direction in which to look for the religious answer, but before we can look an obstacle needs to be overcome. Religious answers vary greatly in scope, ranging from the very general to the quite specific. Specific religious answers are given by Christianity, Buddhism, Islam, and so forth. The general religious answer is based on the belief that there is a cosmic order that is the ultimate source of meaning. Specific religious answers, then, are interpretations of this supposed cosmic order in terms of revelation, religious experience, miracles, sacred books, the deliverances of prophets, sages, mystics, and various gnostics. In trying to understand the religious answer, it is best to begin with the general one, leaving aside the respective merits of different specific interpretations of it.

Part of the general answer is then that there is a cosmic order in reality. The natural world in which we live is a part of reality and it reflects that order. Through science we may discover some aspects of this order, but there are large and deep questions to which there can be no scientific answers. Why is there a natural world? How did it come into being? Why does it have the order it has? Why is it that of the countless alternative possibilities in the natural world it is self-conscious human beings that have been realized? What is the human significance of the cosmic order? Scientific theories about the big bang and evolution do not even begin to answer these questions because the questions can easily accommodate the scientific answers and go beyond them. What was there before the big bang? Why was there one? Why were there natural entities that could evolve? Why were the conditions that shaped the direction of evolution as they were? Science asks and answers questions internal to the natural world. Religion, if it is reasonable, accepts these answers, asks questions external to the natural world, and endeavors to answer them. That some specific religious answers are myths tells no more against the general religious answer than alchemy, astrology, and phrenology tell against science.

Let us suppose for a moment that there is a cosmic order and that the natural world that science aims to understand is but a part of it. Why, if that were so, would it have anything to do with the meaning of life? A Stoic parable will help here. Take a dog tied to a cart drawn by a horse. The dog's position is unenviable, but it can still be made better or worse depending on what the dog does. It can understand its position and act accordingly: move when the cart moves, rest when the cart does. Or, it can try to resist, in which case it will be dragged, and the going will be much rougher than it needs to be. And so it is for us. We can try to understand and live according to the cosmic order, or we can ignorantly or unreasonably pit ourselves against it. The meaning of human lives is given by our place in the cosmic order, and our lives will go well or badly, depending on how well we understand and conform to it.

The Stoics did not think that human beings have a special place in the cosmic order, or that if we live reasonably, then we shall somehow free ourselves from the necessity it imposes on us. They thought that the only freedom we can have is to understand the necessity to which we are subject. Platonists, Jews, Christians, and a host of philosophers and theologians go beyond this and take the more optimistic view that the cosmic order is not just necessary, but also good. If our lives are governed by understanding it, then we shall not only avoid unnecessary suffering, but enjoy positive benefits. This is called salvation, and the hope that its possibility creates is the dominant tradition in religious thought. Ethics is transcendental because whatever has meaning in the natural world has it as a result of being in harmony with the good cosmic order. Meaning is not made, but found, and it is found outside of the natural world. The key to meaningful lives thus is to cultivate our understanding of the necessary and good cosmic order and to bring our projects in harmony with what we have thus understood.

One problem with the religious answer becomes apparent if we reflect on the mythical fate of Sisyphus, as Albert Camus did in *The Myth of Sisyphus*.[7] Sisyphus revealed divine secrets to humanity, and for this he was condemned by the gods to roll a heavy rock uphill to the crest of a mountain until it rolls down, then to roll it up again and again after it rolls down, and to do this for all eternity. Sisyphus's life is the epitome of meaninglessness. Camus's suggestion is that our time-bound lives are like Sisyphus's, albeit on a less heroic scale. The religious answer needs to show that this is not true.

Richard Taylor offers an interesting suggestion that bears on this.[8] He says:

> Let us suppose that the gods, while condemning Sisyphus . . . at the same time, as an afterthought, waxed perversely merciful by implanting in him . . . a compulsive impulse to roll stones. . . . I call this perverse, because from our point of view there is clearly no reason why anyone should have a persistent and insatiable desire to do something as pointless as that. Nevertheless, suppose that is Sisyphus' condition. He has but one obsession, which is to roll stones. . . . Now it can be seen why this little afterthought of the gods . . . was . . . merciful. For they have by this device managed to give Sisyphus precisely what he wants—by making him want precisely what they inflict on him. . . . Sisyphus' . . . life is now filled with mission and meaning, and he seems to himself to have been given an entry to heaven.[9]

Taylor's suggestion provokes a doubt. Sisyphus's belief that his life has meaning is false. He believes that his meaningless life has meaning only because the gods have manipulated him. We may wonder, however, whether meaning can be based on false beliefs. But let us set this doubt aside for the moment and observe that, whatever we may think of Taylor's suggestion, it is not the religious one. Taylor suggests that the meaning of life comes from living the way we want to live, whereas the religious answer is that meaning comes from living according to the cosmic order. A further twist to the myth of Sisyphus, however, will show how it might give rise to the religious answer.

Suppose that Sisyphus's fate remains as before, but when he reaches the crest, the rocks are incorporated into a gigantic monument glorifying the gods. Sisyphus's life then is no longer pointless or futile. He is part of a larger scheme, and his activities, difficult as they are, have a purpose. It may be further supposed that Sisyphus understands this purpose because the gods have explained it to him. This, of course, is the religious answer to the question about the meaning of our own lives as we face the endless struggles our various projects involve. The cosmic order is God's self-designed monument, and the ultimate purpose of all reasonable projects is to enact the small role assigned to us in this monumental scheme. We know that there is such a scheme, and we know that it is good, even if its details remain obscure to our limited intellects, because it has been revealed to us by a sacred book, by prophets, or by our own interpretations of our experiences.

## IV

The religious answer is unpersuasive. In the first place, it is impossible to adduce any evidence in its favor because all evidence available to human beings comes from the natural world. There can thus be no evidence of what may be the case beyond the reach of evidence. Sacred texts and prophets, of course, make various claims about what there is beyond the natural world, but there can be no reason to believe their claims because the authors of the texts and the prophets are human beings who, like us, have access only to the natural world. There undoubtedly are events and experiences that have, at least at present, no natural explanation. But to call the events miracles or the experiences religious is once again to go beyond what the evidence permits. To acknowledge that there are events and experiences in the natural world that we cannot explain lends no support whatsoever for explaining them in terms of a cosmic order. If there is a cosmic order, we cannot know anything about it: not *that* it exists, and even less *what* form it takes. The questions that religion asks about what there is external to the natural world have no rationally defensible answers. This does not make the questions uninteresting or illegitimate, but it does make all answers to them arbitrary. Arbitrary answers can be accepted on faith, but that does not make them less arbitrary. If the meaning of life depends on understanding and being motivated to live according to a cosmic order, then life has no meaning because we cannot understand the cosmic order and consequently cannot be motivated by it.

Assume, however, that these doubts about the religious answer are misplaced. Assume that the natural world points toward a cosmic order. That would still be insufficient to give life meaning. To know that there is a cosmic order is not to know what it is. But assume further that we can extrapolate from features of the natural world and form some views about what the cosmic order is because the natural world reflects the cosmic order. Knowing some things about the cosmic order, however, is still not enough for meaning, as the last twist to the myth of Sisyphus makes it obvious. Why would it make Sisyphus's life meaningful if he knew that the rocks he is rolling help to construct a monument for the glory of the gods? He knows that he is part of a plan, that his endless drudgery has a purpose, but neither the plan nor the purpose is his own. He is, in effect, enslaved by the gods. Having a part in monument building gives no more meaning to Sisyphus's life than having had a part in pyramid building gave to the slaves of the Egyptians. Of course, neither Sisyphus nor the real slaves had a choice in the matter; they both had to do what they had to do—just like the dog tied to the cart. They may resign themselves to it; they may accept the inevitable; but why would that make their lives meaningful? Meaningful lives require more than understanding the uselessness of opposing the immense force that coerces us to do its bidding.

What would have to be added to the cosmic order to make our lives meaningful is that it is not merely necessary, but also good. If we understood this about it, it would motivate us to live according to it. We would then see its necessity as the key to living a good life, and this, of course, is just what the dominant tradition in Western religious thought claims. But is this a reasonable claim? Why should we think that the cosmic order is good? Perhaps it is indifferent; perhaps it is not good, but bad; or perhaps it is a mixture of good, bad, and indifferent. What reason is there for accepting one of these possibilities, rather than the others?

In trying to answer this question, we need to remember the assumption we have accepted for the sake of argument: that it is reasonable to derive inferences from the natural world about the cosmic order. What features of the natural world, then, imply that the cosmic order is good? These features, it might be said, are that the natural world sustains life and the human form of life; that many human beings live happy and beneficial lives; that there are many acts of honor, decency, and self-sacrifice; and that people often strive to be kind and just. In general, we can read back our moral successes into the cosmic order.

This approach, however, is fundamentally flawed. For any form of life that the natural world sustains, there are numerous others that have perished in the struggle for survival. Alongside happy and beneficial human lives there are at least as many that are unhappy and destructive, and, probably more than either, lives that sometimes go one way and sometimes the other. Selfishness, cruelty, greed, aggression, envy, and malice also motivate people and often lead them to cause serious unjustified harm to others. If we extrapolate from how things are in the natural world to what the cosmic order must be like, then we cannot just concentrate on the good and ignore what is bad and indifferent. If the natural world reflects a cosmic order, then there is much that is bad and indifferent in the cosmic order, in addition to what may be good.

If the cosmic order has to be good in order to endow our lives with meaning, then we have no reason to believe that our lives have meaning. For understanding the cosmic order will not then motivate us to try to live according to it, but to try to avoid its malignity or indifference. If Sisyphus had remained reasonable in the midst of what the gods forced him to endure, he would not have concluded that the monument the gods were building to glorify themselves was good or that his enforced contribution to it gave meaning to his drudgery.

There is then no reason to accept the religious answer to the question of whether our lives have meaning, because we have no reason to believe that there is a cosmic order; because if there is one, we have no reason to believe anything about what it is; and because if we hold beliefs about what it is on the basis of what the natural world implies, then reason prompts the belief that the cosmic order is a mixture of good, bad, and indifferent elements.

## V

Let us, then, turn from the religious to the moral approach to the meaning of life. The distinction between the two approaches has been broached by Plato in *Euthyphro*.[10] The subject there is piety or holiness, but it has become customary to pose the question Socrates puts to Euthyphro in more general terms to be about the source of the good. Assuming that there is a God, what is the relation between God and the good? Does God make the good good or does God's will reflect the good that exists independently of it? The religious answer is the first, the moral answer is the second. Because morality is about the good, regardless of whether there is a God whose will could or would reflect the good, the concern of morality is not with God, but with what God's will might reflect.

According to the moral approach, Wittgenstein was wrong to think that "[e]thics is transcendental."[11] It is revealing, however, to bear in mind Wittgenstein's reason for thinking as he did. Commenting on Schlick's view about "two conceptions of the essence of the Good," Wittgenstein says that "according to the superficial interpretation, the Good is good because God wills it; according to the deeper interpretation, God wills the Good because it is good." Wittgenstein, then, goes on: "I think that the first conception is the deeper one: Good is what God orders. For this cuts off the path to any and every explanation of 'why' it is good, while the second conception is precisely the superficial, the rationalistic one, which proceeds as if what is good could still be given some foundation."[12] The moral approach to the meaning of life assumes, for reasons given in the preceding section, the failure of what Wittgenstein thinks of as the deeper conception. Wittgenstein is wrong to regard the moral approach as "the superficial, the rationalistic one," precisely because it recognizes the obligation that Wittgenstein spurns of giving reasons for claims about what the good is, if its pursuit is to endow life with meaning. It is a further feature of the moral approach that it looks for these reasons within the natural world, rather than outside of it.

Before we can address the question of where in the natural world these reasons could be found, clarity requires distinguishing between a wide and a narrow sense of morality. In the narrow sense, the concern of morality is with what is right. In this sense, morality is about the formulation of impersonal, impartial, disinterested rules that ought to govern human interactions. In the wide sense, the concern of morality is not merely with what is right, but also with what is good. In this sense, morality is not only about rules, actions, and obligations, but also about ideals, virtues, conceptions of a good life, personal aspirations, intimate relationships, private projects, supererogation, and so forth. The moral approach to the meaning of life is moral in the wide sense: what gives meaning to life is the pursuit of good projects. Doing what is right is an important part of that, but it is only a part. Right actions are impersonal conditions of a moral life, whereas the meaningfulness of moral lives derives from the personal sphere in which there are great individual variations. (A technical expression of this point is that the meaning of life is to be found in the aretaic/eudaimonist, rather than in the deontological, aspect of morality.)

We can once again begin by returning to the earlier suggestion of Richard Taylor about where in the wide sense of morality (or in the aretaic/eudaimonist aspect of it) the source of meaning may be found. Taylor thought that Sisyphus's life would have meaning if he wanted to pursue the project to which the gods have doomed him. According to Taylor, the crux is the wanting, not the nature of the projects or how we came to have them. Meaning thus comes from us, not from our projects. We confer meaning on them. On this view, meaning is subjective.

The distinction between "subjective" and "objective" can be drawn in a number of different ways, and there is much confusion about the whole question. It is important, therefore, to make it clear that what is meant by the meaning of life being subjective is that its meaning depends wholly on how the agents regard their lives. According to this view, a life has meaning if the agent sincerely thinks so, and it lacks meaning if the agent sincerely denies it. The objective view, then, is that the agents' thinking that their lives have meaning is the necessary and sufficient condition for their lives having meaning. The objective view, by contrast, grants that the agents' attribution of meaning to their lives is necessary for their lives' having meaning, but it denies that it is sufficient. According to the objective view, lives may lack meaning even if their agents think otherwise, for they may be mistaken.

There are three reasons for rejecting the subjective view and accepting the objective one. The first emerges if we recall the doubt we ignored earlier. We may want to pursue a project only because we have been manipulated, just as Sisyphus was by the gods in the last twist to the myth. It seems clear, however, that there is a difference between wanting to pursue a project because of indoctrination or artificial stimulation of the cortex and wanting to pursue it as a result of having reflected and discovered that it makes our lives meaningful. If meaning were subjective, if it were created merely by our wants and beliefs, it would make no difference to meaning whether our wanting to pursue a project is genuine or manipulated. And it would be inexplicable how the discovery of manipulation could lead us to regard as meaningless a project that we regarded as meaningful before the discovery. Wanting to pursue a project is certainly connected with the meaning of life, but there is more to meaningful lives than that we want to pursue some project.

The second reason grows out of the first. Suppose that we genuinely want to pursue a project, so that we have not been manipulated. Suppose that Sisyphus just found himself wanting to roll rocks. That this is not sufficient for meaning is shown by the fact that the bare having of a want is not enough to move us to try to satisfy it. The satisfaction of a want has to matter to us. And its mattering depends on its fitting into the overall causal nexus that connects that want to our other wants, and to our hopes, plans, goals, ambitions, and memories. If we all of a sudden discovered in ourselves an urge to roll rocks, we would not automatically act on it. We would ask ourselves why we want to do that and how it would affect our lives and projects if we did it. There is an explanation that we would want to give ourselves, especially since the want in question is assumed not to be trivial, like scratching one's nose, but a meaning-conferring one, like deciding to make rock rolling one's project in life.

It might be thought, however, that excluding manipulation and having an explanation of why the satisfaction of a want is important to us are requirements that the subjective view can meet. But this is not so. To ascertain whether we have been manipulated, or to explain why something is important to us, inevitably involves reference to objective considerations that exist independently of what we think. Manipulation is interference from the outside by people, the media, the gods, or whatever. To exclude it requires having reasons to believe that we have not been unduly influenced in these ways. And the explanation of why something matters to us must have to do with the influence on us of our upbringing, education, family, society, and so forth. The nature and strength of these influences are independent of what we think about them.

The third reason against the subjective view emerges from the recognition that we want to pursue a project because we believe that it would make our lives better than other available alternatives. But whether this is true depends on whether its pursuit would actually make our lives better. After all, we may pursue a project because we mistakenly believe that it would make our lives better, we may discover that we are mistaken, and we may change our minds about the meaningfulness of the project. If the mere belief that a project is better than the alternatives were sufficient to make the project meaningful, this change of mind could not occur.

It may be said in defense of the subjective view—that the sincere belief that our lives have meaning is necessary and sufficient for our lives' having meaning—that what these three objections show is that the truth of our beliefs may affect how good our projects are, but it will not affect our sense that our lives are meaningful, if we believe them to be so. This is partly right and partly wrong. It is right that we may find our projects meaningful even if, unbeknownst to us, our wants are manipulated and our beliefs in the importance and goodness of our projects are false. But it is wrong to conclude from this that the subjective view that meaning depends merely on our beliefs is correct. The very recognition that meaning requires both that we should fail to know that our wants are being manipulated and that we should fail to realize that our beliefs are false implies the relevance of objective considerations. For the knowledge that our wants are manipulated and beliefs false would destroy our belief in the meaningfulness of our projects. That we may be ignorant of the objective conditions of our projects' having meaning does not show that those conditions are irrelevant to their meaning. It shows that we may be mistaken in believing that our projects have meaning. If we realize that we are mistaken, that our wants are manipulated, or that our beliefs in the importance or goodness of our projects are false, then we would be the first to think that the projects we regarded as meaningful were in fact meaningless. This is just what would happen to Sisyphus if he knew the facts.

We are justified in concluding, therefore, that, in addition to the relevant wants and beliefs, there are objective conditions that must be met by meaningful lives. One of these conditions is that the wants must be genuine; and the other is that the beliefs must be true. Consequently, meaning depends on both subjective and objective conditions. To think otherwise, as Taylor does, is not to suppose that meaning depends on what God wills, as the religious approach claims, but that it depends on what the agent wills. As the religious approach relativizes meaning to God's will, so the subjective moral approach relativizes it to the agent's will. Both leave it unexplained how the subjective state of willing, whether it be God's or human agents', could be sufficient to establish what it is that makes lives meaningful.

The strongest case for the moral approach to the meaning of life will therefore recognize that meaning depends on both the subjective and the objective conditions. The subjective condition requires us to be in the appropriate psychological states of wanting and believing. The objective condition requires that our projects actually make our lives better. Meaning then depends on the coincidence of these two conditions: on our psychological states' being successfully directed toward the appropriate objects. As David Wiggins puts it: "psychological states and their objects [are] equal and reciprocal partners. . . . It can be true both that we desire x because we think x good, and that x is good because we desire x. . . . The quality by which the thing qualifies as good and the desire for the thing are equals and 'made for one another.'"[13]

It need not be supposed that this presupposes commitment to a cosmic order. It is not surprising that in the course of evolution there has emerged something like a correlation between what we want and what is good for us. We would be extinct if it were otherwise. Yet the correlation is less than perfect. Objective conditions both shape and constrain our wants, but within the limits they impose on our projects, there is much scope for experiments in living. Evolutionary success has not freed us from necessity, but it has opened numerous possibilities that we may pursue within the limits of necessity.

We may conclude, then, that according to the moral approach our lives have meaning if the following conditions are met: first, they are not worthless, pointless, misdirected, trivial, or futile; second, we have not succumbed to the view that all human projects are absurd; third, we have identified with projects that we genuinely want to pursue; and fourth, our belief that successful engagement in our projects will make our lives good or better is true.

## VI

The problems of the moral answer begin to emerge if we recognize that the fourth condition of meaningful lives is ambiguous. It may mean that successful engagement in our projects will make our lives *morally* better or that it will make them better in *nonmoral* ways. This ambiguity derives from the ambiguity of the "good" in good lives. Our lives may be good because they conform to the requirements of morality, or they may be good because we find them satisfying. Satisfaction in this context should not be identified either with pleasure or with the feeling that results from having met one's own physiological or psychological needs. To be sure, meeting them is an example of satisfaction, but satisfaction may also be derived from doing our duty at considerable cost to ourselves, imposing hard discipline on ourselves, beholding the success of others that does not reflect on us at all, or seeing that justice is done even though we do not benefit from it. These two constituents of good lives may coincide, or they may not. Morally good lives may not be satisfying, and satisfying lives may not be morally good. It is a moral ideal dating back at least to Socrates that our satisfactions should derive from living in conformity to the requirements of morality. If the ideal holds, the ambiguity of the "good" will disappear. The projects we pursue then will be morally good, and our lives will be at once good and meaningful because we will find our engagement in our morally good projects satisfying. This is the ideal that motivates the moral answer to the meaning of life. The ideal, however, is flawed, and the moral answer fails.

There are two different lines of argument that lead to this conclusion. The first is that morally good projects need not be satisfying. What happened to Mill makes this point obvious. Morally good projects may be tedious or painful; they may involve doing our duty at the cost of self-sacrifice, self-denial, the frustration of our desires, and going against our strong feelings. The modicum of satisfaction we may take in doing what we feel we ought to do is often greatly outweighed by the dissatisfactions that are the by-products of having to act contrary to our nonmoral projects.

The second line of argument that leads to the failure of the moral answer is that even if it were true that morally good projects are satisfying, it would not follow that *only* morally good projects are satisfying. There may be satisfying immoral and nonmoral projects, and successful engagement in them may give meaning to our lives. That immoral lives may be meaningful is shown by the countless dedicated Nazi and Communist mass murderers, by those many sincerely committed terrorists who aim to destabilize one society or another through committing outrageous crimes against innocent civilians, and by people whose rage, resentment, greed, ambition, selfishness, sense of superiority or inferiority give purpose to their lives and lead them to inflict grievous unjustified harm on others. Such people may be successfully engaged in their projects, derive great satisfaction from them, and find their lives as scourges of their literal or metaphorical gods very meaningful.

The moral answer, however, is vitiated not only by moral monsters, but also by lives dedicated to the pursuit of nonmoral projects, which may be athletic, aesthetic, horticultural, erotic, or scholarly, or may involve collecting, learning languages, travel, connoisseurship, the invention of ingenious gadgets, and so forth. The lives of many people are given meaning by projects that are neither morally good nor immoral, but morally indifferent. People engaged in them may by and large conform to morality. The meaning of their lives, however, derives from their engagement in nonmoral projects and not from living in conformity with the requirements of morality. It follows from the possibility that immoral and nonmoral projects may give meaning to lives that the moral answer is mistaken in regarding successful engagement in morally good projects as a necessary condition of meaningful lives.

In sum, the moral answer that meaning derives from living good lives founders because of the ambiguity of the "good." If the "good" is taken to be "morally good," then the claim is false because morally good lives may not be meaningful and meaningful lives may not be morally good. If, on the other hand, the "good" is interpreted as "nonmoral good," then the answer ceases to be moral, since it allows that meaningful lives may be immoral or nonmoral. The moral answer, therefore, turns out to be either false or not moral. Its defenders, of course, normally intend it to be interpreted in the moral sense, so the likely charge they have to contend with is that their answer is false.

## VII

There are, then, strong and independent reasons that show that neither religion nor morality provides a satisfactory approach to the meaning of life. But there is yet another and deeper reason why they both fail: they seek a general answer. Their basic assumption is that finding meaning depends on finding something that applies equally to all lives. The religious approach looks for that something to a cosmic order; the moral approach seeks it in morality. They recognize individual differences, but they treat them as mere variations on the same basic theme. Individual differences matter to them only because they compel us to do different things to conform to the same general meaning-conferring requirement. Given our characters and circumstances, we may have to serve the will of God in different ways, you as an artist, I as a soldier, or we may have to apply the categorical imperative in different situations or pursue the common good by means of different actions. But they both assume that, for all of us, meaning is derived from the same source, be it the will of God or some moral principle. It is this assumption that makes it impossible for both approaches to recognize the possibility that different individuals may derive meaning for their lives from radically different sources. This is the assumption that prevents them from acknowledging that individual differences have a fundamental influence not only on what we must do to pursue a meaning-conferring project, but also on which of many meaning-conferring projects we should aim to pursue. It is the assumption that all meaning-conferring projects must ultimately be variations of some one or few patterns that is responsible for the mistaken view that the phrase "the meaning of life is . . ." can be completed by some general formula that will make the resulting sentence hold true of all lives.

The problem is that if we give up the assumption that there is a general answer to the question of what gives meaning to life, then we seem to be led back to the subjective view that we had three good reasons to reject earlier. But these reasons continue to hold even if no general answer provides the additional necessary and sufficient condition that must be added to the subjective condition. The wants whose satisfaction we seek may be manipulated, self-destructive, trivial, inconsistent, or otherwise detrimental and thus fail to make our lives meaningful. And the beliefs we hold about the kind of life that would be meaningful may be false. Conformity to the subjective condition is necessary, but insufficient, for meaningful lives, and conformity to the objective by searching for a general answer exacts the unacceptable cost of denying that different lives may be made meaningful by conformity to different meaning-conferring requirements.

It is in this way that answering the question: Does life have a meaning? has become a perennial philosophical problem. The problem originates in a disruption of everyday life. Because we are unsuccessful, bored, poor, tired, unlucky, sick, grief-stricken, victims of injustice, or readers of subversive books, we start reflecting on the point of the routine activities we endlessly perform. Once we embark on this reflection, it is hard to stop. Reflection puts an end to the unreflective innocence with which we have unquestioningly lived in accordance to the prevailing conventions. As we question, so we feel the need for answers, and we turn to religion or morality. But the religious answer fails because no reason can be given for thinking that there is a cosmic order that would confer meaning on lives lived in conformity to it. And the moral answer fails because meaningful lives may be immoral or nonmoral and moral lives may not be meaningful. Defenders of the religious answer insist that the problems of morality can be met only by appealing to a cosmic order that would guarantee the identity of good and meaningful lives. Defenders of the moral answer insist that there must be moral reasons for regarding the cosmic order as good and that these reasons are either unavailable, or, if available, cannot themselves be transcendental. The religious and moral answers to this perennial problem agree in seeking a general answer, but they disagree whether it is to be found in the transcendental or in the natural world.

## VIII

The way out of this impasse is to give up the search for a general answer. That brings us to an approach to the meaning of life that is free of the defects of the religious and moral answers. Let us call this approach "pluralistic." Its description is now a simple matter, because it involves no more than assembling the conclusions that have been reached by the preceding arguments. These conclusions may be formulated as conditions of meaningful lives. According to the pluralistic approach, then, lives have meaning if they meet the following conditions:

1. They are not dominated by worthless, pointless, misdirected, trivial, or futile activities.

2. They are not vitiated by the belief that all human projects are absurd.

3. They involve the pursuit of projects with which the agents have genuinely identified; they thus exclude all forms of manipulation.

4. Their agents' genuine identification with their projects is based on their true belief that successful engagement in them will make their lives better by providing the satisfactions they seek; they thus exclude all projects in which the agents' subjective identification is not correlated with objective conditions.

5. Their objective conditions are located in the natural world, not outside of it; they thus exclude the religious answer.

6. Their agents' subjective identifications are based on the pursuit of projects that yield either morally good, or immoral, or nonmoral satisfactions; they thus exclude the moral answer.

7. Their agents' subjective identifications with their projects reflect individual differences; they thus exclude all general answers.

These conditions are individually necessary and jointly sufficient to make lives meaningful. The main purpose of all the preceding arguments has been to attempt to explain and justify them.

The argument has been meant also to make it evident that the proposed approach is pluralistic, not in the trivial sense that there are many conditions that meaningful lives must meet, but in the important sense that meaningful lives may take a wide plurality of forms. The plurality of meaningful lives reflects, in addition to individual differences in our characters and circumstances, also individual differences in the type of projects that we pursue. These projects may be religious or moral, but they may also be scientific, aesthetic, athletic, scholarly, horticultural, military, commercial, political, poetic, and so on. The pluralistic approach recognizes that any project may contribute to making a life meaningful, provided it meets the conditions listed above. Meeting these conditions excludes many possibilities, but for present purposes, the most important among them is the possibility of a general answer to the question of what project or what type of project would make all lives meaningful. The basic difference between the pluralistic approach, on the one hand, and the religious and moral modes of reflection, on the other, is that the first denies and the second asserts that there is a general answer.

It remains to point out that this difference constitutes a radical break between the pluralistic approach and traditional philosophical and religious thinking about the meaning of life. For one central claim of the pluralistic approach is that individuals must make their lives meaningful by genuinely identifying themselves with their projects and that doing so must reflect the differences of their capacities, interests, and preferences. It is because of these differences that there can be no acceptable general answers to questions about the meaning of life. A general answer must apply to all human lives, but if meaningful lives must reflect individual differences, then general answers, by their very nature, are doomed.

Part of the reason why the pluralistic approach constitutes a radical break with traditional philosophical and religious ways of thinking about the meaning of life is that all these ways aim to provide a general answer. This is what all the major religions, metaphysical systems, and moral theories aim to do. For Jews, it is the Covenant; for Christians, it is the life of Christ; for Buddhists, it is the Karma; for Moslems, it is the law as laid down in the Koran; for Platonists, it is the Form of the Good; for Stoics, it is natural necessity; for Hegelians, it is the dialectic; for utilitarians, it is the maximization of general happiness; and so on. If the pluralistic approach is right, then all these, and other, general answers are fundamentally misguided because they are essentially committed to denying individual differences in what lives can be meaningful. The pluralistic approach is an attempt to proceed in a different way.

Another central claim of the pluralistic approach is that meaningful lives may not be morally good and morally good lives may not be meaningful. The fundamental reason for this is that meaningful lives often depend on engagement in nonmoral projects. Such projects may be crucial to making lives meaningful, but engagement in them may violate or be indifferent to the requirements of morality. This claim is also contrary to the traditional ways of thinking about meaningful lives because the traditional assumption is that only morally good projects could make lives meaningful.

The assumption that underlies this tradition is that the scheme of things is such that ultimately only morally good lives will be satisfying and immoral or nonmoral lives cannot be. The pluralistic approach rejects this assumption as groundless. Immoral or nonmoral lives could have sufficient satisfactions to make them meaningful. This is hard to accept because it outrages our moral sensibility, which is deeply influenced by this tradition. Accepting it, however, has the virtue of doing justice to the plain fact that many evil and morally unconcerned people live meaningful lives. It also explains what this tradition has great difficulty with explaining, namely, why so many people live lives in which immoral and nonmoral satisfactions dominate moral ones. The explanation is that such satisfactions may make their lives meaningful. It is thus a consequence of the pluralistic approach that the questions of what makes lives meaningful and what makes them morally good are distinct and should not be conflated as traditionally done.

# NOTES

This paper has been much improved by the criticisms and suggestions of Graeme Hunter, Joel Kupperman, Jonathan Mandle, Wallace Matson, and especially Rachel Cohon. Their help is gratefully acknowledged.

1. John Stuart Mill, *Autobiography* (New York: Columbia University Press, 1924).

2. Thomas Nagel, "The Absurd" in his *Mortal Questions* (Cambridge: Cambridge University Press, 1979), pp. 11–23; quoted passage on p. 13.

3. Nagel, "The Absurd," pp. 14–15.

4. Ludwig Wittgenstein, *Tractatus Logico-Philosophicus*, trans. D. F. Pears and B. F. McGuinness (London: Routledge, 1961), 6.41.

5. Wittgenstein, *Tractatus*, 6.421.

6. Ludwig Wittgenstein, "A Lecture on Ethics," *Philosophical Review*, 74 (1965), pp. 3–12; quoted passage on p. 5.

7. Albert Camus, *The Myth of Sisyphus*, trans. Justin O'Brien (London: Hamish Hamilton, 1955).

8. Richard Taylor, *Good and Evil* (New York: Macmillan, 1970).

9. Taylor, *Good and Evil*, p. 259.

10. Plato, *Euthyphro*, trans. Lane Cooper, in *Plato: The Collected Dialogues*, ed. Edith Hamilton and Huntington Cairns (Princeton: Princeton University Press, 1961).

11. Wittgenstein, *Tractatus*, 6.421.

12. Friedrich Waismann, "Notes on Talks with Wittgenstein," *Philosophical Review*, 74 (1965), pp. 15–16; quoted passage on p. 15.

13. David Wiggins, "Truth, Invention, and the Meaning of Life," *Proceedings of the British Academy*, 62 (1976), pp. 331–378; quoted passage on pp. 348–49.